DATE DUE

MAY 1 5 2008			
6/19/08			
5/51/2010			

Lincoln and Freedom

Thirty-_Eighth_ Congress of the United States of America;

At the _Second_ Session,

Begun and held at the city of Washington, on Monday, the _Fifth_ day of December, one thousand eight hundred and

---

A RESOLUTION

submitting to the Legislatures of the several States a proposition to amend the Constitution of the United States

---

Duplicate

Resolved *by the Senate and House of Representatives of the United States of America in Congress assembled,*

(two thirds of both Houses concurring) That the following article be proposed to the Legislatures of the several States as an amendment to the Constitution of the United States, which, when ratified by three fourths of said Legislatures, shall be valid to all intents and purposes, as a part of the said Constitution, namely: Article XIII. Section 1. Neither slavery nor involuntary servitude, except as a punishment for crime, whereof the party shall have been duly convicted, shall exist within the United States, or any place subject to their jurisdiction. Section 2. Congress shall have power to enforce this article by appropriate legislation.

I certify that this resolution did originate in the Senate
Secretary,

Speaker of the House of Representatives
Vice President of the United States
H. Hamlin and President of the Senate.

Approved

Abraham Lincoln

Lincoln and Freedom

Slavery, Emancipation, and the Thirteenth Amendment

Edited by
Harold Holzer and
Sara Vaughn Gabbard

SOUTHERN ILLINOIS UNIVERSITY PRESS
Carbondale

Published in conjuction with

THE LINCOLN MUSEUM
Fort Wayne, Indiana

10 09 08 07   4 3 2 1

Library of Congress Cataloging-in-Publication Data

Lincoln and freedom : slavery, emancipation, and the Thirteenth Amendment / edited
by Harold Holzer and Sara Vaughn Gabbard ; foreword by Joan L. Flinspach.

    p. cm.

  "Published in conjunction with the Lincoln Museum."

  Includes bibliographical references and index.

  ISBN-13: 978-0-8093-2764-5 (alk. paper)

  ISBN-10: 0-8093-2764-3 (alk. paper)

  1. Lincoln, Abraham, 1809–1865—Political and social views. 2. Lincoln, Abraham,
1809–1865—Relations with African Americans. 3. Slaves—Emancipation—United
States. 4. United States. President (1861–1865 : Lincoln). Emancipation Proclamation.
5. United States. Constitution. 13th Amendment—History. 6. United States—Politics
and government—1861–1865. I. Holzer, Harold. II. Gabbard, Sara Vaughn. III. Lincoln
Museum (Fort Wayne, Ind.)

E457.2.L815 2007
973.7'14—dc22   2006100373

Frontispiece: Senate copy of the Thirteenth Amendment resolution, signed by President
Abraham Lincoln, Vice President Hannibal Hamlin, Speaker of the House Schuyler
Colfax, and thirty-six of the thirty-eight senators who voted for the resolution. Courtesy
of The Lincoln Museum, Fort Wayne, Indiana (Ref. 4600).

Contents

Foreword

In 1995, The Lincoln Museum opened in its current location to much fanfare and the involvement of Lincolnians everywhere. The Gilder Lehrman Institute of American History loaned its copies of the Emancipation Proclamation and the Thirteenth Amendment to the Constitution, both signed by Lincoln, for the opening temporary exhibit. Little did I know then that within the next ten years, The Lincoln Museum would acquire privately held copies of both documents for its own collection.

In 1998, as a departing gift to the retiring CEO of Lincoln Financial Group, Ian Rolland, the company enabled its foundation (Lincoln Financial Foundation) to purchase one of the Leland-Boker editions of the Emancipation Proclamation signed by Abraham Lincoln, which was then added to the museum's collection. Since its installation on the day after Rolland's retirement, thousands of visitors have come to see it.

In 2004, a rare opportunity surfaced to acquire one of the Senate copies of the Thirteenth Amendment to the Constitution, also signed by Lincoln, which formally abolished slavery. Jon Boscia, then CEO of Lincoln Financial Group and president of the foundation, felt that it was only appropriate in celebration of the company's one hundredth anniversary to purchase this important historical document that reflected the company's own values. In a ceremony in which Ernest Green, a member of the Little Rock Nine, told of his experiences in the struggle for equality, we were reminded of the promise of this document to fulfill that "new birth of freedom" and complete that "unfinished work" to achieve true democracy that Lincoln pledged at Gettysburg.

This book is a contribution by The Lincoln Museum to the celebration in 2009 of the bicentennial of the birth of Abraham Lincoln. It would not have been possible without support from the Lincoln Financial Foundation, the M. E. Raker Foundation, the Gilder Lehrman Institute of American History, the Edward M. and Mary McCrea Wilson Foundation, and Jon Boscia. Their assistance in the production of this book was inestimable. I also want to thank the contributing authors. The wisdom of their words will last for years. Finally, I want to thank the editors, Harold Holzer and Sara Gabbard. Although he never met them, they are two of Lincoln's closest friends.

Joan L. Flinspach
President and CEO,
The Lincoln Museum
Fort Wayne, Indiana

Introduction

Harold Holzer

"King's cure for all the evils." With that exuberant assessment, Abraham Lincoln publicly celebrated congressional passage of the Thirteenth Amendment to the U.S. Constitution abolishing slavery.[1] The House and Senate had at last approved and sent the long-awaited amendment to the states. The president's own home state—Illinois—had already acted with breathtaking speed to become the first to approve it. After spending more than twenty years opposing the institution of slavery, and after issuing an Emancipation Proclamation that had hastened, but did not complete, its destruction, Abraham Lincoln was now ready to savor the culmination of a life's work.

With the vast bulk of slaveholding territory still in rebellion against the Union and considered ineligible to participate in the coming ratification process, few observers in Washington doubted that the amendment would quickly win the required three-fourths of the loyal states. Even Maryland—a border state where slavery was still legal—was already, Lincoln proudly calculated, "half way through" the inevitable approval process.

Addressing a crowd of well-wishers who had flocked spontaneously to the White House on the evening of February 1, 1865, to serenade the president—only recently reelected, just four weeks away from his second inauguration, and, though no one would have guessed it, beginning the final ten weeks of his life—Lincoln was in the mood to both rejoice and reflect. "It winds the whole thing up," he declared of the historic moment. Not once, but twice, he told the audience that passage of the amendment resolution represented "the fitting if not indispensable . . . consummation" of the long and bloody Civil War. He "had never shrunk from doing all that he could to eradicate Slavery by issuing an emancipation proclamation," he pointedly reminded the crowd. But even "that proclamation," he admitted, had fallen "far short of what the amendment will be when fully consummated."[2] But this was no time for modesty. Lincoln ended his remarks that night by offering congratulations to the happy crowd, to the country, to the whole world—and rather startlingly, to himself. It was something he seldom did. Famous for his humility, self-aggrandizing statements were ordinarily absent from his vocabulary.

We do not know precisely how he expressed this unusual claim for credit that evening at the White House. Newspaper correspondents on the scene recorded only an imperfect transcript of the president's remarks.[3] But few who read the reports in the press in the days that followed could fail to notice that Lincoln had overtly asked his fellow citizens to recognize his own role in guaranteeing the amendment's success. In fact, that was not all he did. Earlier that day, to be absolutely sure that his name would be enshrined alongside the "King's cure" he had prescribed, Lincoln had taken pen in hand to sign the congressional resolution submitting the amendment to the states. This he did even though he likely knew that his signature was not legally required. In fact, his audacity so miffed some of the senators who had worked for its passage that in less than a week they passed yet another resolution just to go on record complaining that the presidential signature had been, as they put it, "unnecessary."[4]

To Lincoln, it was clearly quite the opposite. Here, at last, was the "great moral victory" for which he had quested all of his adult life. And he was going to make sure that history remembered his role in it.

History, of course, remembered Lincoln. But in a sense, it forgot, or at least neglected, the amendment he had championed. The tidal wave of celebratory literature and art that greeted his death and martyrdom rightly enshrined his declaration of the Emancipation Proclamation as his greatest act, but in so doing, de-emphasized the passage of the Thirteenth Amendment. Perhaps this occurred because the amendment had required that members of Congress and state legislators share the glory; or maybe because Lincoln's behind-the-scenes role in securing Capitol Hill approval was not immediately or widely known; or possibly because the amendment did not officially become part of the Constitution until December 1865—an anticlimactic eight months after his assassination. Executive orders are far easier to comprehend—perhaps also to appreciate—than complex legislative processes that require not only moral pronouncements but unattractive arm-twisting and political trade-offs as well. Whatever the reason or reasons, the result has been a certain, longtime historiographical imbalance regarding the destruction of slavery that has long relegated the Thirteenth Amendment to the status of a Civil War postscript.

Although much new work has appeared in the field in recent years on both the proclamation and the amendment alike, the Thirteenth Amendment has still ranked well behind Lincoln's other widely admired triumphs—winning the war, saving the Union, issuing the Emancipation Proclamation, and achieving rhetorical immortality at Gettysburg—in public consciousness. In an attempt to ameliorate that imbalance, as well as to mark The Lincoln Museum's milestone acquisition of a precious original, autographed Thirteenth Amendment resolution, the museum invited some of the leading Lincoln scholars in the nation to take a fresh look at its enactment, along with the issues, events, and debates that informed it. The result, the editors hope, is a valuable reassessment of its crucial importance by several generations of acclaimed historians.

Where the ledger book of history is concerned, which has long diagnosed the great "consummation" of Lincoln's life as a rather sickly historical step-child, our hope is that this book will not only provide a provocative study for students of the nineteenth century but perhaps also the "King's cure" that the Thirteenth Amendment so richly deserves.

The editors invited these leading scholars to address the issues of slavery and emancipation that once divided the nation and the role that Abraham Lincoln played in the long and complex process that eventually cleansed society of the "peculiar institution."

James Oliver Horton, historical consultant for a highly praised PBS documentary on slavery, describes the introduction and growth of slavery on this continent. His main focus is on the evolution of the institution during the lifetime of Abraham Lincoln and its inevitable, painful consequences on American life.

The *Dred Scott* decision, which denied basic rights to people of color, remains one of the most controversial Supreme Court decisions in history. Political scientist Joseph R. Fornieri examines the life of slave Dred Scott, what the decision meant, the effect it had on public opinion in general and Abraham Lincoln in particular, and the manner in which it served to mobilize public opinion on the slavery issue.

As an attorney and later as the president, Abraham Lincoln was ever mindful of the need to abide by constitutional limits. However, he also believed that his position as commander-in-chief required that he occasionally assume extraordinary executive authority not strictly delineated in the Constitution. Phillip Shaw Paludan offers a comprehensive, thought-provoking assessment of Lincoln's evolving views on presidential powers.

A leading authority on the history of religion and faith, Lucas E. Morel explores the manner in which religious beliefs influenced both the sixteenth president and the abolitionist movement. "The idea of constitutional self-government under the beneficence of God," he notes, "stands as a running theme for Lincoln and a fitting summation of his political reason for being."

Lincoln himself frankly viewed issuing the Emancipation Proclamation as the defining act of his presidency. The leading authority on the subject, Allen

C. Guelzo, addresses the most relevant issues in his first major discussion of the subject since the appearance of his definitive, award-winning book, *Lincoln's Emancipation Proclamation*: What influenced the timing of the proclamation? What effect did it have on the public, the military, and on the slaves themselves? And what was the evolution of Lincoln's thinking on the subject of wartime emancipation?

Historian Matthew Pinsker, whose book on Lincoln's summertime presidential retreat at the Soldiers' Home north of Washington opened new windows onto the sixteenth president's personal life, raises issues that have fascinated, and for the most part eluded, historians for decades: Where and when did Lincoln write the Preliminary Emancipation Proclamation? Many colleagues claimed to have been present and/or consulted. Are their claims true, or are they simply examples of the promotion of self-importance?

The press, of course, was undisguisedly partisan in Lincoln's day and played a huge role in the creation of new heroes—as well as in public acceptance of emancipation and the Thirteenth Amendment. The acclaimed historian of Reconstruction, Hans L. Trefousse, examines both extremes of press coverage on the issues of slavery and abolition, using a wide range of original sources to assess journalism's influence on the debate, the politicians, and the voters.

As a counterpoint, military historian John F. Marszalek provides a fresh and absorbing look at one of the society-altering consequences of freedom: the emergence of the U.S. Colored Troops. As African Americans showed their mettle under fire, did public opinion change? Did these soldiers contribute not only to battle but also to the public debate over slavery?

The central figure of that debate, Abraham Lincoln, proved himself a master of language—arguably one of the great writers of the nineteenth century. Ronald C. White Jr., author of several books on Lincoln's rhetorical craft and creative process, parses his public and private statements on slavery and freedom over the course of his long public career. White examines the questions of whether Lincoln's views changed during his lifetime and how his rhetoric affected public opinion.

Most historians acknowledge that the decisive election of 1864 helped settle the issue of emancipation. Had Lincoln lost that contest, his executive order might well have been overturned by his Democratic successor. David E. Long, author of the most comprehensive book on this hard-fought race, takes a new look at the campaign in an effort to assess whether Lincoln's views on freedom threatened his political future and whether soldiers in the field supported the redefined war against slavery.

Herman Belz's essay addresses the constitutional issues surrounding the long, divisive public debate over slavery, beginning with the original vision of the Framers, their failure to deal with the question of slavery, the provisions they made for future amendments, and the public's evolving view of the Constitution over the next fourscore years. Belz's essay raises a long-ignored issue: Were alternative means available—legislative and executive branch action—to revise constitutional construction and meaning? And should they have been employed earlier?

From the beginning, the Emancipation Proclamation was considered a war measure whose legality might be questioned later, in peacetime. Michael Vorenberg, author of the definitive book on the Thirteenth Amendment, here takes a fresh look at the subject—reexamining his argument that a constitutional change was crucial to preserving black freedom and making it permanent. In the process, he offers a riveting account of the political and moral dimensions of the heated enactment debate on Capitol Hill.

Although deliberative bodies are frequently remembered as single units of change, Ron J. Keller's corollary account of the individual members who voted for passage of the Thirteenth Amendment provides valuable insight into the actions that Congress—and, more to the point, individual congressmen—took to change history. As Keller demonstrates, support for such measures can require enormous political courage.

While the Thirteenth Amendment officially ended slavery, questions persisted regarding the status of freedmen. Rhode Island Chief Justice Frank J. Williams traces the continuing debate that arose over citizenship, civil rights, and equality, and the impact of the subsequent 14th and 15th Amendments to the Constitution. As Williams reminds us, the amendment process may well change the rules of government, but does not always change the heart and soul of its people.

Popular views are often expressed not in legislation but in period iconography, and as a coda to this collection of historical insights, I explore the way art and artists portrayed freedom during the emancipation and amendment processes—presenting the images that not only illustrated public opinion but likely influenced it as well. Picturing freedom may well have helped make it more palatable for white America, at least for a time, in the years after Lincoln's murder.

Abraham Lincoln has been dead for nearly a century and a half, but his spirit continues to animate American history and culture. As we approach the year 2009, which brings the official, national bicentennial celebration of the two hundredth anniversary of his birth, the editors hope that the essays in this book, both individually and collectively, will help to illuminate the manner in which America's greatest president dealt with the greatest challenge of his—and our nation's—time.

Notes

1. *The Collected Works of Abraham Lincoln*, ed. Roy P. Basler, 9 vols. (New Brunswick, N.J.: Rutgers University Press, 1953–55), 8:254–55.

2. Ibid.

3. The most reliable text, though it offered a report, not a transcript, of Lincoln's February 1 remarks, appeared in the *New York Tribune* on February 3, 1865.

4. John Nicolay and John Hay, *Abraham Lincoln: A History*, 10 vols. (New York: Century, 1890), 10:72–90.

1 Slavery during Lincoln's Lifetime

James Oliver Horton

By the time Abraham Lincoln was born, in February of 1809, African bondage in North America was already almost two centuries old. The first Africans were brought to Jamestown, Virginia, in 1619 by Dutch traders. These captives worked in the tobacco fields, saving the struggling colony from extinction. Their labor helped it to become the first permanent British colony in North America. By the mid-eighteenth century, this informal system of forced labor had become legalized racial slavery, the backbone of European American agriculture, and an important source of workers in all the thirteen original British colonies, from New England to Georgia.

By the Revolutionary period, slavery was firmly rooted in American soil as the rhetoric of freedom spurred patriots forward in a quest for national liberty. Slaves heard and understood American claims for natural human rights. They challenged their masters to live up to these declarations by abolishing slavery in the emerging nation. Protesting the oppression they faced daily, slaves petitioned the Massachusetts government, declaring, "We have no property, we have no wives! No Children! We have no City! No Country!"[1] Rhetorically, they sought to expose the hypocrisy of a free nation that tolerated slavery, asking, "do the rights of nature cease to be such, when a Negro is to enjoy them?"[2] Then, confronting the self-image of American patriots, slaves in Boston added, "We expect great things from men who have made such a noble stand against the designs of the fellow-men to enslave them."[3]

These protestations were effective in some Northern states, where slaveholders were less politically powerful than in the South. Throughout New England and in New York, New Jersey, and Pennsylvania, an antislavery spirit pressured government to move against the institution. In these states, constitutions, court rulings, or legislation brought slavery to an end or set it on the road to eventual extinction. There was also strong resistance among many in Congress who believed that slavery should not be allowed to spread into the Northwest Territories east of the Mississippi River and north of the Ohio River. Before the adoption of the U.S. Constitution, while the nation was still governed by the Articles of Confederation, Congress passed the Northwest Ordinance of 1787, legislation under which that territory might be organized into states for admission into the Union. In addition to guaranteeing the free inhabitants of the region full citizenship rights, including religious freedom, the Congress also ruled that "There shall be neither slavery nor involuntary servitude in the said territory, otherwise than in the punishment of crimes whereof the party shall have been duly convicted."[4]

During the early nineteenth century, the free states of Ohio, Indiana, Illinois, Michigan, and Wisconsin were carved from this region. In the South, however, slavery was becoming more entrenched. After the invention of the cotton gin in 1793 made cotton processing more efficient, and once the addition of the Louisiana Territory in 1803 provided the rich fertile soil for the expansion of cotton agriculture, Southern slavery grew stronger than ever. By 1815, as cotton textile manufacturing in Europe and in New England expanded, the value of the cotton produced in the new plantation areas of the Deep South also rose dramatically, making that region the economic powerhouse of the nation. In that year, cotton became the single most valuable U.S. export.[5]

The Upper South grew far less cotton and was generally less wealthy than the Deep South. This was true of Lincoln's home state of Kentucky, which was originally part of the western region of Virginia. It was more agriculturally diverse than eastern, tobacco-growing Virginia and grew little cotton. Still, the region's residents held more than twelve thousand slaves by 1790. When Kentucky became a state two years later, it retained slavery, and the slave population grew substantially. By 1800, there were more than forty thousand slaves in the new state, and that number more than doubled by the time of Lincoln's birth.[6] Although there were few large slaveholders in Hardin County where the Lincolns lived, the percentage of slaves there was substantial. By 1811, there were 1,007 slaves in the county, almost two-thirds the number of white males above sixteen years of age (1,627).[7] Slaveholding was greatest in the central, bluegrass region of the state. There, slaves raised livestock and grew cereal and other food crops. They also grew hemp and tobacco. Some Kentucky slaveholders worked their slaves in salt mines, in ironworks, and on bridge and road construction throughout the state.

Lincoln later recalled that his father was troubled by the growth of slavery around him, opposing it on religious grounds, but also for important economic reasons. Apparently, Thomas Lincoln, who worked as a carpenter and laborer to supplement his farm income, was forced to compete with slave labor.[8] He was also plagued by recurring difficulties in gaining clear title to the land he farmed because of disputes over land boundaries that resulted from the confusion of the old English system employed under previous Virginia law. At one point, he lost thirty-eight acres as a result of a lawsuit brought against him by a former owner of the land. Under this pressure, Thomas moved the family to another area of Hardin County, where he purchased a small farm. Then again in 1815, he was confronted by the unstable land-title system when the heirs of a land speculator sought to claim his thirty acres as part of a ten-thousand-acre parcel willed to them. This conflict, combined with his discomfort over slavery's expansion, encouraged Thomas to move the family to Indiana, a territory that became a free state in 1816.[9]

The Kentucky that the Lincolns left behind was changing, as was the South generally during this period. As was typical of Upper South slavery, holdings in Kentucky remained relatively small. Only 12 percent of the state's slaveholders owned twenty or more slaves, the lower limit for being considered a planter, and only seventy people in the entire state held fifty or more slaves. Yet slavery became an ever more important part of the political and economic life of the state, as Kentuckians assumed an increasingly significant role in supplying slaves to the Deep South.[10]

While the Lincoln family was moving to Indiana and away from slavery, Kentucky was becoming an important slave-trading center. Slaves imported from the border states and the eastern South were gathered in Kentucky for shipment to the plantations of the Mississippi Delta, Louisiana, and other regions of the Deep South where king cotton and sugarcane demanded ever-increasing numbers of slaves. In the wake of the War of 1812, the South expanded westward. As early as 1818, Lexington, Kentucky, became a principal transit point from which slave traders loaded their human cargo on flatboats to be sold in New Orleans and on the lower Mississippi River. Large numbers of slaves, chained together and marching along the roads to Lexington and through the streets of the city, were common sights during the 1820s. By then, Kentucky had become a major contributor to the changing economic and political world of the cotton kingdom.[11]

Even those from free states might expect to encounter slavery on occasion and to confront the unsettling sight of human bondage firsthand. Young Abraham Lincoln had strong memories of his earliest racial encounters in the Deep South, when he came face to face with the stark inhumanity of slavery. John Hanks, Lincoln's mother's cousin, remembered that he and Lincoln piloted a flatboat to New Orleans, where they saw slaves at auction, "Negroes chained, maltreated, whipped and scourged." Hanks reported that this had a strong effect. "Lincoln saw it, his heart bled, said nothing much, was silent from feeling, was sad, looked bad, felt bad, was thoughtful and abstracted."

Hanks was confident, as he said, "that it was on this trip that [Lincoln] formed his opinions of slavery; it ran its iron in him then and there."[12]

One sight Lincoln especially remembered and related in many accounts was that of a young mixed-race woman being sold. Prospective buyers handled her as they might a farm animal or an inanimate piece of property. Their close inspection showed no respect for her gender or her humanity. Lincoln was angered by the inhumanity of the entire process, and his emotional response helped shape his lifelong hatred of slavery and of those who profited from it. "If I ever get a chance to hit that thing," he said aloud, "I'll hit it hard."[13] Although those who related this story were not present at the moment of this statement, and some have questioned this account of Lincoln's strong reaction to this experience, years later Lincoln told this story to a number of his fellow attorneys. He was "disgusted," he said, when he "saw young women, as white as any that walked these streets to-day, sold on the auction-block simply because they had some Negro blood in their veins."[14] Lincoln was not alone in finding the enslavement of human beings a revolting sight. During the early 1830s, the movement against slavery took on new strength when white radical reformer William Lloyd Garrison and his Boston-based newspaper, the *Liberator,* joined black abolitionists, facilitating an interracial abolition movement. The movement was banned in the South, but by the 1840s, in New England, parts of Pennsylvania and New Jersey, areas of the Middle West, and New York State, especially upstate, where the fires of reform were said to have burned over the western region, antislavery sentiment was a growing political force. In mass meetings, abolitionists attacked slavery as inhumane and unchristian. Garrison indicted the U.S. Constitution for its role in protecting slavery and, on occasion, in a display of abolitionist theater, burned copies of that document. In 1843, the Massachusetts Antislavery Society adopted a resolution crafted by Garrison that denounced the Constitution as a "covenant with death and an agreement with hell." Radical abolitionists argued that the national union that sanctioned human slavery violated the very principles of the nation's founding and involved both slaveholders and non-slaveholders in "atrocious criminality." Garrison argued that such a union should be "immediately annulled." The cry of "no union with slaveholders" went up from those increasingly unwilling to compromise American freedom.[15]

Clearly, as the mid-nineteenth century approached, slavery was one of the most potentially dangerous issues to national unity. Americans had already struck a number of compromises in an effort to stave off the massive sectional showdown that some white reformers and many free African Americans were starting to predict. From the beginning, slavery had been the subject too hot to handle, debated but not written into the Constitution except in the most indirect manner. Using euphemistic phrases such as "those not free," or "those owing service," the Founders insured the constitutional protections of slave property, while not actually calling it by name. As the nation expanded, the growing political and economic power of the slave South forced other compromises, such as in the summer of 1821, when the new slave state of Missouri was admitted to balance the free state of Maine admitted to the Union a few months before.

The slave South was appeased again in the early 1830s when South Carolina flexed its muscles, opposing the rise in national tariff rates. Although the tariff policy occasioned the Nullification Crisis, as it was dubbed, South Carolina argued that its stand was ultimately a show of force against the federal power to impose its will on the South, a power that might ultimately threaten Southern slavery.[16]

The federal government seemed to give in to Southern concerns by instituting a lower compromise tariff in 1833, demonstrating slavery's powerful influence on federal policy. Yet, the issue would not rest, surfacing frequently and with ever-increasing intensity. The addition of territory to the nation as a result of Texas statehood in 1845 and substantial land acquisitions in the aftermath of the Mexican war once again introduced the possibility of the spread of slavery westward. Another important compromise in 1850 abolishing slave trading in Washington, D.C., and admitting the new state of California to the Union as a free state seemed to some a victory for abolitionists. Yet, it also opened the possibility of slaveholding in the Southwest, newly acquired from Mexico, should settlers in the area chose to tolerate the institution. It also established the most restrictive fugitive slave law in national history.[17]

Incensed by the willingness of the federal government to bend to slaveholder demands, some abolitionists called for disunion and violence in support of slaves attempting to escape from bondage. Frederick Douglass, the abolitionist and former slave, posed the question "Is It Right and Wise to Kill a Kidnapper?" He answered by saying that a federal officer slain while defending slavery against abolitionist forces had "forfeited his right to live" when he took on the "revolting business of kidnapping." Expressing the sentiments of many in the free black community who feared that the South was exercising intolerable power over federal policy, Douglass argued that every "slavehunter who meets a bloody death in his infernal business is an argument in favor of the manhood of our [African American] race."[18] Lincoln was not willing to go that far, but he did express his distaste for the bondage that exploited human beings and treated them like so much commodity.

The increasingly determined abolitionist attack on slavery was challenged by an equally aggressive proslavery defense. Supporters of slavery rejected the relatively apologetic stance of the old Jeffersonian claim that slavery had been forced on the American colonies by Great Britain's slave traders and was maintained in the new American nation simply as a necessary evil. Jefferson had argued that with tens of thousands of Africans held in bondage within its borders, America was caught in a dangerous quandary. It was, he explained like "holding a wolf by the ears." The nation could neither hold on nor let go without endangering all that it sought to become.[19]

Although this defensive stance may have been sufficient to salve the consciences of early slaveholders, as the sectional differences widened in the decades before the Civil War, Southerners mounted an offensive against the abolitionists using a racial argument. They pictured Africans as inferior, degraded, and childlike creatures in need of constant supervision. These subhumans, they argued, were designed by God and nature to labor under the guidance of, and for the benefit of, higher society, and they profited greatly from the experience. Thus, according to this argument, slavery was a "positive good," a system that provided great advantages for all involved, including the slaves.[20]

Lincoln, although not an abolitionist in the Garrisonian mold, was nevertheless appalled by such proslavery claims. He rejected these arguments, responding with characteristic wit. To argue that slavery worked to the advantage of both the slave and the slave master, he observed, was to suppose that the lambs benefited equally with the wolves that devoured them. "Whenever I hear any one arguing for slavery," he remarked, "I feel a strong impulse to see it tried on him personally."[21] Beneath this wit, however, Lincoln's antislavery position was built on his compassion for those who suffered. He reacted strongly to humanitarian appeals against this evil system that broke up families and destroyed lives for the profit of wealthy and powerful planters in the South and of Northern business interests that financed much of the Southern slave system.[22]

Among those who skillfully brought the abolitionist message to Northern audiences were former slaves who played a powerful role as antislavery speakers relating their personal stories of horror at the hands of this evil system. Their accounts brought the terrifying reality of slavery to many white Northerners who had not themselves witnessed its heartbreak and brutality. These former slaves became the solid backbone of the abolitionist movement and a vital part of its fund-raising efforts.

By the 1840s, Frederick Douglass, who had escaped from bondage in Maryland in 1838, became one of the most powerful voices of abolition in the world. Like Lincoln, this former slave had fallen in love with words and the world of ideas. From an early age, he had displayed a native intelligence and an impressive facility with language. Garrison first heard Douglass address an audience in Nantucket, Massachusetts, in the summer of 1841 and was struck by the force of his message. He asked the former slave, still a fugitive at that time, to serve the antislavery cause as a speaker for the American Antislavery Society, the reform organization that Garrison had founded in 1836.

Douglass became one of the most effective antislavery speakers of his generation, telling his personal story of bondage not only in the United States but in Europe as well. A favorite in England and the British Isles, his message that the evil of slavery must be eradicated as a service to Christian principles and to those of America's founding was one that appealed to Lincoln as well. Yet both men saw slavery expanding its reach and power in the decades before the Civil War. Cotton grew in national importance as America's single most valuable export, more valuable than all others combined by 1840. Slavery's political power also grew to a formidable force, influencing both Southern politics and national politics, including every presidential election of the period. In fifty of the seventy-two years between the presidential elections of George Washington and Lincoln, a slaveholder served as president of the United States. Significantly, during those years, only slaveholding presidents were elected to a second term of office.

The institution also played a critical role in the formation of the social structure even in the free states, but especially in the South. It clearly designated the importance of race in American society and provided a social floor below which no white person, no matter how economically deprived, could ever fall. Lincoln believed that the presence of slavery worked to the disadvantage of many in white society, even as it exploited the labor of blacks to the great advantage of the planter class. While visiting southern Ohio in 1855, he explained to a friend the differences he observed between the characteristics of white people in the slaveholding society in Covington, Kentucky, on the south side of the Ohio River, and those in free society in Cincinnati. Although Covington was settled before Cincinnati and had as good a location for trade and commerce, it remained a small town compared to what Lincoln described as "this fine city of Cincinnati." He asked why and then suggested an answer: "just because of slavery, and nothing else." He reasoned that the institution robbed the white population of its ambition and discouraged respect for industriousness and intellectual pursuit, leaving little incentive for business expansion or economic progress. "That is what slavery does for the white man," he argued. Thus, for Lincoln, the system of slavery posed a hardship for the slave and threatened to retard white society. He feared that the institution might very well lower white people to the level of black people.[23]

Like most white people of his day, Lincoln assumed and accepted white supremacy as a part of the natural order. In a series of debates with Stephen A. Douglas during the Illinois senate race of 1858, Lincoln laid out his position on race and slavery, saying that "there is a physical difference between the white and black races which I believe will forever forbid the two races living together on terms of social and political equality." He strongly believed, as he said in Charleston, that if the races were to live together, "there must be the position of superior and inferior." He then went on to make his racial position clear to his white, Midwestern audience: "I as much as any other man am in favor of having the superior position assigned to the white man."[24]

Lincoln was responding to an attack by Stephen Douglas, his political opponent, claiming that Lincoln was in favor of a racial equality that would support and encourage interracial marriage. Clearly, he was not, but neither was he willing to leave the spread of slavery to the democratic choices of the voting public. Lincoln made an important distinction between his stand on white supremacy and his stand on slavery. "I say upon this occasion," he told his listeners, "I do not perceive that because the white man is to have the superior position the [N]egro should be denied everything." Still, he left no doubt that he was not in support of full citizenship rights for any black person, slave or free. "I am not nor ever have been in favor of making voters or jurors of [N]egroes, nor of qualifying them to hold office." He also added his disapproval of interracial marriage. Then, as reported in the *Chicago Daily Press and Tribune*, to more directly respond to Douglas's charge, Lincoln added, "I do not understand that because I do not want a [N]egro woman for a slave I must necessarily want her for a wife."[25]

Herein lay a thorny problem for the abolitionist movement, for many of their members shared Lincoln's views on race, even as they attacked the racist institution of slavery. Frederick Douglass and other black abolitionists often felt the sting of racial prejudice even from antislavery colleagues. On this question, Garrison stood out as one of a relatively small number of white reformers who professed and acted on the principle of racial equality. Thus, Lincoln was not alone in his racial views among those who opposed slavery. Yet, he would change his position during the Civil War as he was presented with evidence that contradicted his earlier assumptions about race.

During the decades leading to the Civil War, it was becoming clear to those who would see the truth that slavery was tearing the nation apart. Would America ultimately be the land of the free or the land of the free supported and made prosperous by the toil of slaves? This question became ever more significant as the nation faced the dilemma of its continued expansion. The limitation on the spread of slavery established under the Missouri Compromise of 1820 was challenged when Congress adopted the Kansas-Nebraska Act in 1854 that opened areas north of Missouri's southern boundary to the institution if those settling in that region desired it. Under this proposition, there might be no predetermined limits to the spread of slavery. Lincoln could imagine no "more apt invention to bring about collision and violence on the slavery question."[26]

He was right to worry. The settlement of Kansas was contentious to the brink of war as the antislavery and proslavery forces clashed over the future of the territory. Lincoln attempted to calm his colleagues in the Whig Party, urging against violence in Kansas. "Physical rebellion and bloody resistance," he argued, were not only wrong but also unconstitutional.[27] Yet, especially for the so-called conscience Whigs, who were said to put their conscience before their economic concerns, the prospect of slavery spreading into the Western territories was unacceptable. Those of the more conservative "cotton Whigs" wing of the party were far more driven by their business investments in the Southern plantation system. To complicate matters even further, yet another wing of the party, those calling themselves Know-Nothings, stood against immigrants, especially Irish Catholics. Lincoln saw the party coming apart and struggled to define his own position. He opposed both slavery and efforts to discriminate against immigrants. Perhaps by the mid-nineteenth century, he suggested, the Declaration of Independence had come to be read "all men are created equal except [N]egroes, and foreigners, and catholics [sic]." If America had moved that far from its origins, he told a friend, he might prefer to leave the country for someplace like "Russia, for instance, where despotism can be taken pure, and without the base alloy of hypocrisy."[28]

The question of Kansas's settlement and the dispute over the spread of slavery splintered the Whig Party. During the mid-1850s, Lincoln played a leading role in the construction of the new Republican Party that united those who opposed the expansion of slavery. Clearly, in the decade before the Civil War, slavery had become the central point of contention dividing the nation, threatening to sever the slaveholding South from the free-labor North. Lincoln stood on a precarious middle ground, not demanding the abolition of slavery in the South, but determined to limit its expansion. While he did not favor an abolitionist to head the Republican presidential ticket in 1856, he did believe that the party and its candidate must take a stand on slavery. He was infuriated by the violence in Kansas and by the attack on Massachusetts senator Charles Sumner by South Carolina representative Preston Brooks, who had taken exception to Sumner's antislavery position and his verbal attack on a South Carolina senator. Historian Michael Burlingame reports that, after hearing the news of Brooks's assault on the senator on the floor of the U.S. Senate, Lincoln, who saw this as yet another proslavery aggression, "stepped cleanly out of his character and became . . . a different person—fiery, emotional, reckless, violent, hotblooded—everything which at other times he was not."[29]

Lincoln's anger and reported loss of self-control mirrored the reaction of many Americans to the growing national confrontation over slavery. When he ran for the presidency as the Republican candidate in 1860, he did so not as an abolitionist but as one committed to containing what he had grown to see as a cancerous institution. When he won election, he attempted to reassure the slave states that had declared their separation from the nation, as well as those that had remained loyal, that he had no intention of interfering with slavery in the states where it currently existed. Despite his earlier antislavery statements, his main concern, Lincoln told the nation, was to hold the Union together, and he would do that with or without slavery. In a letter to newspaper editor Horace Greeley in 1862, he explained his position in detail: "My paramount object in this struggle *is* to save the Union, and is *not* either to save or to destroy slavery. If I could save the Union without freeing *any* slave I would do it, and if I could save it by freeing *all* the slaves I would do it; and if I could save it by freeing some and leaving others alone I would also do that. What I do about slavery, and the colored race, I do because I believe it helps to save the Union."[30]

The newly formed Confederate States of America did not believe Lincoln's reassurances, however. The original seven seceding states of South Carolina, Mississippi, Florida, Alabama, Georgia, Louisiana, and Texas argued that the new president was an abolitionist—what they called a "black Republican"—who could not be trusted to respect the rights of slaveholders. After the Confederates fired on the federal Fort Sumter on April 12, 1861, Lincoln issued a call for seventy-five thousand volunteers for the U.S. military. Within days, another four states, Virginia, Arkansas, Tennessee, and North Carolina, withdrew from the United States to fill out the eleven states of the Confederacy. Slavery was the central issue. Its defense motivated Southern secession, and that secession moved Lincoln and the nation to action to save the United States from disunion.[31]

Slavery deeply affected Lincoln's presidency, as it had affected much of his life and the life of the nation. It drove the movement for southern secession and shaped his efforts to save the nation. He was willing to reassure the slave South by supporting constitutional protection of slavery in states in which it was legal. He also favored the colonization of African Americans outside the United States. He sought to encourage free blacks to leave voluntarily and hosted a meeting of black leaders at the White House to discuss his plan. They gathered in mid-August 1862, the first time African Americans had ever met with a president of the United States in the White House to discuss a matter of state. Colonization was the only practical means of ending slavery in America, Lincoln argued. It was thus inevitable. Black leaders must set an example for the good of their people, he told his African American guests. They must support and personally adopt his plan for colonizing American blacks, those free and those who might be freed, in West Africa. "You and we are different races," he observed. "We have between us a broader difference than exists between almost any other two races. . . . This physical difference is a great disadvantage to us both." He then told these black men what they already knew: that their race had suffered "the greatest wrong inflicted on any people." There was no real chance for racial justice in America, he argued. It would be best both for blacks, slave and free, and for white Americans if African Americans left America and settled in what he called their "homeland." This would allow for the abolition of slavery in America, and Lincoln believed that "without the institution of Slavery and the colored race as a basis, the war could not have an existence."[32]

Although a few of his African American guests endorsed his argument, the vast majority of the nation's free blacks vigorously condemned Lincoln's plan to remove them from their homes in the only country most had ever known. A meeting of free blacks in Philadelphia asked rhetorically if they should be expected to "leave our homes, forsake our birthplace, and flee to a strange land, to appease the anger and prejudice of traitors now in arms against the Government?"[33] Frederick Douglass, with typical Lincolnian pointed humor, likened the president's attributing the outbreak of the war to the presence and suffering of black slaves to a thief blaming his crime on the money carried in his victim's pocket.[34]

Congress provided funding for Lincoln's colonization efforts in Africa, in Haiti, and in Central America, but the overwhelming black opposition helped to foreclose any such possibility. They were Americans, black leaders argued, and as the war dragged on year after year and U.S. casualties mounted, they were called upon to help save their nation. By the fall of 1862, Lincoln turned to the abolition of slavery and the recruitment of African American soldiers as a means of winning the war against the slaveholding power. Although his Emancipation Proclamation, which took effect on January 1, 1863, only applied to slaves then under the control of Confederate forces, leaving slavery alone in areas controlled by the United States or in states that had not withdrawn from the nation, it was a critical step toward ending the slave system. It also extinguished the thin black support Lincoln had for his colonization efforts and gave all African Americans hope for freedom in their native land. After Lincoln's proclamation, the tens of thousands of slaves who had escaped the Confederacy and flocked to Union lines found immediate freedom.

Meanwhile, the more than two hundred thousand blacks who served in the Union military during the war became instrumental in the ultimate victory and impressed Lincoln greatly. Their service helped to change his mind on slavery, colonization, and many racial issues. His meetings with Frederick Douglass and other African American leaders also profoundly affected him. His Second Inaugural Address in 1865 gave evidence of the modification of his ideas. In it, Lincoln linked the hardships of the war to God's retribution for America's sin of tolerating slavery. "Yet, if God wills that [the war] continue until all the wealth piled by the bondsman's two hundred and fifty years of unrequited toil shall be sunk, and until every drop of blood drawn with the lash shall be paid by another drawn with the sword, as was said three thousand years ago, so still it must be said 'the judgments of the Lord are true and righteous altogether.'"[35] Despite his earlier belief that African Americans were unfit for the rights and privileges of full citizenship, by 1865 Lincoln called not only for black freedom but also for a measure of political equality. He was, in fact, assassinated because of his support for the idea that black soldiers and educated blacks should be allowed full voting rights, a prospect that his murderer, John Wilkes Booth, found intolerable. By the end of his life, Lincoln had shown a capacity for personal growth. He had set slavery on the road to extinction by his proclamation and his advocacy of the Thirteenth Amendment to the U.S. Constitution. He was martyred for his willingness to end slavery and to move beyond freedom toward racial equality. American slavery had preceded Lincoln, and although he did much to bring it to an end, he did not live to see its demise. Yet, African Americans generally gave him the credit for their freedom. Many at the time, however, were realistic about his racial views. They, like Frederick Douglass himself, were impressed at Lincoln's transformation on those issues as the war progressed. For generations after his assassination, Abraham Lincoln remained to them the man who ended slavery, the Great Emancipator.

Notes

1. Petition of the Africans, living in Boston, 1773, Boston Athenaeum (Library and Archives).

2. Philip Foner, *History of Black Americans: From Africa to the Emergence of the Cotton Kingdom* (Westport, Conn.: Greenwood, 1975), 1:297.

3. Circular letter, Boston, April 20, 1773, New-York Historical Society.

4. Theodore C. Pease, "The Ordinance of 1787," *Mississippi Valley Historical Review* 25 (1938): 167–80; Christine Compston and Rachel Filene Seidman, eds. *Our Documents: 100 Milestone Documents from the National Archives* (New York: Oxford University Press, 2003), 27.

5. The cotton gin, invented by Eli Whitney, made it possible for a slave to process fifty pounds of cotton per day by removing cotton seeds from the fiber, an increase of fiftyfold. It received a patent on March 14, 1794. See Angela Lakwete, *Inventing the Cotton Gin: Machine and Myth in Antebellum America* (Baltimore: Johns Hopkins University Press, 2003).

6. *Negro Population in the United States, 1790–1915* (New York: Arno Press and the New York Times, 1968), 57.

7. Paul Simon, *Lincoln's Preparation for Greatness: The Illinois Legislative Years* (Urbana: University of Illinois Press, 1971), 128.

8. See David Herbert Donald, *Lincoln* (New York: Simon & Schuster, 1995), 23–24.

9. Allen C. Guelzo, *Abraham Lincoln: Redeemer President* (Grand Rapids, Mich.: William B. Eerdmans, 1999), 29.

10. James C. Klotter, ed., *Our Kentucky: A Study of the Bluegrass State*, 2nd ed. (Lexington: University Press of Kentucky, 2000), 108.

11. T. D. Clark, "Slave Trading between Kentucky and the Cotton Kingdom," *Mississippi Valley Historical Review* 21 (December 1934): 331–42.

12. Douglas L. Wilson and Rodney O. Davis, eds., *Herndon's Informants: Letters, Interviews, and Statements about Abraham Lincoln* (Urbana: University of Illinois Press, 1997), 457. Allen Guelzo finds Hanks's account suspect and argues that Hanks never completed the trip to New Orleans and may have confused this trip with an earlier one in 1828. See Guelzo, *Abraham Lincoln*, 128.

13. Benjamin Quarles, *Lincoln and the Negro* (New York: Oxford University Press, 1962), 18.

14. Michael Burlingame, *The Inner World of Abraham Lincoln* (Urbana: University of Illinois Press, 1994), 22–23.

15. Paul Boller, *Not So! Popular Myths about America from Columbus to Clinton* (New York: Oxford University Press, 1995), 63.

16. See William W. Freehling, *Prelude to Civil War: The Nullification Controversy in South Carolina, 1816–1836* (New York: Harper & Row, 1966).

17. See James Oliver Horton and Lois E. Horton, "A Federal Assault: African Americans and the Impact of the Fugitive Slave Law of 1850," in *Slavery and the Law*, ed. Paul Finkelman (New York: Madison House, 1996).

18. James Oliver Horton and Lois E. Horton, *Black Bostonians: Family Life and Community Struggle in the Antebellum North*, 2nd ed. (New York: Holmes and Meier, 1999), 111–13.

19. See John Chester Miller, *Wolf by the Ears: Thomas Jefferson and Slavery* (New York: Free Press, 1977).

20. See Paul Finkelman, *Defending Slavery: Proslavery Thought in the Old South* (Boston: Bedford/St. Martin's, 2003).

21. Burlingame, *Inner World of Abraham Lincoln*, 33; Lincoln's Speech to 140th Indiana Regiment, March 17, 1865, in *The Collected Works of Abraham Lincoln*, ed. Roy P. Basler, 9 vols. (New Brunswick, N.J.: Rutgers University Press, 1953–55), 8:361.

22. See Anne Farrow, Joel Lang, and Jenifer Frank, *Complicity: How the North Promoted, Prolonged, and Profited from Slavery* (New York: Ballantine Books, 2005).

23. Burlingame, *Inner World of Abraham Lincoln*, 30.

24. Fourth Debate with Stephen A. Douglas at Charleston, Illinois, September 18, 1858, in *Collected Works*, 3:145–46; Harold Holzer, ed., *The Lincoln-Douglas Debates: The First Complete, Unexpurgated Text* (New York: Harper Collins, 1993), 189.

25. Holzer, *Lincoln-Douglas Debates*, 189.

26. Donald, *Lincoln*, 188.

27. Ibid.

28. Lincoln to Joshua F. Speed, August 24, 1855, in *Collected Works*, 2:323.

29. Burlingame, *Inner World of Abraham Lincoln*, 159.

30. Lincoln to Horace Greeley, August 22, 1862, in *Collected Works*, 5:388.

31. See Edward L. Ayers, *In the Presence of Mine Enemies: The Civil War in the Heart of America, 1859–1863* (New York: W. W. Norton, 2003).

32. *Collected Works*, 5:372.

33. See David W. Blight, *Frederick Douglass' Civil War: Keeping Faith in Jubilee* (Baton Rouge: Louisiana State University Press, 1989).

34. Quarles, *Lincoln and the Negro*, 118.

35. *Collected Works*, 8:332–33; James Tackach, *Lincoln's Moral Vision: The Second Inaugural Address* (Jackson: University Press of Mississippi, 2002), 138.

2 Lincoln's Critique of *Dred Scott* as a Vindication of the Founding

Joseph R. Fornieri

The least initial deviation from the truth is multiplied later a thousandfold.—Aristotle

*T*he *Dred Scott* case placed on trial the very moral foundations of the American regime. This pivotal event during the Civil War era compelled a pointed reexamination of the republic's origins and ends. The very soul of the nation was on trial, not to mention the legitimacy of the Republican Party and its core principle: the containment and ultimate extinction of slavery.

The unresolved status of slavery and its incompatibility with a regime dedicated to the principles of liberty and equality had plagued the republic from its founding. Ever since the Constitutional Convention of 1787, the dilemma of slavery had necessitated a series of compromise measures to preserve the Union. Still, the agitation continued. The crisis reached critical mass with the acquisition of new territories after the Mexican War and the repeal of the Missouri Compromise by the Kansas-Nebraska Act of 1854. Should the federal government allow slavery to spread into the territories, or should it contain the institution to the Southern states? The future character and destiny of the Union was at stake.

From the bench, Chief Justice Roger B. Taney sought to resolve definitively the constitutional status of slavery and its relationship to the Union. The essence of Taney's ruling may be summarized by two of his most notorious assertions: the first, that "the right of property in a slave is distinctly and expressly affirmed in the Constitution";[1] and the second, that those of the African race were "so far inferior, that they had no rights which the white man was bound to respect."[2] In brief, Taney ruled that the Constitution enshrined a national right to property in a slave; that it precluded federal restriction of the institution; and that it mandated federal protection of it. His ruling thus divested the entire African race—whether freeborn or not—of both constitutional and inalienable rights. According to historian Don E. Fehrenbacher, the Republican Party clearly recognized the profound implications of *Dred Scott*: "Slavery, previously considered legal only where authorized by positive local law, had been made legal throughout the country, except where forbidden by positive local law. In other words, slavery, once local, was now national; and freedom, once national, was now local."[3]

If Taney was correct, then the founding principles of the American regime pointed not to the aim of human equality but to the affirmation of racial supremacy. It would also follow that Lincoln's antislavery policies were not an extension of these principles but, instead, a radical departure from them—as certain critics (and even some defenders) of his legacy contend.[4] It is worth recalling that during the Civil War era, Northern and Southern disunionists alike concurred with the major premise of *Dred Scott*—namely, that the Constitution was a proslavery document committed to the nationalization of human servitude.

Today, the idea stubbornly persists that Taney was technically correct; that despite our repugnance for the result, he drew the proper conclusion, given the Founders' concessions to slavery in 1787.[5] To be sure, this view is reflected among prominent members of our own ruling and intellectual elite, who invoke Taney's opinion in *Dred Scott* as if it were the authoritative interpretation of the Constitution and the Founders' intent. The following examples reveal the extent to which Taney's opinion has become ingrained. In his "Reflections on the Bicentennial of the Constitution in 1987," Supreme Court Justice Thurgood Marshall cited Taney's opinion to illustrate the poverty of original intent and the subsequent need to remedy it through a "living Constitution."[6] In her remarks to the International Institute for Strategic Studies in London, Condoleeza Rice inadvertently repeated one of the core elements of Taney's decision. "When the Founding Fathers said 'We the People,'" she explained, "they did not mean me."[7] And the scholar Samuel P. Huntington uncritically borrowed from Taney's opinion when he noted that the entire African race, not just slaves, was viewed by the Founders as "'a subordinate and inferior class of beings,' unentitled to 'the rights and liberties of citizens, and hence not part of the 'people of the United States.'"[8] Huntington cited Taney's statement as proof that the Founders, and, indeed, Americans of the mid-nineteenth century, expected "high levels of racial, religious, and ethnic homogeneity" to maintain the republic.[9]

While conceding far too much ground to Taney's opinion, the foregoing nonetheless make valid points that are worth acknowledging. Marshall is correct in emphasizing that praise of the Founders should neither blind us to their limitations nor obscure the contributions of those who actually achieved equal rights during the Civil Rights movement. Rice is correct in pointing out that earlier generations of African Americans were unjustly and shamefully denied the American dream of equal opportunity. Huntington is correct in warning us against the dangers of a pluralism that is divorced from a common national identity. However, by (a) simply conflating Taney's proslavery reading of the Constitution with that of the Founders, and (b) failing to mention Lincoln's critique of this reading, Marshall, Rice, and Huntington have all permitted Taney to have the last word, thereby reinforcing the mistaken impression upon the public mind that his opinion in *Dred Scott* was correct.

Was Taney correct? In view of the Founders' concessions to slavery, did the letter and spirit of America's political institutions commit the federal government to the affirmation, perpetuation, and even the nationalization of human servitude? By invoking *Dred Scott* without challenging its legal reasoning, we blithely permit Taney to have "the last word" on the very essence of our republic and its first principles. Furthermore, it means that we have disregarded Lincoln's sustained critique of the decision and his inclusive reading of the Declaration of Independence, the Founders' intent, and the Constitution.

Lincoln's sustained attack upon *Dred Scott* figures prominently in his major speeches and writings from his first public response to the decision at Springfield on June 26, 1857, to his debates with Douglas in 1858; the "speech that made him president" at Cooper Union in 1860; his First Inaugural Address on March 4, 1861; and his crucial support for the Thirteenth Amendment—the inspiration for this volume.[10]

It is my purpose to present Lincoln's critique of *Dred Scott* as a vindication of the founding principles of the American republic vis-à-vis Taney's proslavery reading of the Constitution. As will be seen, Lincoln's critique of *Dred Scott* involved a point-by-point refutation of three key aspects of Taney's opinion: (1) his denial of Negro citizenship and natural rights; (2) his denial of federal authority to restrict slavery in the territories; and (3) his affirmation of a national right to property in a slave based upon the Fifth Amendment's due process clause.[11]

In addition to these three aspects, Lincoln's critique also exposed the sinister motives behind the decision. This is most evident in his "House divided against itself" speech in which Lincoln named Taney as a co-conspirator in a plot to nationalize slavery. Though the claim was perhaps exaggerated, we do know that President James Buchanan had corresponded with the chief justice about the decision, that he had pressured Justice Grier from his home state of Pennsylvania to go along with it, and that he had prior knowledge of its outcome. In his inaugural address of March 4, 1857, Buchanan alluded to a forthcoming decision by the Supreme Court that would definitively resolve the controversy over slavery. Only two days later, on March 6, *Dred Scott* was decided. This coincidence is highly suspicious. Buchanan almost certainly had foreknowledge of the decision.[12] A fuller treatment of the conspiracy charge, however, is beyond the scope of this essay.

As an experienced lawyer himself, a seasoned veteran of forensic combat, Lincoln was well poised for a constitutional duel with Chief Justice Taney.[13] Bringing to bear the full force of his incisive legal mind, Lincoln dissected each part of Taney's decision in light of the plain language of the Constitution, history, precedent, logic, and the Founders' intent. In sum, Lincoln concluded that *Dred Scott* was based on *"assumed historical facts which were not really true"*[14] (emphasis added). This damning verdict is worth remembering as a remedy for our political and historical amnesia concerning Taney's proslavery *reinterpretation* of the Constitution.

To understand Lincoln's critique of *Dred Scott*, we must first recognize that Taney divested the entire black race of both constitutional and natural (inalienable) rights. That is to say, he first denied that blacks had any legal claim to rights of national citizenship under the Constitution. He then further denied that they had any moral claim as human beings, even in principle, to those inalienable rights enshrined in the Declaration of Independence.

Taney unequivocally and categorically denied American citizenship to the entire black race—regardless of whether they were freeborn or manumitted. His opinion also precluded a foreign, free black person from becoming *a naturalized citizen* of the United States. At best, Taney conceded that, although a person of the African race might be considered narrowly as a citizen of the particular state in which he resided, he was not entitled to American citizenship and the corresponding federal guarantee that "The Citizens of each State shall be entitled to all Privileges and Immunities of Citizens in the several States" (Article IV, Section 2). Thus, insofar as a free black person enjoyed any rights at all, these rights were entirely relative to the discretion of the state in which he resided and were forfeited upon leaving that state's jurisdiction. More specifically, this meant that free blacks venturing outside the boundaries of their free state could be stripped of the few liberties they enjoyed as free citizens within that state. Because they were denied federal protection against those agents of slaveholding states seeking to reclaim them as fugitives, African Americans were vulnerable to being reenslaved.

Rather inconsistent with his usual commitment to the principle of states' rights, Taney rejected the discretionary authority of state governments to confer American citizenship upon blacks. Barring passage of a constitutional amendment, he thus foreclosed any possibility that blacks could be entitled to the corresponding rights and protections guaranteed to American citizens under the federal Constitution.

Indeed, Taney clearly posed the question of black citizenship in these terms: "Does the Constitution of the United States act upon him [the Negro] whenever he shall be made free under the laws of a State, and raised there to the rank of a citizen, and immediately clothe him with all the privileges of a citizen in every other State, and in its own courts?"[15] Answering this question in the negative, he enumerated those privileges and immunities enjoyed by white citizens but denied to blacks:

> More especially, it cannot be believed that the large slaveholding States regarded them [African Americans] as included in the word citizens, or would have consented to a Constitution which might compel them to receive them in that character from another State. For if they were so received, and entitled to the privileges and immunities of citizens, it would exempt them from the operation of the special laws and from the police regulations which they considered to be necessary for their own safety. It would give to persons of the negro race, who were recognized as citizens in any one State of the Union, the right to enter every other State whenever they pleased, singly or in companies, without pass or passport, and without obstruction, to sojourn there as long as they pleased, to go where they pleased at every hour of the day or night without molestation, unless they committed some violation of law for which a white man would be punished; and it would give them the full liberty of speech in public and in private upon all subjects upon which its own citizens might speak; to hold public meetings upon political affairs, and to keep and carry arms wherever they went.[16]

Taney reached this conclusion despite that fact that American citizenship for whites was conferred by birth or residency in a state within the Union. The sum of Taney's opinion in regard to Negro citizenship thus divested all blacks—whether free, enslaved, or manumitted—of federal protection, enshrining racial discrimination as a principle of the Constitution. It bears repeating that, in Taney's judgment, if states did confer personal liberties upon blacks, these liberties extended no further than state boundaries. Furthermore, the logic of *Dred Scott* seemed to eviscerate state laws restricting and interfering with slavery since they would be infringing upon the federal right to property in a slave.[17]

Taney's denial of federal protection to freeborn blacks was itself based upon a novel and contradictory definition of the term *citizenship*—one that equated it with the exercise of sovereign power on the part of a particular group of people and their descendants. More specifically, Taney identified citizenship with those Anglo-Americans at the time of the founding and their descendants who voted and ruled at the time of the Constitutional Convention in 1787. This novel definition made no distinction between free blacks and slaves, even though the Constitution itself distinguished between blacks as "free persons" and "other persons"—the latter term being an oblique reference to slaves. Thus, Taney's definition of citizenship was tailored to exclude free blacks altogether and was synonymous with the narrow class of white, property-owning, male citizens of Anglo-American ancestry who could vote and exercise power in government at the time of the Constitution. Throughout his decision, Taney was at pains to emphasize that "We the People" of the Preamble to the Constitution and "All men are created equal" of the Declaration of Independence did not include blacks. In Taney's mind, the fundamental principles of equal consent and popular sovereignty applied exclusively to the narrow class of white people described above.

In response to this narrow reading of the term, Lincoln repudiated Taney's definition of citizenship as internally contradictory, contrary to precedent, and absurd in its consequences. Throughout his critique, he exposed Taney's definition as a thinly veiled subterfuge, a judicial contrivance, designed to reach the preordained and arbitrary conclusion that blacks were not included as "people" in the Preamble nor as human beings in the Declaration of Independence.

Drawing on historical fact, Lincoln first demonstrated that American citizenship was traditionally associated with free birth or free residency in a state. He then used an internal argument against Taney. If applied consistently, Taney's definition would not only exclude the entire black race from citizenship but also women, children, and propertyless white males as well—a counterfactual conclusion, since even though members of these groups were denied the right to vote, they were nevertheless considered citizens of the United States.

Indeed, in his First Inaugural Address, Lincoln directly challenged Taney's ruling on Negro citizenship by applying the privileges and immunities clause to free blacks. This important detail of the First Inaugural has received scant attention.[18] It suggests that, in bold defiance of *Dred Scott*, Lincoln was willing to extend federal protection to free blacks, thereby refusing to comply with Taney's ruling.

Furthermore, Lincoln showed that Taney's equation of citizenship with the narrow class of Anglo-Americans at the time of the founding and their descendants led to absurd consequences. If applied consistently, Taney's peculiar definition of citizenship would inevitably deny citizenship to those who were the descendants of immigrants—a class of people who neither exercised sovereign power at the time of the founding nor were of Anglo-American ancestry. This was yet another counterfactual conclusion, since those descended from immigrants were always considered American citizens.

But even more devastating to Taney's opinion was the historical fact that some African Americans had indeed exercised sovereign power in Taney's own narrow sense of the term: voting and participating in government at the time of the Constitution. Relying on Justice Benjamin Curtis's dissent in *Dred Scott*, Lincoln revealed that in five states at that time—New Hampshire, Massachusetts, New York, New Jersey, and North Carolina—free blacks enjoyed the right to suffrage and voted in the state ratifying conventions that adopted the Constitution. Thus, by Taney's own novel definition, free blacks had exercised sovereign power and were therefore included under the Preamble's "We the People." As a result, they and their posterity were entitled to bona fide American citizenship.

Taney extended his denial of Negro citizenship in *Dred Scott* to the sweeping rejection of their inalienable rights as well. In his words, blacks "had no rights which the white man was bound to respect." He explained:

> The general words [of the Declaration] would seem to embrace the whole human family. . . . But it is too clear for dispute that the enslaved African race were not intended to be included, and formed no part of the people who framed and adopted this declaration, for if the language, as understood in that day, would embrace them, the conduct of the distinguished men who framed the Declaration of Independence would have been utterly and flagrantly inconsistent with the principles they asserted, and instead of the sympathy of mankind to which they so confidently appealed, they would have deserved and received universal rebuke and reprobation.[19]

Taney would later argue that the above statement was lifted out of context and that it was merely a factual description of public opinion at the time of the founding. However, not only was this statement wrong as to historical fact, it also represented the inescapable conclusion of his train of thought, supported by his own words, as when he said, "In the opinion of the court, the legislation and histories of the times, and the language used in the Declaration of Independence . . . neither . . . slaves, nor their descendants . . . were then acknowledged as part of the people."[20]

Thus, in one broad sweep, Taney consigned the entire African race to an indefinite servile status. Neither the protections of the Constitution nor the rights of the Declaration of Independence applied to them. This feat was accomplished, in part, as we have seen, by conflating the status of three different groups of African Americans: enslaved, freeborn, and manumitted. Taney's denial of inalienable rights to African Americans followed logically from his dehumanization of the entire race. He regarded blacks as "far below [whites] in the scale of created beings" and claimed that a "stigma, of the deepest degradation, was fixed upon the whole race."[21]

By contrast, Lincoln affirmed and defended the common humanity of African Americans, insisting that, as human beings, they were entitled to the inalienable rights of "life, liberty and the pursuit of happiness" asserted in the Declaration of Independence.[22] In his seventh debate with Douglas at Alton, Illinois, on October 15, 1858, Lincoln decried those policies and opinions that paved the way for the dehumanization of the African American: "I *combat it* as having an evil tendency, if not an evil design; I combat it as having a tendency to dehumanize the negro—to take away from him the right of ever striving to be a man. I combat it as being one of the thousand things constantly done in these days to prepare the public mind to make property, and nothing but property, of the *negro in all the States of this Union.*"[23]

While Lincoln conceded that blacks did not enjoy equality with whites at the time of the Declaration of Independence, he further argued that it did not necessarily follow from this point of fact that they were *never* entitled to such rights in principle, or that they could never gain such rights in practice at some future point. Exposing Taney's argument as a non sequitur, Lincoln retorted, "Now this grave argument comes to just nothing at all, by the other fact, that [the Founders] did not at once, *or even afterwards*, actually place all white people on an equality with one or another."[24] How, then, did Lincoln understand the meaning of *equality* in the Declaration?

Lincoln interpreted the Declaration as a normative standard, an aspiration that should guide the regime and that should be approximated as much as possible under the circumstances, even if it could not be fully realized in practice. Lincoln's first official reply to the *Dred Scott* decision on June 26, 1857, was clearly intended as a rebuttal to Taney's view of the Declaration:

> The [Founders] did not mean to assert the obvious untruth, that all were then actually enjoying . . . equality, nor yet, that they were about to confer it immediately upon them. In fact, they had no power to confer such a boon. They meant simply to declare the *right*, so that the *enforcement* of it might follow as fast as circumstances should permit. They meant to set up a standard maxim for free society, which should be familiar to all, and revered by all; constantly looked to, constantly labored for, and even though never perfectly attained, constantly approximated, and thereby constantly spreading and deepening its influence, and augmenting the happiness and value of all life to all people *of all colors* everywhere.[25] (emphasis added)

Here, we have two alternative views of the Declaration of Independence and the founding. Whereas Taney believed that the Declaration applied exclusively to white males, Lincoln viewed it as an inclusive "standard maxim for free society" whose universal principles applied in the abstract to "all people of all colors everywhere." The Declaration, according to Lincoln, articulated the broad goals to which the regime was dedicated; and it provided a yardstick to rule and measure the moral progress or decline of the country.[26] It contained positive injunctions to uphold human dignity and negative prohibitions, or immunities, forbidding the degradation of human beings. It was a moral beacon and a "stumbling block" to those who would turn America back toward the odious path of despotism, whether it took the form of the divine right of kings or slavery, which Lincoln viewed in principle as one and the same.

Lincoln's reading of the Declaration is of enduring significance in revealing the connection between law and morality.[27] Though he did not equate law and morality, he nonetheless maintained that there was a coincidence between the two in fundamental matters relating to human dignity, liberty, and the public good. The most important legal claims necessarily presume moral claims. Throughout his public life, Lincoln measured the legitimacy of human laws and policies in terms of their conformity to the precepts of the natural law promulgated in the Declaration, known by human reason, affirmed by republican tradition, and confirmed by God's revelation in the Bible.[28]

Unlike abolitionist William Lloyd Garrison, who repudiated the Constitution for its concessions to slavery, Lincoln saw the Declaration and the Constitution as complementary charters of freedom. The abstract principles of the Declaration were to be prudently actualized within the concrete legal framework of the Constitution.[29]

Rather than undertaking a refounding of the American regime by superimposing a radical understanding of equality upon the Constitution, as Garry Wills has claimed,[30] Lincoln clearly saw himself as *affirming, defending* and *extending* the Founders' legacy of freedom and equality. He believed that the Declaration "contemplated the progressive improvement in the condition of all men everywhere"[31] and that the Constitution authorized the restriction of slavery in the territories.

Lincoln blamed Taney for propounding a novel view of the Declaration that was incompatible with the Founders' universal intent and America's mission to serve as the standard bearer of democracy to the world. If Taney's view were correct, Lincoln argued, then it followed that the Declaration of Independence was something merely of antiquarian interest, and the Fourth of July did not deserve a sacred place in the hearts of the American people. Prompting his fellow citizens to recall what America ultimately stood for, Lincoln rhetorically drew the logical, if irreverent, conclusion of Taney's argument: "The Declaration is of no practical use now—merely rubbish—old wadding left to rot on the battle-field after the victory is won." It is merely an "interesting memorial of the dead past . . . shorn of its vitality, and practical value; and left without the *germ* or even the *suggestion* of the individual rights of man in it."[32]

Lincoln also challenged Taney's assertion in *Dred Scott* that the public's estimation of the black race had improved since the time of the Founding. On the contrary, he maintained, the public perception of the African race had deteriorated. Plans for the gradual abolition of slavery in the Southern states had been arrested and reversed. Gag rules prevented even the consideration of abolitionist proposals. And some of the strides toward the expansion of black freedom in the Northern states had been reversed as well. New York, for example, had dramatically increased the property qualification for black suffrage; and Illinois had passed a black exclusion law prohibiting free blacks from even entering the state.

Altogether, Lincoln decried the steady debauching of public opinion on slavery since the time of the Founders. A new generation now embraced the institution as a positive good to be extended and perpetuated indefinitely, rather than a necessary evil to be contained and tolerated insofar as its forcible extinction would cause greater evils. Whereas Thomas Jefferson had warned that slavery would bring the wrath of God upon the nation, Senator John Pettit from Indiana now repudiated the declaration that "all men are created equal" as a self-evident lie. Tracing the gradual and steady corruption of the national ethos, Lincoln exclaimed:

> In those days, our Declaration of Independence was held sacred by all, and thought to include all; but now, to aid in making the bondage of the Negro universal and eternal, it is assailed, and sneered at, and construed, and hawked at, and torn, till, if its framers could rise from their graves, they could not at all recognize it. All the powers of the earth seem rapidly combining against [the Negro]. *Mammon* is after him; ambition follows, and *philosophy* follows, and the *Theology* of the day is fast joining the cry.[33] (emphasis added)

The references in the quote manifest Lincoln's scorn for the proslavery philosophy and theology of his time that sanctioned slavery as an institution ordained of God. The fact that human servitude was being preached from Southern pulpits and seminaries made the prospects of peaceful emancipation increasingly dim in comparison to the hopes of previous generations.

In addition to the wholesale denial of black citizenship and inalienable rights, the second element of Taney's opinion rejected the authority of the federal government to restrict slavery in the territories, thereby striking at the core principle of the Republican Party. *Dred Scott*, which declared the Missouri Compromise null and void, was the first exercise of judicial review to strike down an act of Congress since *Marbury v. Madison* in 1803. In effect, Taney's decision prohibited all federal and state interference with slavery while mandating federal protection of it.

In response, Lincoln appealed to Article IV, Section 3 of the Constitution, which grants Congress the "Power to dispose of and make all needful Rules and Regulations respecting the Territory or other Property belonging to the United States." Taney sought to evade this explicit provision through a narrow reading of Article IV that tortured both the letter and spirit of the Constitution. He argued that the clause only referred to territory held by the national government at the time of the Constitution's adoption in 1787; therefore, it had no future applicability to newly acquired territories. This argument, however, defied not only the plain language of the text but also Madison's explication of the territory clause in the *Federalist Papers (#38).*[34] Moreover, it ran counter to John Marshall's precedent in *Canter v. Insurance Company*, which affirmed the authority of the federal government to regulate the territories based on Article IV, Section 3.[35]

Demonstrating his superior command of both history and law, Lincoln cited myriad precedents over seventy years in which the federal government had either restricted or interfered with slavery.[36] Most notably, he pointed to the Northwest Ordinance of 1787 as a compelling precedent of the Founders' intention to prohibit slavery. Indeed, Lincoln regarded the Northwest Ordinance as a kind of blueprint for discerning the Founders' intent: it testified to their clear preference for freedom under ideal circumstances untainted by the actual presence of servitude. In 1784, Jefferson himself had proposed an original version of the ordinance that authorized the ultimate abolition of slavery in these territories. The final version, passed under the Articles of Confederation in 1787 and then reconfirmed by the First Congress under the Constitution, was even more stringent. Article 6 of the ordinance prohibited the very introduction of slavery into the territories, fortuitously ensuring that they would enter the Union as free states.

Lincoln conceded that the Founders had allowed slavery to spread into the Southwest Territories; however, he distinguished this precedent from the Northwest Ordinance by the fact that "it was made a condition by the ceding States that the Federal Government should not prohibit slavery in the ceded country."[37] In other words, the prohibition of a ban on slavery was agreed to as a binding condition *before* the territory was ceded to the federal government. The ban was to remain in effect thereafter. Nonetheless, even in the case of the Southwest, Lincoln demonstrated that while Congress did not ban slavery outright, it did interfere with and regulate it there. For example, it imposed limits on the migration and importation of slaves to and from these same territories.

Lincoln then cited congressional actions in regard to the Mississippi Territory in 1798, the Territorial Act of 1804 (dealing with the Louisiana Purchase), and the Missouri Compromise of 1820 as further examples of federal interference with slavery. But did these precedents accord with the Founders' intent, or were they arbitrary exercises of power warranting judicial condemnation?

At Cooper Union in 1860, Lincoln provided a magisterial exposition of the Founders' intent to restrict slavery in the territories and to place it on a path of ultimate extinction.[38] After identifying the thirty-nine signers of the Constitution as the Founders, Lincoln then cross-examined them on the question of slavery's extension. As historian Harold Holzer has shown, Lincoln devoted several months to poring over all the relevant law and history books that he could lay his hands on to ascertain the voting records and opinions of the Founders. He revealed that of the thirty-nine men who signed the Constitution, twenty-three left a clear voting record on the subject. Of these, twenty-one voted in favor of restriction. And of the remaining sixteen who left no explicit voting record, fifteen were known to have clear antislavery convictions on the subject—among them some of the most renowned antislavery figures, including Gouverneur Morris, Alexander Hamilton, and Benjamin Franklin. Thus, as Holzer has shown, Lincoln's cross-examination of the Founders' intent to restrict slavery culminated with the final tally: "thirty-six to three."[39]

To provide final validation, Lincoln appealed to the most revered figure among the Founders: George Washington. Replying to the charge of radicalism against the Republican Party, Lincoln reminded his opponents that Washington both "approved and signed" the Northwest Ordinance. Further appealing to Washington's testimony, he noted that the Founding Father "wrote to Lafayette that he considered the prohibition [of slavery] a wise measure, expressing in the same connection his hope that we should at some time have a confederacy of free States."[40]

The final aspect of Taney's opinion, while perhaps the most egregious in doing violence to the plain language of the Constitution, is also the one that is most commonly perceived to be true—namely, that "the right of property in a slave is distinctly and expressly affirmed in the Constitution." This erroneous conclusion is reached through the following train of thought: because the Founders made concessions to slavery in the Constitution, it follows that they expressly affirmed a federal right to property in a slave.

Assuming the validity of Taney's argument, Lincoln first established that the chief justice did not merely claim that the right to property in a slave was implied in the Constitution but emphatically asserted that it was distinctly and expressly affirmed by the Constitution. After establishing the saliency of this fact, Lincoln then analyzed the three provisions of the Constitution dealing with slavery—Article I, Section 2, counting slaves toward representation; Article I, Section 9, regulating the foreign slave trade; and Article IV, Section 2, mandating the return of fugitives. Lincoln then pointed out: the words *slave* or *slavery* are nowhere to be found in the Constitution; the word *property* is never mentioned in connection to slaves or slavery; and the document never makes any reference to *race* or *color*. In fact, blacks are referred to as "persons," not property. Lincoln thus accused Taney of doing violence to the plain language of the text:

> An inspection of the Constitution will show that the right of property in a slave is not "*distinctly* and *expressly* affirmed" in it. Bear in mind the Judges [in *Dred Scott*] do not pledge their judicial opinion that such right is *impliedly* affirmed in the Constitution; but they pledge their veracity that it is "*distinctly* and *expressly*" affirmed there—"distinctly," that is, not mingled with anything else—"expressly," that is, in words meaning just that, without the aid of any inference, and susceptible of no other meaning.[41]

Indeed, three years prior to *Dred Scott*, in his 1854 Peoria address, Lincoln had argued that the Founders deliberately avoided using the words *slave* or *slavery* because they did not wish to saddle posterity with the kind of Constitution that Taney envisioned. At Peoria, Lincoln metaphorically described slavery as a "cancer" or a "wen" that a patient shamefully conceals, but which he dares not cut out at once lest he bleed to death. This, according to Lincoln, was the situation of the Founders. They had inherited the cancer of slavery and could not get rid of it without causing a greater evil—the dissolution of the American republic and the end of the great experiment in self-government. Slavery was thus tolerated as a necessary evil that constrained the possibilities of the founding generation. The concessions to slavery in the Constitution were therefore concessions to state authority under the federal system. According to Lincoln, the lengths to which the Founders went to avoid using either *slave* or *slavery* in the document implicitly conveyed their view of the moral dubiousness of the institution and their reticence to affirm it as a national right.

In sum, the Founders' deliberate refusal to use these words in the Constitution pointed to the hope that one day the institution would be placed on a path of ultimate extinction; that the Constitution and the nation would one day outlive the anachronism of human servitude. Lincoln maintained that an inspection of the Constitution not only failed to affirm a distinct and express right to property in a slave, as Taney contended, but also implied a moral stance against slavery in the oblique language used by the Founders to conceal the institution. In terms that are both clear and profound, Harry V. Jaffa explains that "The American Founding, in its principles, was antiracist to the core. But the antiracism of the Constitution—and its original intent—can only be understood if one distinguishes the principles of the Constitution from the compromises of that Constitution."

On what basis, then, did Taney derive a fictitious right to property in a slave? In manufacturing such a right, Taney was the first judge in American history to make use of the controversial legal doctrine of *substantive due process*. This doctrine, which still haunts us today, maintains that the word *liberty* in the due process clause of the Fifth and Fourteenth Amendments entails substantive requirements of freedom that are not found in the actual text of the Constitution itself, in contrast to those procedural requirements that are found in the document. It then falls upon the Court to decide what these substantive requirements are.

In *Dred Scott*, writes constitutional scholar Robert Bork, "[t]he substance that Taney poured into the [Fifth Amendment's due process] clause was that Congress cannot prevent slavery in a territory because a man must be allowed to bring slaves there."[42] Lincoln was astute enough to recognize the implication of Taney's maneuver. Exposing the underlying rationale of the right to property in a slave, Lincoln noted, "The Supreme Court . . . plant themselves upon the Fifth Amendment, which provides that no person shall be deprived of 'life, liberty, or property without due process of law.'"[43]

Taney's substantive interpretation of the due process clause was discredited further by the Founders' actions in banning slavery from the Northwest Territories: How could they, Lincoln asked, have affirmed a national right to property in a slave and at the same time denied this same right to the only territories then under their control?

Contrary to Taney's assertion that the right to property in a slave was expressly and distinctly found in the Constitution, Lincoln cited James Madison at the convention in 1787, who "thought it wrong to admit in the Constitution the idea that there could be property in men."[44] Lincoln further buttressed his case against a national right to slavery by appealing to the testimony of several other Founders at the convention who condemned slavery in principle.[45] For example, William Patterson of New Jersey observed that the Founders "had been ashamed to use the term 'slaves' & had substituted a different description" when framing the Articles of Confederation.[46] Roger Sherman of Connecticut "was against . . . acknowledging men to be property, by taxing them as such under the character of slaves."[47] Gouverneur Morris of Pennsylvania characterized slavery as "a nefarious institution. . . . the curse of heaven on the States where it prevailed."[48] Luther Martin of Maryland regarded slavery as "inconsistent with the principles of the revolution and dishonorable to the American character to have such a feature in the Constitution."[49] And George Mason, author of the Virginia Declaration of Rights, forthrightly proclaimed that "Every master of slaves is born a petty tyrant. They bring the judgment of heaven on a Country."[50]

If treated as an authoritative precedent, Lincoln contended, Taney's opinion in *Dred Scott* would lead to the imposition of a permanent and inflexible racial categorization that is nowhere to be found in the text of the Constitution.

Lincoln believed that this clearly portended the nationalization of slavery, and he ominously warned of a forthcoming decision that would extend the precedent, thereby prohibiting free states from interfering with the transportation and even permanent residence (or domicile) of slaves within their borders.

Far from quieting sectional discord, *Dred Scott* had the unintended consequence of escalating it. It may be argued that the decision hastened disunion by giving credence to the South's claim of a constitutional right to extend slavery. This meant that the South could now claim, with the blessing of the Supreme Court, that Northern opposition to the extension of slavery was a flagrant violation of the rule of law, thereby leaving them with secession as the only recourse to preserve their liberty.

As a vindication of the founding principles of the American regime, Lincoln's critique of *Dred Scott* provides a concrete example of how future leaders may respond to the raw exercise of judicial power unhinged from natural and constitutional law. In an era that has become accustomed to legislating from the bench, Lincoln's critique of *Dred Scott* may inspire contemporary leaders to challenge the Court on its own terms. This, however, would require a democratic statesmanship that both educates and elevates the public. Let us hope that in confronting new challenges to the republic, our future leaders will look to Abraham Lincoln, not Roger B. Taney, as the best expositor of our founding principles and Constitution. It is therefore fitting to conclude this essay by giving Lincoln the last word, rather than Taney: "[I]f the policy of the government, upon vital questions, affecting the whole people, is to be irrevocably fixed by decisions of the Supreme Court, the instant they are made . . . the people will have ceased, to be their own rulers, having, to that extent, practically resigned their government, into the hands of that eminent tribunal."[51]

Notes

1. *Scott v. Sanford*, 60 U.S. 393 (1857), 393–425. For the opinion, see http://supct.law.cornell.edu/supct/html/historics/USSC_CR_0060_0393_ZO.html.

2. *Scott v. Sanford*, 400–454.

3. Don E. Fehrenbacher, *The Dred Scott Case: Its Significance in American Law and Politics* (New York: Oxford University Press, 1978), 437.

4. Garry Wills, *Lincoln at Gettysburg: The Words That Remade America* (New York: Simon & Schuster, 1992), 38. For an overview of the debate over Lincoln's political legacy, see Kenneth L. Deutsch and Joseph R. Fornieri, *Lincoln's American Dream: Clashing Political Perspectives* (Washington, D.C.: Potomac Books, 2005), 4–12.

5. On the Founders' concessions to slavery, see George Anastaplo, "Slavery and the Constitution: Explorations," *Texas Tech Law Review* 20 (1989): 677–786.

6. Remarks of Thurgood Marshall at the Annual Seminar of the San Francisco Patent and Trademark Law Association, Maui, Hawaii, May 6, 1987.

7. Remarks of Condoleeza Rice at the International Institute for Strategic Studies. London, June 26, 2003. See http://www.whitehouse.gov/news/releases/2003/06/20030626.

To her credit and as a testament to her intellectual integrity, it should be noted that Rice subsequently emended and clarified her statement.

8. Samuel P. Huntington, *Who Are We: The Challenges to America's National Identity* (New York: Simon & Schuster, 2004), 55.

9. Ibid., 54.

10. *The Collected Works of Abraham Lincoln*, ed. Roy P. Basler, 9 vols. (New Brunswick, N.J.: Rutgers University Press, 1953–55), 2:387–88, 400–409, 462–67, 494–502, 539–41, 545–47; 3:21–24, 27–30, 47–48, 89–90, 230–33, 250–51, 277–79, 282–83, 298–300, 315–18, 404–5, 423–26, 449–50, 543–46.

11. In his Pulitzer Prize–winning book, *The Dred Scott Case*, Fehrenbacher provides an in-depth analysis of each aspect of Taney's decision.

12. Fehrenbacher, *Dred Scott Case,* 311–13.

13. Frank J. Williams, *Judging Lincoln* (Carbondale: Southern Illinois University Press, 2003), 34–59. Williams describes how Lincoln masterfully combined the dual roles of politician and lawyer.

14. *Collected Works*, 2:404.

15. *Scott v. Sanford*, 4.

16. Ibid., 9.

17. The pending case was *Lemmon v. the People*. See Fehrenbacher, *Dred Scott Case*, 60–61, 444–45, 692.

18. I have attempted to remedy this gap by tracing the development of Lincoln's defense of black citizenship from his first critique of *Dred Scott* in Springfield on June 26, 1857, to the Emancipation Proclamation in 1863. See Joseph R. Fornieri, "Lincoln on Negro Citizenship," *Lincoln Lore*, no. 1885 (Summer 2006). Harry V. Jaffa and Herman Belz have both recognized the import of Lincoln's suggestion in his First Inaugural Address that the privileges and immunities clause applied to African Americans. See Harry V. Jaffa, *A New Birth of Freedom and the Coming of the Civil War* (Lanham: Rowman and Littlefield, 2000), 266–67; and Herman Belz, "Lincoln's Construction of the Executive Power in the Secession Crisis," *Journal of the Abraham Lincoln Association* 27 (Winter 2006): 34–35.

19. *Scott v. Sanford*, 5.

20. Ibid., 6.

21. Ibid.

22. See William Lee Miller, *Lincoln's Virtues: An Ethical Biography* (New York: Alfred A. Knopf, 2002), 340–74.

23. *Collected Works*, 3:304.

24. Ibid., 2:406.

25. Ibid., 2:407.

26. Harry V. Jaffa, *Crisis of the House Divided, An Interpretation of the Lincoln-Douglas Debates* (Garden City, N.Y.: Doubleday, 1959), 370–83; Joseph R. Fornieri, "Lincoln's View of Equality in the Declaration," in *Abraham Lincoln: Sources and Style of Leadership*, ed. Frank J. Williams and William Pederson (Westport, Conn.: Greenwood, 1994), 45–69.

27. Joseph R. Fornieri, *Abraham Lincoln's Political Faith* (DeKalb: Northern Illinois University Press, 2005), 104–32.

28. Ibid. In "The False Prophets of American Conservatism," Jaffa characterizes the "laws of nature and nature's God" in the Declaration as "a distillation of a tradition of more than two thousand years. They—and the American Founding generally—represent the culmination of the attempt by Socrates, described by Cicero, to bring philosophy down from the heavens. They also represent the agreement of reason and revelation—of

Athens and Jerusalem—on the moral ground of human government" (www.claremont. org/writings/980212jaffa.html [posted February 12, 1998]).

29. Allen C. Guelzo, *Lincoln's Emancipation Proclamation: The End of Slavery In America* (New York: Simon and Schuster, 2004), 157–81; Joseph R. Fornieri, "Lincoln and the Emancipation Proclamation: A Model of Prudent Leadership," in *Tempered Strength: Studies in the Nature and Scope of Prudential Leadership,* ed. Ethan Fishman (Lanham: Rowman and Littlefield, 2002), 125–49; Ethan Fishman, "Under the Circumstances: Abraham Lincoln and Classical Prudence," in Williams and Pederson, *Abraham Lincoln,* 3–15; Ethan Fishman, "On Professor Donald's Lincoln," in Deutsch and Fornieri,

30. *Lincoln's American Dream,* 232–42. Wills, *Lincoln at Gettysburg,* 38. For a more extensive discussion of this controversy, see Deutsch and Fornieri, *Lincoln's American Dream,* chapter 1.

31. *Collected Works,* 2:408.

32. Ibid.

33. Ibid., 2:405.

34. Paper no. 38 in Alexander Hamilton, James Madison, and John Jay, *The Federalist Papers,* ed. Clinton Rossiter, with a new introduction and notes by Charles R. Kesler (New York: Mentor Books, 1999), 206–8; Fehrenbacher, *Dred Scott Case,* 82.

35. Fehrenbacher, *Dred Scott Case,* 144, 372–73.

36. Speech at Peoria, October 16, 1854, in *Collected Works* 2:247–83; speech at Springfield, Illinois, June 26, 1857, ibid., 2:399–410; address at Cooper Union, February 27, 1860, ibid., 3:522–50. See also Harold Holzer, *Lincoln at Cooper Union: The Speech That Made Abraham Lincoln President* (New York: Simon and Schuster, 2004).

37. *Collected Works,* 3:529.

38. Holzer, *Lincoln at Cooper Union,* 119–31.

39. Ibid., 128.

40. *Collected Works,* 3:538.

41. Ibid., 3:545–46.

42. Robert H. Bork, *The Tempting of America: The Political Seduction of the Law* (New York: Free Press, 1990), 31.

43. *Collected Works,* 3:534.

44. James Madison, *Notes of the Debates in the Federal Convention of 1787* (New York: Norton, 1987), 532.

45. *Collected Works,* 3:522–50; Holzer, *Lincoln at Cooper Union,* 119–48.

46. Madison, *Notes of the Debates,* 259.

47. Ibid., 532.

48. Ibid., 431.

49. Ibid., 502.

50. Ibid., 504.

51. *Collected Works,* 4:268.

3 Lincoln and the Limits of Constitutional Authority

Phillip Shaw Paludan

braham Lincoln was a lawyer. He practiced law longer than he did anything else in his fifty-six years of life. Furthermore, the law was not just his profession. It was the means for his escape from rural poverty, his climb to social respectability, and the creation of his identity. In the legal profession, Lincoln found acceptance, friendship, and affirmation of his abilities. Certainly, politics was a career he enjoyed, but by the time of Lincoln's maturity, politics and lawyering were intimately connected. Lawyers dominated the legislative halls of states and of the nation, and politics was consistently about constitutional and legal questions. Lincoln easily combined politics and law.

It is also highly likely that Lincoln's personal psychological needs were satisfied by practicing law. The profession provided a sense of order and discipline in his changing world. When Lincoln was a teenager, one of his friends, Matthew Gentry, went insane. Lincoln was so haunted by that experience that twenty-one years later he wrote a poem describing Gentry's insanity and claiming that madness was worse than death.[1] Lincoln also worked to bring order to his thinking by reading the books of Euclid on geometry.

Lincoln's first major speeches extolled the virtues of law and order and the Constitution in a rapidly changing society. His 1838 address to the Young Men's Lyceum of Springfield, Illinois, told the story of the founding generation no longer able to guide the country. The nation needed guidance as the excesses of Jacksonian democracy, often equated with mob rule, showed themselves. With the Founders gone, Lincoln insisted, preserving the institutions that they had established, the Constitution and the rule of law, were imperative if the nation was to survive. "Let reverence for the laws, be breathed by every American mother, to the lisping babe, that prattles on her lap. . . . Let it become the political religion of the nation and let the old and the young, the rich and the poor, the grave and the gay of all tongues and colors and conditions sacrifice unceasingly upon its altars."[2]

Lincoln spoke in tune with the nation that he would one day lead. While the Whig Party spoke more often of order, Democrats, too, promised that they would bring stability by restoring the purer world of the Founders. Most of this discussion centered on interpreting the meaning of the Constitution.

Constitutional discussion permeated the United States. Alexis de Tocqueville noted that every question facing the country ultimately became a constitutional question. The nation's history demonstrated the fact. The American Revolution was in large part a struggle over the meaning of the English constitution. Alexander Hamilton and Thomas Jefferson claimed that the Constitution blessed their diverse positions. New Englanders challenged Jefferson's embargo in the name of the Constitution. Northern and Southern congressmen debated the meaning of union under the Constitution. And, of course, the slavery debate, which permeated the polity from 1820 to the Civil War, was about the meaning of national power and local rights in the territories, among other things. Lincoln and Stephen A. Douglas debated that issue memorably.

Almost all of this latter debate rested on the fundamental question of the extent to which the Constitution was a proslavery document. White Southerners almost unanimously insisted that it was. Most abolitionists agreed with them, echoing William Lloyd Garrison, who called the Constitution a "covenant with death and an agreement with hell."[3] Only a few of the abolitionist band argued that the Constitution opposed slavery; after all, the Fifth Amendment did hold that property could not be taken without compensation, and if slaves were property . . . Besides, the word *slavery* never appears anywhere in the document.

Of course, at its root, slavery was more than a constitutional question. The white South remembered the slave rebellion led by Nat Turner (1830–31) and its fifty-five white casualties, most of them women and children. And throughout the region, the terror lingered that blacks might remember him, too. The Southern commitment to state sovereignty was not abstract; it dripped with blood.

The more moderate majority of Americans recognized that the Constitution did provide protections for slavery: its three-fifths clause gave extra congressmen to slave states; its fugitive slave clause stopped free states from freeing runaways; and it forbade Congress from outlawing the international slave trade before 1808. Most fundamentally, the Constitution, in establishing a federal union, gave the states full authority to determine whether there would be slavery within their borders.

This respect for states' authority was not only a Southern crop. Northerners sowed it, too. It rested in large measure on the powerful respect for local
self-government within the country. The United States was a nation of small
communities. As late as 1860, 80 percent of the population lived in places with
fewer than twenty-five hundred inhabitants. Within these communities, citizens
acted as jurors and filled other local government positions. If necessary, their
posses upheld local law and custom. They rotated offices frequently so every
man (almost always men), except the village idiot (and there was some dispute
here), was in some very personal way the government itself. Voting habits further
reinforced this self-governing concept. Voter turnout might reach as high as 90
percent. The elections of 1860 and 1864 saw voter turnout hit 80 percent and
above. American government was self-government at a very deep level.[4]

Lincoln recognized how the deeply admired Constitution protected slavery,
a system that personally he despised. He wrote to his friend Joshua Speed, "I
. . . acknowledge your rights and my obligations under the Constitution. [But]
in regard to your slaves . . . you ought . . . to appreciate how much the great
body of the Northern people do crucify their feelings in order to maintain their
loyalty to the Constitution and the union."[5] But loyalty to the Constitution
might cut both ways. If the "great body" tolerated slavery out of respect for the
Constitution, their tolerance might weaken should slavery somehow threaten
the Constitution. On several levels, this is exactly what happened in the prewar
years, and it would set the stage for the Civil War constitutional debate.

First of all, Southern defenses of slavery in terms of the Constitution began
to threaten the union that the Constitution had created. John C. Calhoun
was only the most notable of white Southern thinkers who argued that states
were sovereign, the final authorities on the meaning of the Constitution, and
that they could nullify federal laws and, if necessary, leave the union with the
blessings of the Constitution itself. Countless times in the antebellum years,
Southern leaders threatened the union. Their threats not only persuaded many
that slavery endangered the Constitution but also inspired constitutional argument that spoke of national power connecting liberty and unity.

Defenses of slavery also threatened civil liberties in the North and the South.
Of course, the slaves had no rights, but even white Southerners who spoke
out too vigorously against slavery were shunned and threatened. People who
could tolerate the attacks on civil liberties in the South became disturbed when
the North also came under fire. Abolitionist speakers were silenced by pro-
Southern mobs as far north as Utica, New York, and Boston, Massachusetts.
An abolitionist editor, Elijah Lovejoy, was killed by a mob in Alton, Illinois.
United States Senator Charles Sumner was beaten almost to death on the floor
of the Senate for making an antislavery speech. Territorial elections in Kansas
resulted in a civil war between pro- and antislavery settlers.

Then national institutions seemed to be corrupted by slavery. In 1850, Congress passed the Fugitive Slave Law, which allowed federal officials to break into the homes of Northern citizens in search of escaping slaves. "A filthy enactment," Ralph Waldo Emerson said. "I will not obey it!"[6] The presidency itself seemed implicated when Presidents Pierce and Buchanan both supported the proslavery legislature in Kansas Territory, despite antislavery majorities there. Then, in 1857, the Supreme Court of the United States showed how far slavery's evil influence had reached. Overturning a law of Congress for the first time in fifty-four years, the Court in *Dred Scott v. Sanford* ruled that Congress could not outlaw slavery in the territories and that black Americans were not, and could never be, citizens of the United States. These events exposed slavery's danger to the Constitution's concept of union and many of the liberties it protected. Opponents helped to crystallize the antislavery argument by offering rebuttals and by demonstrating the self-serving vision of Southern constitutionalism. Make no mistake, however: this prewar argument did not discredit the idea that states controlled slavery. Americans everywhere remained devoted to the Constitution and its federal union. But now they were less willing to accept the idea that slavery had to be protected in all circumstances; the seeds of more flexible constitutional concepts were being planted.

But when war broke out, traditional constitutional ideas held sway. They did so because the only legal justification that the Union had for challenging secession was dependent upon the Constitution. That document established that the only way of changing governments in the United States was through the electoral process. But the Confederacy defied the election results. The Constitution established federal powers in Article I, Section 8, that could be exercised within the states. But the rebels closed their borders to such laws, calling them invasions. They set up their own constitution and defied the Republican government to challenge their new nation. Lincoln replied that nothing in the Constitution allowed states individually or collectively to leave the Union. Secession was anarchy. Rallying the North, Lincoln emphasized these constitutional violations; by doing so, he helped establish a constitutional yardstick for the conflict.

Conservative opponents demanded that Lincoln be judged by that same yardstick. The case of John Merryman in Maryland provided an early test of the president's authority. Lincoln had suspended the privilege of the writ of habeas corpus in the area between Washington and Philadelphia. The suspension allowed military authorities to capture and hold suspected rebels and prevented judges from issuing writs to inquire into the legality of these arrests.

But one judge tried: Roger B. Taney, chief justice of the Supreme Court, issued a writ of habeas corpus to the commander of the military prison demanding that Merryman be released so that Taney could rule on the legality of his capture. When the commander refused and cited Lincoln's order, Taney attacked the president as a lawbreaker. Presidents, he argued, were not above the law, and Lincoln had defied the law by suspending the privilege of the writ, which the Constitution gave Congress alone the power to do; Lincoln was acting outside his constitutional authority. Taney's argument rested on the fact that the suspension of the writ is discussed in the so-called congressional article of the Constitution.

But Lincoln argued for a bit more flexibility, stretching the yardstick a bit. Yes, the suspension is discussed in Article I, he conceded, but the Constitution did not clearly give the power to Congress. What it said was, "The Privilege of the Writ of Habeas Corpus shall not be suspended, unless in Cases of Invasion or Rebellion the public Safety may require it" (Art. 1, Sec. 9). Congress was not in session when the rebellion began, Lincoln argued; he, the president, had had to act before the rebels took advantage of the situation. If that happened, several laws would have been broken and the Union itself imperiled. Lincoln asked, "Are all the laws, but one, to go unexecuted, and the government itself go to pieces, lest that one be violated?"[7] He insisted that he had not violated the Constitution, and he made a constitutional argument in doing so. Lincoln accepted the idea that debate over war powers and the goals of the war would be a constitutional one and that he would be restrained by the Constitution. But, as would often be the case throughout the war, Lincoln found it possible to do what he wanted, and to do it with the Constitution's blessing. He would show that he was bound by the Constitution but not strangled by it.

At times, in fact, he sounded as though he would not be restrained at all. Speaking of Midwestern Democrats, Lincoln said, "The man who stands by and says nothing, when the peril of his government is discussed, can not be misunderstood. If not hindered, he is sure to help the enemy."[8] But Lincoln was barking, not biting. No one was arrested for remaining silent. A few newspapers were closed, a few speakers went to military jails, and most of these were tried by military commission and not by civil courts. Several thousand people fell under military control, but these were overwhelmingly people near the scene of battle who tried to cross Union lines, who cheated Union army supply sergeants, or who were simply there in occupied territories as the army advanced.[9] Most of the people who were deprived of their liberties received a trial, one in which military rules were followed, but a trial nonetheless. Of course, legal rights were not always obeyed. Occasionally, in the early days of the war, a newspaper might be closed and an editor jailed, and then, after a time determined by Secretary of State William H. Seward, who supervised loyalty questions, the editor would be released. No trials interfered with these security sweeps. This was done to intimidate opposition newspapers, and it usually worked, at least for a while. But as the war went on, legal proceedings replaced executive whims. Thousands of newspapers, at the top of their voices, spoke their minds, pro and con.

The staple of Democratic opposition was constantly to charge Lincoln with being a dictator. But the charge was excessive. Despite the few arrests, Democrats gave hundreds, perhaps thousands, of speeches calling Lincoln a dictator, a bloodthirsty, insane gorilla, a man better off dead—all without noting the irony in their exercise of free speech. And most significantly, the electoral process went on throughout the war. No county, state, and, especially, no national election was put off for the duration. The Republican "dictator-ship" was vulnerable to removal every time ballots were cast. Democrats won seats in the 1862 election, but the majority of the Northern population ap-proved of Lincoln's "reign." Apparently, they believed in his commitment to the Constitution.

Lincoln was also given latitude by the United States Supreme Court. After the Merryman episode, the justices stayed out of Lincoln's way. Taney disap-proved of practically everything Lincoln did. But his disapproval appeared in dissents. Court majorities stayed on Lincoln's side. In the *Prize* cases, the justices approved warlike actions taken by the president before Congress had formally declared war. In *ex parte Vallandigham*, the Court refused to intervene in the actions of military commissions, even those behind the lines.

Congress also supported the exercise of Lincoln's authority. In March of 1863, it passed a law endorsing Lincoln's activities in the early days of the con-flict. Members clashed with him on the question of how the states should be reconstructed and how fast emancipation should proceed. But the legislative and executive branches of government were in sufficient harmony that, during his presidency, Lincoln vetoed only two minor acts and pocket vetoed two others. Lincoln had few limits on his constitutional authority so far as Con-gress and the Court were concerned. Apparently, his eloquence and behavior persuaded them and the non-Democratic Northern majority that he respected the document and the institutions they were engaged in war to save.

But this relative harmony broke down when the question of slavery in the states was raised. Overwhelming majorities believed that states should control their own domestic institutions. But did the rebellious states continue to have the Constitution's protection? They claimed to have left the Union, antislav-ery leaders said; why not take them at their word? Furthermore, government power expanded during time of war; surely that power was broad enough to liberate a black population whose work assisted the Confederacy. General Benjamin Butler, commanding near Fortress Monroe, hit upon an ingenious constitutional weapon. As slaves ran away from their Southern masters and into Butler's lines, he began calling them "contraband" of war. As such, they could be confiscated like other forms of property, such as lands and factories.

Congressmen were attracted by Butler's device but wanted to mold it closer to constitutional requirements. On August 6, 1861, Congress passed what is now known as the First Confiscation Act. It declared that slaves used to advance the rebellion could be confiscated. But the act still allowed loyal masters to reclaim runaway slaves. Why this distinction? First of all, congressmen thought border state loyalties were still in question, and they feared alienating potential allies. The goal of restoring the Union, the Union that still allowed slavery, remained in sight. The act punished those clearly making war against the nation but was meant to appeal to loyal Southerners (no one knew how large a group that was) with the promise of being allowed to keep their slaves if they abandoned the Confederacy. Lincoln signed the First Confiscation Act.

This signature showed a willingness to stay as close to constitutional boundaries as possible. The Union remained the home of slaves as well as free men and women. But more than constitutional commitment was on display here. War strategy required that a narrow path be taken. "I think to lose Kentucky is nearly the same as to lose the whole game. Kentucky gone, we can not hold Missouri, nor, as I think, Maryland. These all against us, and the job on our hands is too large for us."[10]

The Bluegrass State sat strategically between the old Northwest and the heart of the Confederacy. Kentucky also had thousands of potential Union soldiers and resources to supply them. It could influence events in the other border states. Lincoln and many other Republicans believed that there were loyal Unionists behind Confederate lines. Moreover, the influence of the border states was not confined to state boundaries. The southern half of the states of Ohio, Indiana, and Illinois had been settled from the South. Hundreds of thousands of people had followed the same path that the Lincolns had taken out of Kentucky into central Illinois. Indeed, Springfield, Illinois, was frequently called "Old Kentuck." Influenced by their familiarity with slavery, people of this region believed strongly in states' rights. In fact, the state motto of Illinois praised both state sovereignty and national union.

As the war unfolded, the president faced pressure from antislavery forces to attack slavery. Frederick Douglass envisioned a war "in which not a slave would be left a slave in the returning footprints of the American army going to put down the slave holding rebellion. Sound policy not less than humanity demands the instant liberation of every slave in the rebel states. We are striking the guilty rebels with our soft white hand when we should be striking with the iron hand of the black man," he added.[11] Other Radical Republicans pointed out that it was slavery that caused the war, reinforced the Southern economic system, and allowed more white Confederates to be on the battle line. Union soldiers advancing southward finally saw, many for the first time, what slavery was like and turned against it. General John C. Frémont, commanding in

Missouri, freed all the slaves there. A few months, later General David Hunter in South Carolina freed the slaves in the Sea Islands. Radical Republicans rejoiced. Even some conservative Democrats were coming to see the benefits to them of freeing black men to fight for the Union. One of them wrote a song that said he would be ready to let "Sambo be killed in place of meself on any day of the year."[12]

But Lincoln knew that Kentucky, with its states' rights traditions, would find emancipation intolerable. Kentucky friends wrote that ten thousand soldiers might switch their loyalties. Lincoln heeded the warning and revoked the liberation that these generals had granted. The antislavery forces, in turn, attacked the president. Moncure Conway said, "We don't have a president of the United States[;] we have a president of Kentucky."[13] But Lincoln was unmoved. He knew the importance of Kentucky and its constitutional standpoint. He also knew that many in the North had similar views, and that included much of the army. Union generals like George McClellan ordered their troops to return runaway slaves to loyal masters. Echoing the sentiment, after the first battle of Bull Run, Congress passed the Crittenden-Johnson resolutions, promising that the war was not being fought "for any purpose of conquest, or subjugation, nor purpose of overthrowing or interfering with the right or established institutions of those [Confederate] states."[14]

But that sentiment began quickly to fade. When the war had been projected as a ninety-day romp, it was easy to imagine the Union and the Constitution unchanged. But as the casualties mounted, hostility grew toward Southern culture as well as rebel soldiers. As lives were lost and the Confederates fielded larger armies, belief in hidden loyalty to the Union in Dixie was harder to sustain. And when Union armies occupied much of Kentucky, that state's allegiance to the Confederacy was more problematic.

And yet, when Lincoln turned to the emancipation question, what is remarkable is that he showed considerable tenderness about invalidating states' rights. Throughout the first half of 1862, Lincoln tried to persuade the border states to free their slaves. In March, May, and July, the president used all his powers of eloquence to persuade these states that by freeing their slaves they would substantially end the rebellion. His rhetoric was passionate: "I do not argue. I beseech you to make the arguments for yourselves. You can not if you would, be blind to the signs of the times. I beg of you a calm and enlarged consideration of them, ranging, if it may be, far above personal and partizan politics. . . . So much good has not been done, by one effort, in all past time, as, in the providence of God is now your high privilege to do. May the vast future not have to lament that you have neglected it."[15]

But all three times, Maryland, Delaware, Kentucky, and Missouri rejected Lincoln's request. Their states' rights allegiances were too strong. Lincoln accepted their decision, for he knew the power of those sentiments. He also recognized another fundamental fact: all these states were still within the Union. And the Constitution allowed states within the Union to make their own decisions about slavery. He respected that Constitution.

But as the war continued, efforts for emancipation accelerated. In mid-July 1862, Congress passed the Second Confiscation Act. This act dropped the limitation in the First Confiscation Act that only property used to help the rebellion could be seized. Now the slaves of all rebel masters would be set free. But the enforcement of the act showed how bound to constitutional process the lawyers in Congress were. In order to determine who were rebel masters, individual trials would have to be held, tens of thousands of them. Emancipation under this law would have made glaciers seem speedy. More effective was legislation that outlawed slavery in the territories and forbade soldiers to return runaway slaves to their masters. Still, these laws merely nibbled around the edges of the peculiar institution. Lincoln was ready to make a full attack wherever the Constitution allowed.

Days after Congress had passed the Second Confiscation Act, Lincoln decided that he would free the slaves held in Confederate territory. He told his cabinet he was ready to act. But Secretary of State William H. Seward raised a powerful objection: the Union had been losing battles recently; to announce emancipation now might seem like a desperate last gasp. Lincoln agreed and began a propaganda campaign to prepare the North for an act that would come as soon as someone gave him a victory. He told Horace Greeley, the editor of the largest-circulation newspaper in the country, that should emancipation be announced, it would be done to save the Union. He told visiting ministers his concerns that the act might not be effective. He told a delegation of black citizens that colonization would be the proper solution for any freedom they gained. Lincoln was covering the bases. Saving the Union was the almost unanimous goal of every group in the North. His meeting with the ministers rehearsed public dialogue that was sure to take place once emancipation happened. Colonization of blacks to Africa or the Caribbean soothed racist fears of four million blacks being unleashed.

Then on September 17, 1862, in the bloodiest single day in American history, General George B. McClellan's army won the day at Antietam. It was enough of a victory to allow a proclamation of emancipation to be issued. Five days later, Lincoln announced his proclamation, covering all of those states and those places in states that were still in rebellion as of January 1, 1863. The response was enormous. Abolitionists, Republicans, and people who had been recently persuaded of abolitionist principles cheered wildly. Throughout the Confederacy, Lincoln was maligned for seeking a race war in which innocents would be slaughtered. Conservatives attacked him for hypocrisy as well as for threatening the Constitution. How could he claim to be fighting to save the Union while violating the constitutional principle that states alone controlled slavery? The *Times* of London attacked him for freeing slaves where he could not touch them while leaving those he could touch in bondage.[16] This latter charge continued to be heard throughout the late twentieth and into the early twenty-first centuries.

But Lincoln was limited in his constitutional options. His only power to free slaves was the war power that allowed him to do what was necessary to end the rebellion and save the Union. He believed that the war power did not operate in loyal states, as his border state campaign had demonstrated. It did operate where war was still being waged. Lincoln freed the slaves in the only place where he constitutionally could free them. But the impact on slavery was enormous; for with Lincoln's proclamation, the Union army became an army of emancipation and not only a Union-saving force. Every step taken by Union soldiers after January 1, 1863, expanded the domain of freedom. Approximately two-and-a-half million slaves ultimately were freed by his proclamation.

Yet, even in Dixie, this momentous act was still wrapped in respect for the federal system. During the hundred days between the first announcement and the actual emancipation on January 1, states were given the chance to rejoin the Union and escape having their slaves freed. Did Lincoln believe that any of these states would grab that option? It seems highly unlikely, given that he knew they would be outraged over the proclamation. Perhaps Lincoln wanted, hoped, that in those hundred days factions would form in the Confederacy that would struggle over whether to accept the option he offered. A little dissent in Dixie would certainly help the Union.

But Lincoln probably had his eye on the North as much as on the South. His hundred-day option respected the existence of the states, even those within the Confederacy. It bowed in the direction of the strong states' rights sentiment that still existed during war, even north of Dixie. It was similar to his proclamation on reconstruction, which also recognized the states in describing the ways in which they could return to the Union. In the midst of war's many changes, Lincoln was providing assurance that the constitutional structure still lived. It was hardly surprising that he did so. When a few Radical Republican legislators suggested turning the Confederacy into territories, the measure was soundly defeated. No serious attempt was made to reconstruct anything other than states. After the war, in *Texas v. White,* the Supreme Court would declare that the nation consisted of an indestructible union comprised of indestructible states.[17]

The war had shown that the United States was a federal union in which local government thrived even as the national government preserved itself and made the nation's prosperity possible. Americans were a people who respected their system of self-government because they were involved so intimately in it. Lincoln seldom felt shackled by this Constitution. Within it, he found the authority and the flexibility to fight four years to maintain it. Slavery, protected within the document of 1787, had endangered the constitutional system and opened up constitutional options. The Thirteenth Amendment to the Constitution, proposed by Lincoln as his party's emblem in 1864, marked the beginning of a federal union free of the corrosions of slavery. But states had to ratify it, as the Constitution required.

Living in a nation in which the Constitution was its abiding guide, Lincoln surprised no one by appealing, as he did constantly, to that document and the rule of law. Occasionally his opponents also used the document, or tried to use it, to limit his authority. But Lincoln found in it the power he needed to preserve the Union that he and most of the nation treasured.

Notes

1. Douglas Wilson, "Young Man Lincoln," *The Lincoln Enigma: The Changing Faces of an American Icon,* ed. Gabor Boritt (New York: Oxford University Press, 2001), 20–35.

2. *The Collected Works of Abraham Lincoln*, ed. Roy P. Basler, 9 vols. (New Brunswick, N. J.: Rutgers University Press, 1953–55), 1:112, 115.

3. *Liberator*, July 7, 1854.

4. Phillip Paludan, "The American Civil War Considered as a Crisis in Law and Order," *American Historical Review* 77 (October 1972): 1013–34.

5. *Collected Works*, 2:320–21 (August 24, 1855).

6. Len Gougeon and Joel Myerson, eds., *Emerson's Antislavery Writings* (New Haven: Yale University Press, 1995), 60.

7. *Collected Works,* 4:430.

8. Ibid., 6:265.

9. Mark E. Neely Jr., *The Fate of Liberty* (New York: Oxford University Press, 1991).

10. Lincoln to Orville H. Browning, September 22, 1861, *Collected Works*, 4:532.

11. Speech of Frederick Douglass on the War, Delivered in National Hall, Philadelphia, January 14, 1862, printed in *Douglass' Monthly*, February 1862. See "Documents of 1860–1865" in *American History Sources* (New York: Blackwell, 2006), http://www.brandywinesources.com.

12. Song quoted in Phillip Paludan, *A People's Contest* (New York: Harper & Row, 1988), 212.

13. Conway quoted in James M. McPherson, *The Struggle for Equality* (Princeton: Princeton University Press, 1964), 73–74.

14. Henry Steele Commager, ed., *Documents of American History* (New York: Appleton, 1949), 395.

15. *Collected Works*, 5:223–24.

16. *Times* (London), October 7, 1862, quoted in *Abraham Lincoln: A Press Portrait*, ed. Herbert Mitgang (Chicago: Quadrangle Books, 1971), 319–20.

17. 7 Wallace 700.

4 Lincoln, God, and Freedom: A Promise Fulfilled

Lucas E. Morel

Men are not flattered by being shown that there has been a difference of purpose between the Almighty and them. To deny it, however, in this case, is to deny that there is a God governing the world. It is a truth which I thought needed to be told; and as whatever of humiliation there is in it, falls most directly on myself, I thought others might afford for me to tell it.—Abraham Lincoln to Thurlow Weed, March 15, 1865

Had he put the abolition of slavery before the salvation of the Union, he would have inevitably driven from him a powerful class of the American people and rendered resistance to rebellion impossible. Viewed from the genuine abolition ground, Mr. Lincoln seemed tardy, cold, dull, and indifferent; but measuring him by the sentiment of his country, a sentiment he was bound as a statesman to consult, he was swift, zealous, radical, and determined.—Frederick Douglass, "Oration in Memory of Abraham Lincoln," April 14, 1876

When Abraham Lincoln assumed the office of the presidency, he declared at the outset of his inaugural address that he had "no purpose, directly or indirectly, to interfere with the institution of slavery in the States where it exists." He was quoting from his first debate with U.S. Senator Stephen A. Douglas in August 1858 and added, "I believe I have no lawful right to do so, and I have no inclination to do so." Appealing to "the people of the Southern States," he went on to remind them of Congress's oath to support the fugitive slave clause (as part of "the whole Constitution") and of his own oath taken "with no mental reservations." He even endorsed a possible amendment specifying "that the federal government shall never interfere with the domestic institutions of the States, including that of persons held to service."[1] Simply put, in his first official statement as president, Lincoln showed no intention of disturbing America's "peculiar institution" and gave little indication he would go down in history as the Great Emancipator.

None of this was lost on the famous escaped slave and abolitionist orator Frederick Douglass. He read Lincoln's inaugural address as a declaration of "his complete loyalty to slavery in the slave States" and declared, "what an excellent slave hound he is." Douglass concluded, "If we held the Constitution, as held by Mr. Lincoln, no earthly power could induce us to swear to support it."[2] Moreover, after the firing upon Fort Sumter, Douglass wrote that "war for the destruction of liberty must be met with war for the destruction of slavery." In his mind, emancipation and the enlistment of black troops were the surest means of ending the war.[3] Lincoln would resist both as explicit war measures until he issued the Emancipation Proclamation on January 1, 1863.[4]

On August 22, 1862, exactly one month before he announced his Preliminary Emancipation Proclamation, Lincoln put the abolition of slavery in its proper constitutional and wartime context. In a now famous reply to *New York Tribune* editor Horace Greeley's "Prayer of Twenty Millions," Lincoln declared, "My paramount object in this struggle *is* to save the Union, and is *not* either to save or to destroy slavery." While he did close his public letter to Greeley by affirming "my oft-expressed *personal* wish that all men everywhere could be free," his reply focused on his "*official* duty": to wit, "I would save the Union. I would save it the shortest way under the Constitution."[5] This was an apt summation of Lincoln's policy throughout the war: namely, to save the constitutional union of the American states first and foremost, with emancipation of slaves viewed only as a means to that end, only if necessary, and only under certain circumstances. Lincoln did eventually seek to destroy slavery in rebel-held territory (through the Emancipation Proclamation) and then throughout the United States (through the Thirteenth Amendment), but the path to these objectives would illustrate what he understood about the nature of self-government and the ways of Divine Providence.

Abraham Lincoln was a constitutionalist first and last, devoted to the rule of law as manifested in the slow but deliberate processes of laws and courts and with public opinion as the ultimate driver of political progress. This meant that what the public thought of its government, especially the principles that informed its foundation and operation, was essential to the survival of free government. Lincoln also saw self-government as a tenuous possession of the American people and hence something that required the effort of statesmen and general citizenry alike to perpetuate and maintain. As early as his 1838 lyceum address, he explained the necessity of a free people to secure justice by means of laws and courts and not through vigilante action: "Let every

American, every lover of liberty, every well wisher to his posterity, swear by the blood of the Revolution, never to violate in the least particular, the laws of the country; and never to tolerate their violation by others."[6] What he hoped would become "the *political religion* of the nation"—namely, "reverence for the laws" and the Constitution—would remain a political priority for Lincoln as he sought to preserve the American union as president of the United States. Thus, emancipating slaves was never simply a matter of morality for Lincoln but of political authority.

Lincoln was not honest

Lerone Bennett, who argues that Lincoln does not deserve the title of "Great Emancipator" because he was "forced into glory," claims that Lincoln deliberately undermined his own Emancipation Proclamation by its selective application: "What Lincoln did—and it was so clever that we ought to stop calling him honest Abe—was to 'free' slaves in Confederate-held territory where he couldn't free them and to leave them in slavery in Union-held territory where he could have freed them."[7] This argument implies that what Lincoln should have done regarding slavery concerned only military might, and not constitutional right. But Lincoln omitted the so-called border slave states of Missouri, Kentucky, Maryland, and Delaware from the Emancipation Proclamation because they were not in rebellion against the federal government and therefore their citizens deserved the full protection of their constitutional rights, which included the state-supported institution of slavery. As he put it in his December 1863 annual message to Congress, "According to our political system, as a matter of civil administration, the general government had no lawful power to effect emancipation in any State."[8]

The explicit exceptions Lincoln made of Southern, slaveholding areas under Union army control prior to January 1, 1863 (i.e., the counties constituting West Virginia and portions of Virginia and Louisiana) also fell into this category. When Secretary of the Treasury Salmon P. Chase argued for applying the Emancipation Proclamation to the exempted areas of Virginia and Louisiana, Lincoln replied he could only do so "without the argument of military necessity, and so, without any argument, except the one that I think the measure politically expedient, and morally right." He added, "Would I not give up all footing upon the constitution or law? Would I not thus be in the boundless field of absolutism?"[9] Lincoln showed that a president, even acting as commander-in-chief, must exercise authority not as a dictator—benevolent or otherwise—but within the limits set forth by the Constitution. If and when Lincoln decided to abolish slavery, he would do so by virtue of the power vested in him by the consent of the people and not at the cost of free government.

Two years earlier, Lincoln shared a similar view with Senator Orville H. Browning, who had complained of Lincoln's revoking General Frémont's military proclamation freeing the slaves of rebels in Missouri. Without "military

necessity" as a basis for the order, Lincoln saw the proclamation "as to confiscation of property, and the liberation of slaves" as "*purely political.*" Their "permanent future condition" must be "settled according to laws made by law-makers,
and not by military proclamations. The proclamation in the point in question,
is simply 'dictatorship.'" Lincoln concluded: "You speak of it as being the only
means of *saving* the government. On the contrary it is itself the surrender of
the government. Can it be pretended that it is any longer the government of
the U.S.—any government of Constitution and laws,—wherein a General, or
a President, may make permanent rules of property by proclamation?" Lincoln
did not believe a military subordinate or the president himself possessed the authority to "do *anything* he pleases."[10] More than a year after Lincoln proclaimed
emancipation of slaves held in rebel territory, he said to Kentucky newspaper
editor Albert G. Hodges that despite his personal animus against slavery, he
"never understood that the Presidency conferred upon me an unrestricted right
to act officially upon this judgment and feeling." He added that the presidential
oath of office "forbade me to practically indulge my primary abstract judgment
on the moral question of slavery. I had publicly declared this many times, and
in many ways. And I aver that, to this day, I have done no official act in mere
deference to my abstract judgment and feeling on slavery."[11]

Although he was not an abolitionist, Lincoln always considered himself
antislavery. In his 1864 letter to Hodges, he wrote, "I am naturally anti-slavery.
If slavery is not wrong, nothing is wrong. I can not remember when I did not
so think, and feel."[12] Furthermore, Lincoln saw the existence of slavery in a
self-governing nation as contrary to divine intention: "We [Northerners] think
Slavery a great moral wrong, and while we do not claim the right to touch
it where it exists, we wish to treat it as a wrong in the Territories, where our
votes will reach it. We think that a respect for ourselves, a regard for future
generations and for the God that made us, require that we put down this wrong
where our votes will properly reach it."[13] That the injustice of slavery would
"require" men to treat it as "a great moral wrong" follows from the Declaration of Independence insofar as it called Americans to revolt from despotic
government not only out of "right" but out of "duty."[14]

In another reflection on the basis of self-government found in the Declaration of Independence, Lincoln said, "This was their majestic interpretation
of the economy of the Universe. This was their lofty, and wise, and noble
understanding of the justice of the Creator to His creatures. Yes, gentlemen,
to *all* His creatures, to the whole great family of man. In their enlightened
belief, nothing stamped with the Divine image and likeness was sent into the
world to be trodden on, and degraded, and imbruted by its fellows."[15] The
question was how best to rid the nation of slavery, given its status as a state-
protected institution.

Lincoln believed that upholding the Constitution—even with its slavery provisions—was the safest way to promote the demise of slavery over the long haul. For example, in a March 1860 speech in Connecticut, Lincoln said, "If, then, we of the Republican party who think slavery is a wrong, and would mould public opinion to the fact that it is wrong, should get the control of the general government, I do not say we would or should meddle with it where it exists; but we could inaugurate a policy which would treat it as a wrong, and prevent its extension."[16] Moreover, Lincoln's respect for the Constitution entailed a commitment to restrict the extension of slavery because the Constitution stood for the equality of men. He considered this the "philosophical cause" of the birth of the American nation and its subsequent prosperity: "The assertion of that *principle* ['Liberty to all'], at *that time*, was *the* word, *'fitly spoken'* which has proved an "apple of gold" to us. The *Union*, and the *Constitution*, are the *picture* of *silver*, subsequently framed around it. The picture was made, not to *conceal*, or *destroy* the apple; but to *adorn*, and *preserve* it. The *picture* was made *for* the apple—*not* the apple for the picture.[17] Thus, he believed that to not restrict the spread of slavery would "subvert the first principle of free government."[18] Lincoln went so far as to exclaim at an 1856 Republican rally that "we have an interest in the maintenance of the principles of the Government, and without this interest, it is worth nothing. . . . [C]ome to the rescue of this great principle of equality. Don't interfere with anything in the Constitution. That must be maintained, for it is the only safeguard of our liberties."[19] To uphold the Constitution was to uphold the free principles that gave it legitimacy and to strengthen the means of securing freedom for all.

Lincoln always believed that the will of the people as expressed through constitutional government was the only legitimate form of rule. As he put it in his First Inaugural Address, "A majority, held in restraint by constitutional checks, and limitations, and always changing easily, with deliberate changes of popular opinions and sentiments, is the only true sovereign of a free people."[20] However, he also believed that "the will of God prevails" and that in some way the Almighty worked out His purposes through "human instrumentalities."[21]

However, one should not reduce Lincoln's political philosophy to the crude formulation *vox populi vox Dei* (the voice of the people [is] the voice of God), which is not quite what Lincoln thought. Rather, as he put it, "Let us diligently apply the means, never doubting that a just God, in his own good time, will give us the rightful result."[22] Or, as he once remarked, "So true is it that man proposes, and God disposes."[23] He expressed it most poignantly to Eliza P. Gurney in an 1864 letter that foreshadowed the central theme of his Second Inaugural Address: "The purposes of the Almighty are perfect, and must prevail, though we erring mortals may fail to accurately perceive them in advance. We hoped for a happy termination of this terrible war long before this; but God knows best, and has ruled otherwise. We shall yet acknowledge His wisdom and our own error therein. Meanwhile we must work earnestly in the best light He gives us, trusting that so working still conduces to the great ends He ordains."[24] "God knows best, and has ruled otherwise" became a Civil War refrain for Lincoln as he grappled with the prolonged conflict and its unanticipated emancipation of Southern slaves.

How was emancipation connected to Lincoln's view of the will of God as expressed in the politics of free human beings? Lincoln held firmly to both horns of the dilemma between man's free will and God's superintendence of human affairs. Historian Allen C. Guelzo writes that "there seems no easy way to reconcile the man who believed that all human action was decided by powers beyond human control and the president who reiterated his faith in the capacity of individuals to improve themselves *via* a free-labor system that 'gives hopes to all, and energy, and progress, and improvement of condition to all.'"[25] And so we have Lincoln's longtime law partner William Herndon commenting that Lincoln "held most firmly to the doctrine of fatalism all his life," while observing that Lincoln "was always calculating, and always planning ahead. His ambition was a little engine that knew no rest."[26] Lincoln's belief in fate implies a passivity belied by his own vigorous activity as a lawyer and politician on the rise.[27] It also suggests a deistic view of the world that contradicts Lincoln's belief that God directed the affairs of men not only through impersonal laws and forces but also in response to their prayers and through their very actions.

Lincoln expressed this belief in a personal God when he responded to a serenade the day he was reelected to the presidency. After thanking a crowd of supporters, he said, "I am thankful to God for this approval of the people. . . . It is no pleasure to me to triumph over any one; but I give thanks to the Almighty for this evidence of the people's resolution to stand by free government and the rights of humanity."[28] He repeated the sentiment two days later to another group of serenaders: "I am deeply sensible to the high compliment of a re-election; and duly grateful, as I trust, to Almighty God for having directed my countrymen to a right conclusion, as I think, for their own good."[29]

Throughout his political career, Lincoln made a habit of uniting a concern for his "final account to God" with a consideration of his duty to "the American people." This was made clear in a brief address he delivered to the New Jersey Senate en route to his first inauguration, where he commented on the role he sought to play as president of the United States. The occasion was peculiar for Lincoln, for he faced an assembly whose majority had not voted for him but for his longtime rival, Democrat Stephen A. Douglas. What Lincoln chose to highlight was his sympathy for the historic location of Trenton, New Jersey, as a pivotal locale of the American Revolutionary War. Lincoln observed that there was something special, something beyond mere "National Independence," for which the colonists fought. It contained "a great promise" not only to the Americans who fought for independence but "to all the people of the world to all time to come." That promise was a form of government that would secure "the liberties of the people" consistent with the equality of mankind that was its only legitimate basis.[30] If the nation could not or would not perpetuate itself "in accordance with the original idea for which that struggle was made," the American union, the Constitution, and the Revolutionary struggle that produced it would all have been in vain. This was a premise Lincoln would return the nation to most famously in his 1863 address at Gettysburg, when he called the Civil War a test of "whether that nation, or any nation so conceived and so dedicated, can long endure."[31]

The idea of constitutional self-government under the beneficence of God stands as a running theme for Lincoln and a fitting summation of his political reason for being. A chief example is his well-known reference to the American people as God's "almost chosen people," which he made in his address to the New Jersey Senate. In relating the early Revolutionary efforts of New Jersey to his present objective as president-elect, Lincoln remarked, "I shall be most happy indeed if I shall be an humble instrument in the hands of the Almighty, and of this, his almost chosen people, for perpetuating the object of that great struggle."[32] Here, he provides a political parallel for the biblical representative of God's will, the Hebrew nation. But where the Jews of the Old Testament were chosen by God to be a spiritual "light unto the nations," Lincoln suggests that the American people could very well be God's elect to offer political light unto the world.

Lincoln is careful not to substitute the American people for the biblical chosen. He calls them God's "almost" chosen people, at minimum respecting the religious sensibilities of Jewish Americans. More to the point, in a political sense the American people could only be God's "chosen" if they succeeded in perpetuating "this Union, the Constitution, and the liberties of the people" according to "the original idea for which that struggle was made"; an idea "that held out a great promise to all the people of the world to all time to come."[33] With the nation divided over slavery, Lincoln could scarcely call them God's chosen people without qualification. Recall the Old Testament promise to Abram (Abraham), the original "chosen" one: "And I will make thee a great nation, and I will bless thee, and make thy name great; and thou shalt be a blessing: And I will bless them that bless thee, and curse him that curseth thee: and in thee shall all families of the earth be blessed" (Gen. 12:2–3). Lincoln hoped to be the instrument of God and the American people in leading them to secure the principle of human equality for themselves and hence for humankind, thereby blessing all the families or nations of the earth.

He saw in the success of the American experiment in self-government a success for all humanity. In his message to Congress in special session of July 4, 1861, Lincoln reflected that the attempt at secession "embraces more than the fate of these United States. It presents to the whole family of man, the question, whether a constitutional republic, or a democracy—a government of the people, by the same people—can, or cannot, maintain its territorial integrity, against its own domestic foes. It presents the question, whether discontented individuals, too few in numbers to control administration [can] . . . break up their Government, and thus practically put an end to free government upon the earth."[34] In Lincoln's mind, nothing less than the survival of self-government was at stake in his response to the formation of the Confederate States of America.

Thus, on February 21, 1861, Lincoln appreciated that a good portion of his New Jersey audience were not what we would call today "sore losers." Although the majority of the New Jersey state senators had voted for a man who lost the election, they abided by the results of the election and paid deference to President-elect Lincoln. Lincoln could think of no greater proof of the practical demonstration of self-government than being hosted at a reception of men who did not vote for him. Their peaceful submission to "the *constitutional* President of the United States" (emphasis added), unlike the armed aggression of Southern citizens he sought to resist, showed an adherence to the rule of law and the principle of majority rule necessary for the successful perpetuation of a republican government. For this, Lincoln accepted their reception "more gratefully than I could do did I believe it was tendered to me as an individual."[35] He admired their republican souls despite the fact that they voted for a Democrat.

However, Lincoln came to discover that his much-vaunted devotion to the rule of law and the Constitution, even his leadership of a war effort to preserve what he considered "the last best, hope of earth," apparently fell short of the purposes of the Almighty. As he put it in his Second Inaugural Address, his original intentions for the war (as well as those of "the insurgents") would have produced "an easier triumph, and a result less fundamental and astounding." Even presiding over a nation that "read the same Bible" and "pray[ed] to the same God" did not ensure that the divine will would be manifest in the actions of one or the other party to the great contest of the American Civil War. Lincoln concluded, "The Almighty has his own purposes."[36]

As late as September 13, 1862, Lincoln continued to make the case for his "political religion" of reverence for the Constitution and laws, telling a group of ministers who called for a national emancipation proclamation, "I think you should admit that we already have an important principle to rally and unite the people in the fact that constitutional government is at stake. This is a fundamental idea, going down about as deep as any thing." For Lincoln, the cause of constitutional government was the cause of liberty; to speak of liberty without providing for its practical security was utopian. Nevertheless, at the time of his meeting with this group, he had already drafted the Preliminary Emancipation Proclamation and was awaiting an opportune time for its announcement. He even gave them a subtle hint to this effect: "I have not decided against a proclamation of liberty to the slaves, but hold the matter under advisement. And I can assure you that the subject is on my mind, by day and night, more than any other. Whatever shall appear to be God's will I will do."[37] Four days later, with the Battle of Antietam's repulse of General Robert E. Lee's invasion into Maryland, Lincoln saw in the Union victory a sign of God's will for the slaves. He would issue the Preliminary Emancipation Proclamation the following week and surprise his cabinet by sharing a vow he had made to God regarding the war and emancipation.

According to Salmon P. Chase's diary, Lincoln made the following remark to his cabinet the day he announced the Preliminary Emancipation Proclamation: "When the rebel army was at Frederick, I determined, as soon as it should be driven out of Maryland, to issue a Proclamation of Emancipation such as I thought most likely to be useful. I said nothing to any one; but I made the promise to myself, and (hesitating a little)—to my Maker. The rebel army is now driven out, and I am going to fulfill that promise."[38] This account is confirmed by the diary of Secretary of the Navy Gideon Welles: "[Lincoln] remarked that he had made a vow, a covenant, that if God gave us the victory in the approaching battle, he would consider it an indication of Divine will, and that it was his duty to move forward in the cause of emancipation. . . . God had decided this question in favor of the slaves."[39]

In April 1864, Lincoln acknowledged publicly what Chase and Welles noted privately in September 1862 about his vow to God to free the slaves upon a Union victory. In Baltimore, Lincoln addressed the following words to a sanitary fair: "Upon a clear conviction of duty I resolved to turn that element of strength [the use of colored troops] to account; and I am responsible for it to the American people, to the christian world, to history, and on my final account to God."[40] Lincoln confessed that he owed a reckoning to the Almighty for the Emancipation Proclamation, which included a provision "that such [freed] persons of suitable condition, will be received into the armed service of the United States."[41] What makes this all the more instructive is how Lincoln decided it was time to issue the proclamation. Not only had he sworn a vow to free the slaves upon a Union victory but also had come to believe that fighting the war merely to preserve the constitutional union was an insufficient rationale for his presidential administration. As Gideon Welles recorded it, "God had decided this question in favor of the slaves."

Lincoln believed that his prosecution of the war to preserve the Union and not to free the slaves fell short of God's intentions for resolving the crisis of the house divided. In his letters to Eliza P. Gurney and Albert G. Hodges (spanning the years 1862 and 1864), and most especially in his 1865 Second Inaugural Address, Lincoln confessed that Civil War events had not unfolded exactly as he had planned them. Fundamentally, he prosecuted the war effort to save the Union, even "as it was," which was a union of free and slave states. But he perceived, through the historical logic of events, that God apparently willed otherwise. As he put it, around the time of his Preliminary Emancipation Proclamation, "I am almost ready to say that this is probably true; that God wills this contest, and wills that it shall not end yet." What puzzled Lincoln, at least at first, was why God would tarry in bringing about His will for America through the Civil War. "By his mere great power on the minds of the now contestants, he could have either saved or destroyed the Union without a human contest. Yet the contest began. And, having begun, he could give the final victory to either side any day. Yet, the contest proceeds."[42]

This belief about God's power over the minds of men, what Lincoln once referred to as the "Doctrine of Necessity,"[43] led him to conclude that the protracted war and his eventual need to free slaves to prosecute that war indicated a greater power at work and a grander aim being pursued than he originally discerned. Throughout his public career, Lincoln had viewed the emancipation of American slaves not as a near-term possibility but as the eventual product of an ever-progressing, ever-liberating American union devoted to restricting the spread of slavery and placing it "where the public mind shall rest in the belief that it is in course of ultimate extinction."[44] Emancipation became a near-term objective for Lincoln only when the war dragged on longer than either side expected. He found his way to a legitimate, federal policy of emancipation only as "a fit and necessary war measure for suppressing said rebellion."[45] Once he stepped down the path of emancipation, Lincoln never turned back.

This was demonstrated on several occasions when Lincoln surmised that others sought an end to the war, even at the price of returning the freedmen to their previous bondage. To a rally of "unconditional Union-men" in Springfield, Illinois, to be held on September 3, 1863, Lincoln sent a letter to be read by his friend James C. Conkling. As the body of the letter makes clear, Lincoln was aware that many in the audience did not favor the Emancipation Proclamation, and so he devotes most of his message to addressing their lack of concern for the freedmen: "Why should they do anything for us, if we will do nothing for them? If they stake their lives for us, they must be prompted by the strongest motive—even the promise of freedom. And the promise being made, must be kept."[46] Lincoln later reflected upon this letter to Conkling, reiterating his commitment to keep the freedmen free: "I am sure you will not, on due reflection, say that the promise being made, must be *broken* at the first opportunity. I am sure you would not desire me to say, or to leave an inference, that I am ready, whenever convenient, to join in re-enslaving those who shall have served us in consideration of our promise. As matter of morals, could such treachery by any possibility, escape the curses of Heaven, or of any good man?"[47]

He also expressed this sentiment a year earlier in a letter: "For my own part I think I shall not, in any event, retract the emancipation proclamation; nor, as executive, ever return to slavery any person who is free by the terms of that proclamation, or by any of the acts of Congress."[48] In addition, in his 1863 and 1864 annual addresses to Congress, using much the same language, Lincoln declared he would not renege on the Emancipation Proclamation: "I may add at this point, that while I remain in my present position I shall not attempt to retract or modify the emancipation proclamation; nor shall I return to slavery any person who is free by the terms of that proclamation, or by any of the acts of Congress."[49] And: "I retract nothing heretofore said as to slavery. . . . If the people should, by whatever mode or means, make it an Executive duty to re-enslave such persons, another, and not I, must be their instrument to perform it."[50]

In a draft of a letter responding to an invitation to speak at a Union meeting in New York, Lincoln again linked the strength of the freedmen in arms to his own determination not to see them reenslaved: "Any different policy in regard to the colored man, deprives us of his help, and this is more than we can bear. . . . Keep it and you can save the Union. Throw it away, and the Union goes with it. Nor is it possible for any Administration to retain the service of these people with the express or implied understanding that upon the first convenient occasion, they are to be re-inslaved. It *can* not be; and it *ought* not to be.[51] Fundamentally, Lincoln believed that he was duty-bound not only to fulfill his vow to God but also to act in good faith toward the men freed by his Emancipation Proclamation.[52] What Lincoln practiced, he would preach to the nation as their charge upon the conclusion of the war.

With his Second Inaugural Address, Lincoln distilled a lifetime of political, philosophical, and religious musings that proposed a connection between slavery, the Civil War, Divine Providence, and the future of American self-government. "May one be pardoned and retain th' offence?" So asks King Claudius as he struggles to pray as a sinner "still possessed / Of those effects" for which he murdered Hamlet's father: namely, "My crown, mine own ambition, and my queen." They were lines the president knew well. This abortive prayer of repentance may have suggested a way of examining the problem the United States faced at the close of the Civil War. In Lincoln's mind, the abolition of slavery had become a necessary consequence of the war, with the nation, both North and South, paying for the national sin of slavery. However, the true fruit of this national repentance over slavery would need to take two forms: for the North, no triumphal revenge against its defeated Southern brethren for the evil of slavery, because both North and South had reaped its profits; for the South, admission that slavery was an evil that came "in the providence of God" for which it now receives (with the North) its due retribution through "this mighty scourge of war." Only a common memory of the war and its significance for the nation's future—"a just, and a lasting peace"—could produce what Lincoln called at Gettysburg "a new birth of freedom." Only a nation reborn in its devotion to union and liberty could be asked to bear "malice toward none" and extend "charity for all."[53] Lincoln's Second Inaugural Address stands as a profound reflection upon America's peculiar theodicy, a theological conundrum that strengthened his faith in the purposes of the Almighty. The address served as the culmination of Lincoln's lifelong pursuit to understand what Hamlet called the "Divinity that shapes our ends, / Rough-hew them as we will."[54]

Notes

1. First Inaugural Address—Final Text, March 4, 1861, in *Collected Works of Abraham Lincoln,* ed. Roy P. Basler, 9 vols. (New Brunswick, N.J.: Rutgers University Press, 1953–55), 4:263, 264, 270. Lincoln also cited a plank from the 1860 Republican Party platform that affirmed "the right of each State to order and control its own domestic institutions according to its own judgment exclusively" as "essential to that balance of power on which the perfection and endurance of our political fabric depend" (ibid., 4:263).

2. Frederick Douglass, "The Inaugural Address," April 1861, in *The Life and Writings of Frederick Douglass*, ed. Philip S. Foner, 4 vols. (New York: International Publishers, 1975), 3:72, 74, 75.

3. Frederick Douglass, "How to End the War," May 1861, in *Life and Writings of Frederick Douglass*, 3:94. Later that summer, Douglass wrote, "To fight against slave holders, without fighting against slavery, is but a half-hearted business, and paralyzes the hands engaged in it" ("Notes on the War," July 1861, in ibid., 3:116).

4. For example, on August 4, 1862 (seven weeks before his Preliminary Emancipation Proclamation), Lincoln met with two Indiana congressmen and others who wanted him to enlist "two colored regiments" from their state. As the *New York Tribune* reported, "The President received them courteously, but stated to them that he was not prepared to go the length of enlisting negroes as soldiers. He would employ all colored men offered as laborers, but would not promise to make soldiers of them." Lincoln feared that he would lose Kentucky and that "to arm the negroes would turn 50,000 bayonets from the loyal Border States against us that were for us" (Lincoln, Remarks to Deputation of Western Gentlemen, August 22, 1862, in *Collected Works*, 5:356–57). The Emancipation Proclamation of January 1, 1863, unlike the preliminary proclamation of September 22, 1862, stipulated

"that such persons of suitable condition, will be received into the armed service of the United States to garrison forts, positions, stations, and other places, and to man vessels of all sorts in said service" (ibid., 6:30). Cf. Lincoln's 1864 letter to Albert G. Hodges, where he explains that he "believed the indispensable necessity for military emancipation, and arming the blacks would come, unless averted by" compensated emancipation programs in the border states, which Lincoln had suggested a few times between March and July 1862 (ibid., 7:282).

5. Lincoln to Horace Greeley, August 22, 1862, in ibid., 5:388, 389 (emphasis in original unless otherwise noted).

6. Address before the Young Men's Lyceum of Springfield, Illinois, January 27, 1838, in ibid., 1:112.

7. Lerone Bennett Jr., *Forced into Glory: Abraham Lincoln's White Dream* (Chicago: Johnson Publishing, 2000), 7–8.

8. Annual Message to Congress, December 8, 1863, in *Collected Works*, 7:49. Lincoln added that "for a long time it had been hoped that the rebellion could be suppressed without resorting to it as a military measure."

9. Lincoln to Salmon P. Chase, September 2, 1863, in ibid., 6:428–29.

10. Lincoln to Orville H. Browning, September 22, 1861, in ibid., 4:531, 532.

11. Lincoln to Albert G. Hodges, April 4, 1864, in ibid., 7:281.

12. Ibid. Near the start of his 1858 campaign against Stephen A. Douglas, Lincoln said, "I have always hated slavery, I think as much as any Abolitionist" (Speech at Chicago, Illinois, July 10, 1858, in *Collected Works*, 2:492).

13. Speech at New Haven, March 6, 1860, in ibid., 4:16.

14. The relevant sentence of the Declaration of Independence reads: "But when a long train of abuses and usurpations, pursuing invariably the same Object evinces a design to reduce them under absolute Despotism, it is their right, it is their duty, to throw off such Government, and to provide new Guards for their future security."

15. Speech at Lewistown, Illinois, August 17, 1858, in *Collected Works*, 2:546. He would say just one month later, "Our reliance is in the *love of liberty* which God has placed in our bosoms" (Speech at Edwardsville, Illinois, September 11, 1858, in ibid., 3:95).

16. Speech at Hartford, Connecticut, March 5, 1860, in ibid., 4:5.

17. Fragment on the Constitution and the Union, ca. January 1861, in ibid., 4:168, 169.

18. Fragment: Last Speech of the Campaign at Springfield, Illinois, October 30, 1858, in ibid., 3:334.

19. Speech at Kalamazoo, Michigan, August 27, 1856, in ibid., 2:364, 366. Lincoln said as much later that year at another Republican meeting: "That '*central idea*' in our political public opinion, at the beginning was, and until recently has continued to be, 'the equality of men.' And although it was always submitted patiently to whatever of inequality there seemed to be as matter of actual necessity, its constant working has been a steady progress towards the practical equality of all men" (Speech at a Republican banquet, Chicago, Illinois, December 10, 1856, in ibid., 3:385).

20. First Inaugural Address—Final Text, March 4, 1861, in ibid., 4:268.

21. Meditation on the Divine Will, ca. September 2, 1862, in ibid., 5:403, 404. An example of how Lincoln believed "human instrumentalities" could work out divine intentions can be found in a well-known revision of his First Inaugural Address. Lincoln showed a draft to Secretary of State William Seward, who thought the address concluded on too harsh a note. Seward suggested a kinder, gentler conclusion to Lincoln's first official speech

to the nation as president. He suggested the president close the address by speaking of the "mystic chords" of the nation once again harmonizing "in their ancient music when breathed upon by the guardian angel of the nation." Instead of "the guardian angel of the nation," Lincoln chose a deleted phrase from Seward's draft, "better angel," so the last sentence would read: "The mystic chords of memory, stretching from every battle-field, and patriot grave, to every living heart and hearthstone, all over this broad land, will yet swell the chorus of the Union, when again touched, as surely they will be, by the better angels of our nature." Lincoln wanted to emphasize that responsibility for mending the "strained . . . bonds of affection" reposed in the citizenry and not divine intervention. First Inaugural Address—First Edition and Revisions, March 4, 1861, in ibid., 4:262 and n99, and First Inaugural Address—Final Text, March 4, 1861, in ibid., 4:271. In response to a delegation of Chicago ministers who urged him to issue an emancipation proclamation, Lincoln stated, "These are not, however, the days of miracles, and I suppose it will be granted that I am not to expect a direct revelation. I must study the plain physical facts of the case, ascertain what is possible and learn what appears to be wise and right" (Reply to Emancipation Memorial Presented by Chicago Christians of All Denominations, September 13, 1862, in ibid., 5:420).

22. Lincoln to James C. Conkling, August 26, 1861, in ibid., 6:411.

23. Address at Sanitary Fair, Baltimore, Maryland, April 18, 1864, in ibid., 7:301.

24. Lincoln to Eliza P. Gurney, September 4, 1864, in ibid., 7:535. In the fall of 1862, Lincoln met with Mrs. Gurney and fellow Quakers, to whom he acknowledged the providence of God in the same manner he would do in 1864. As in his 1861 Farewell Address at Springfield, Illinois, he called himself "a humble instrument in the hands of our Heavenly Father," adding that "we all are": namely, instruments "to work out his great purposes" (Lincoln to Eliza P. Gurney, October 26, 1862, in ibid., 5:478).

25. Allen C. Guelzo, "Abraham Lincoln and the Doctrine of Necessity," *Journal of the Abraham Lincoln Association* 18, no. 1 (Winter 1997): 79.

26. William H. Herndon and Jesse W. Weik, *Herndon's Life of Lincoln*, intro. Paul Angle, new intro. Henry Steele Commager (New York: Da Capo, 1983), 354, 304. Herndon goes on to say, "he did not believe, except in a very restricted sense, in the freedom of the will" (ibid., 354). The recent biography of Lincoln by Richard Carwardine is one in a long line that demonstrates the truth of Herndon's claim about Lincoln's ambition. See Richard J. Carwardine, *Lincoln* (London: Pearson Education Limited, 2003), esp. chap. 1, "Inner Power: Lincoln's Ambition and Political Vision, 1809–54."

27. In an 1842 letter to close friend Joshua Speed, in which he attempted to remove the doubts Speed expressed regarding his imminent marriage, Lincoln wrote, "I almost feel a presentiment that the Almighty has sent your present affliction expressly for that object." Speed had shared with Lincoln that he was uncertain about his feelings for Fanny but now was saddened by the thought that she was, as Lincoln put it, "destined to an early grave" (Lincoln to Joshua F. Speed, February 3, 1842, in *Collected Works*, 1:267). This reflects a view of God that is less deistic than the typical reference to "Lincoln the fatalist" would suggest. So, too, does a subsequent letter Lincoln wrote to Speed, where he referred to himself as being used by God: "I was drawn to it as by fate; if I would, I could not have done less than I did. I always was superstitious; and as part of my superstition, I believe God made me one of the instruments of bringing your Fanny and you together, which union, I have no doubt He had fore-ordained. Whatever he designs, he will do for *me* yet" (Lincoln to Speed, July 4, 1842, in ibid., 1:289).

28. Response to a Serenade, November 8, 1864, in ibid., 8:96.

29. Response to a Serenade, November 10, 1864, in ibid., 8:101.

30. Address to the New Jersey Senate at Trenton, February 21, 1861, in ibid., 4:236. A year earlier, Lincoln observed, "We understand that the 'equality of man' principle which actuated our forefathers in the establishment of the government is right; and that slavery, being directly opposed to this, is morally wrong" (Speech at Hartford, Connecticut, March 5, 1860, in ibid., 4:3).

31. Gettysburg Address, November 19, 1863, in ibid., 7:23.

32. Address to the New Jersey Senate at Trenton, February 21, 1861, in ibid., 4:236. See also Lincoln to Eliza P. Gurney, October 26, 1862, in ibid., 5:478, where he refers to himself as "a humble instrument in the hands of our Heavenly Father, as I am," adding, "and as we all are, to work out his great purposes." See also John Dos Passos, "Lincoln and His Almost Chosen People," in *Lincoln and the Gettysburg Address: Commemorative Papers*, ed. Allan Nevins (Urbana: University of Illinois Press, 1964), 15–37.

33. Address to the New Jersey Senate at Trenton, February 21, 1861, in *Collected Works*, 4:236.

34. Message to Congress, July 4, 1861, in ibid., 4:426. In an 1862 meeting with a Lutheran committee, he reflected that the American Civil War involved "not only the civil and religious liberties of our own dear land, but in a large degree the civil and religious liberties of mankind in many countries and through many ages." Lincoln added that "if it shall please the Divine Being who determines the destinies of nations that this shall remain a united people, they will, humbly seeking the Divine guidance, make their prolonged national existence a source of new benefits to themselves and their successors, and to all classes and conditions of mankind" (Reply to Evangelical Lutherans, May 13, 1862, in ibid., 5:212–13).

35. Address to the New Jersey Senate at Trenton, February 21, 1861, in ibid., 4:236. New Jersey gave four electoral votes to Lincoln and three to Stephen Douglas. See John Niven, *The Coming of the Civil War, 1837–1861* (Arlington Heights, Ill.: Harlan Davidson, 1990), 120. Given that the senate of New Jersey represented a state that split its electoral college votes between Stephen Douglas and himself, Lincoln reflected upon the requirements of self-government: "I learn that this body is composed of a majority of gentlemen who, in the exercise of their best judgment in the choice of a Chief Magistrate, did not think I was the man. I understand, nevertheless, that they came forward here to greet me as the constitutional President of the United States—as citizens of the United States, to meet the man who, for the time being, is the representative man of the nation, united by a purpose to perpetuate the Union and liberties of the people. As such, I accept this reception more gratefully than I could do did I believe it was tendered to me as an individual." Lincoln affirmed the majority's vote for Douglas as following from "their best judgment" and hence worthy of respect. Although Lincoln did not receive all of the state's electoral college votes, he acknowledged that differences of opinion are to be expected in politics and are especially not to be condemned by those who win. The votes of the people must be considered by all as faithfully cast and, therefore, faithfully respected, regardless of who won.

36. Second Inaugural Address, March 4, 1865, in *Collected Works*, 8:333. Earlier in the address, Lincoln stated his prewar presidential aim as "*saving* the Union without war" and then added that he "would *accept* war rather than let it perish." Regarding slavery, he went on to state that "the government claimed no right to do more than to restrict the territorial enlargement of it" (ibid., 8:332).

37. Reply to Emancipation Memorial Presented by Chicago Christians of All Denominations, September 13, 1862, in ibid., 5:423–24, 425.

38. David Donald, ed., *Inside Lincoln's Cabinet: The Civil War Diaries of Salmon P. Chase* (New York: Longmans, Green, 1954), 150.

39. Edgar T. Welles, ed., *The Diary of Gideon Welles*, 3 vols. (Boston: Houghton Mifflin, 1911), 1:143.

40. Address at Baltimore Sanitary Fair, April 16, 1864, in *Collected Works*, 7:302.

41. Emancipation Proclamation, January 1, 1863, in ibid., 6:30.

42. Meditation on the Divine Will, September 2 [?], 1862, in ibid., 5:404.

43. Handbill Replying to Charges of Infidelity, July 31, 1846, in ibid., 1:382. "It is true that in early life I was inclined to believe in what I understand is called the 'Doctrine of Necessity'—that is, that the human mind is impelled to action, or held in rest by some power, over which the mind itself has no control." While Lincoln goes on to say that the "habit of arguing thus however, I have, entirely left off for more than five years," he does not say he gave up believing in this doctrine. His 1862 "Meditation on the Divine Will" seems to confirm that he held to this view into adulthood. For an examination of Lincoln's purposes in releasing the handbill during his 1846 campaign for Congress, see Lucas E. Morel, *Lincoln's Sacred Effort: Defining Religion's Role in American Self-Government* (Lanham, Md.: Lexington Books, 2000), 86–92.

44. House Divided Address, June 16, 1858, in *Collected Works*, 2:461. In his famous 1854 Peoria Address, in which he criticized Stephen Douglas's Kansas-Nebraska Act for its policy of popular sovereignty, Lincoln remarked, "If all earthly power were given me, I should not know what to do, as to the existing institution [of slavery] . . . It does seem to me that systems of gradual emancipation might be adopted; but for their tardiness in this, I will not undertake to judge our brethren of the south" (ibid., 2:255).

45. Emancipation Proclamation, January 1, 1863, in ibid., 6:29.

46. Lincoln to James C. Conkling, August 26, 1863, in ibid., 6:409. See Allen C. Guelzo, "Defending Emancipation: Abraham Lincoln and the Conkling Letter, 1863," *Civil War History* 48 (2002): 313–37.

47. Lincoln to Charles D. Robinson, August 17, 1864, in *Collected Works*, 7:500. Two versions of this letter are extant, with no indication that either was ever sent.

48. Lincoln to Nathaniel P. Banks, August 5, 1863, in ibid., 6:365.

49. Annual Message to Congress, December 8, 1863, in ibid., 7:51.

50. Annual Message to Congress, December 6, 1864, in ibid., 8:152.

51. Lincoln to Isaac M. Schermerhorn, September 12, 1864, in ibid., 8:2.

52. Lincoln's desire to fulfill his commitment to emancipation reflects a lifelong concern that he stick to a decision once he made it. As early as 1842, Lincoln wrote Joshua Speed that he considered "my own ability to keep my resolves when they are made" as "the only, or at least chief, gem of my character" (Lincoln to Speed, July 4, 1842, in ibid., 1:289). For an illuminating discussion of how Lincoln anguished over losing this "gem" of his character, and how he proposed to regain it, see Douglas L. Wilson, *Honor's Voice: The Transformation of Abraham Lincoln* (New York: Alfred A. Knopf, 1998), esp. 317–23. Lincoln took this personal resolution all the way to the White House. Upon taking the presidential oath of office for the first time, Lincoln contrasted his constitutional responsibility with the violent intention of his "dissatisfied fellow countrymen" to break the American union: "*You* have no oath registered in Heaven to destroy the government, while *I* shall have the most solemn one to 'preserve, protect and defend' it" (First Inaugural Address, March 4, 1861, in *Collected Works*, 4:271). Lincoln shows that his swearing an oath to God was no light matter. Whereas fighting for "secession" is at minimum a debatable proposition, taking the oath of office is explicitly spelled out in the Constitution and hence a legitimate public

expectation of their president. See the U.S. Constitution, Article II, Section 1, for the text of the presidential oath of office—the only oath literally spelled out in the Constitution.

53. Second Inaugural Address, March 4, 1865, in *Collected Works*, 8:333. For an exegesis of this address, see Lucas E. Morel, *Lincoln's Sacred Effort: Defining Religion's Role in American Self-Government* (Lanham, Md.: Lexington Books, 2000), chap. 5.

54. William Herndon cited this quotation from *Hamlet* as a favorite of Lincoln's. Herndon and Weik, *Herndon's Life of Lincoln*, 352n8.

5 "Sublime in Its Magnitude": The Emancipation Proclamation

Allen C. Guelzo

hich would you rather memorize? This sentence: "Four score and seven years ago our fathers brought forth upon this continent, a new nation, conceived in Liberty, and dedicated to the proposition that all men are created equal." Or this:

Whereas, on the twenty-second day of September, in the year of our Lord one thousand eight hundred and sixty-two, a proclamation was issued by the President of the United States, containing, among other things, the following, to wit:

"That on the first day of January, in the year of our Lord one thousand eight hundred and sixty-three, all persons held as slaves within any State or designated part of a State, the people whereof shall then be in rebellion against the United States, shall be then, thenceforward, and forever free; and the Executive Government of the United States, including the military and naval authority thereof, will recognize and maintain the freedom of such persons, and will do no act or acts to repress such persons, or any of them, in any efforts they may make for their actual freedom. That the Executive will, on the first day of January aforesaid, by proclamation, designate the States and parts of States, if any, in which the people thereof, respectively, shall then be in rebellion against the United States; and the fact that any State, or the people thereof, shall on that day be, in good faith, represented in the Congress of the United States by members chosen thereto at elections wherein a majority of the qualified voters of such State shall have participated, shall, in the absence of strong countervailing testimony, be deemed conclusive evidence that such State, and the people thereof, are not then in rebellion against the United States."

> Now, therefore I, Abraham Lincoln, President of the United States, by virtue of the power in me vested as Commander-in-Chief, of the Army and Navy of the United States in time of actual armed rebellion against authority and government of the United States, and as a fit and necessary war measure for suppressing said rebellion, do, on this first day of January, in the year of our Lord one thousand eight hundred and sixty-three, and in accordance with my purpose so to do publicly proclaimed for the full period of one hundred days, from the day first above mentioned, order and designate as the States and parts of States wherein the people thereof respectively, are this day in rebellion against the United States, the following, to wit . . .

Both passages are by the same author—Abraham Lincoln—and were written in the same year—1863. But no explaining is needed to conclude that they couldn't be more different. The first sentence, from the Gettysburg Address, is arresting and eloquent, and it begins an appeal that soars to the very top of American political rhetoric; the other, the opening of the Emancipation Proclamation, is so pedestrian as almost to make the word *boring* fail on the lips. And thereby hangs a tale of contradictions: the Gettysburg Address was, after all, only a few simple words uttered at the dedication of a national cemetery, while the proclamation was a long-awaited, headline-bursting emancipation of more than three million slaves, based on a highly contentious, thin-ice reading of the presidential war powers. Lincoln's own estimate (if we can believe Ward Hill Lamon) of the Gettysburg Address was that it "fell on the audience like a wet blanket" and was a "flat failure" that "wouldn't scour."[1] But he thought the Emancipation Proclamation was "the central act of my administration, and the great event of the nineteenth century."[2] So, shouldn't the proclamation be more dramatic, its language more powerful, and its effect more electric than a mere cemetery dedication? And what should people conclude when instead the proclamation sounds, as Karl Marx unfeelingly put it, like "ordinary summonses sent by one lawyer to another on the opposing side."[3]

The puzzlement that results from the contrast between Lincoln the Eloquent and Lincoln the Emancipator has, over the years, generated three suspicions:

1. The blandness of the proclamation's language is so thoroughly out-of-character that it must be revelatory of Lincoln's personal intentions, and that in turn must mean that he was not in earnest when he wrote it. If he had been, he could have been as eloquent an emancipator as he was a cemetery dedicator. That he wasn't demonstrates a clear lack of interest and enthusiasm in emancipation and therefore in the liberation of black people. "Cold, forbidding, with all the passion and eloquence of a real estate deed, the Proclamation doesn't contain

a single quotable sentence and doesn't enumerate a single principle hostile to slavery," complains Lerone Bennett, Lincoln's most searing (and reckless) modern critic.[4]

2. Looked at closely, the proclamation is filled with legal loopholes, the most glaring being the exemption of the slaves in the border states and the Union-occupied portions of the Confederacy, where Lincoln left them in bondage "precisely as if this proclamation were not issued." This created an incongruity which the *Times* of London was swift to mock: "Where he has no power Mr. Lincoln will set the negroes free; where he regains power he will consider them as slaves."[5] And once again, it suggests that Lincoln was more interested in legalistic niceties than he was in the oppression suffered by slaves whom it was perfectly within his power to liberate.

3. Lincoln took elaborate care to explain the proclamation, not as a cry for deliverance or the triumph of liberty, but as a military strategy. He was, in other words, more interested in undermining the Southern rebellion than in freeing black people from bondage, and his principal aim was not to bestow freedom but to convert the slaves into yet another Northern war asset, or to rally Northern public opinion, or to bluff the European powers into standing down from intervention in what Lincoln was cynically portraying as a crusade against slavery. The proclamation was, to use Walter D. Kennedy's phrase in his recent anti-Lincoln essay, "Lincoln: The Un-Emancipator," merely "a propaganda ploy to influence abolitionist England and France not to recognize the Confederacy."[6]

As a result, it has now become commonplace to say that Lincoln had no great intentions in view when he issued the Emancipation Proclamation, that his real aim was to restore the Union and use emancipation as a tool to whip up public fervor for a military cause that was flagging, and that he never really wanted to emancipate any slaves but was forced into it by the exigencies of the war.

Yet, there is no solid reason to doubt Lincoln's claim in 1864 that "I am naturally anti-slavery. If slavery is not wrong, nothing is wrong. I can not remember when I did not so think, and feel."[7] Slavery "was a great & crying injustice an enormous national crime," Lincoln argued to his Illinois political ally, Joseph Gillespie, in the 1850s.[8] It violated natural law, by robbing the worker of the fruits of his labor: "The ant, who has toiled and dragged a crumb to his nest, will furiously defend the fruit of his labor, against whatever robber assails him." In exactly the same way, even "the most dumb and stupid slave that ever toiled for a master, does constantly know that he is wronged."[9] Almost as bad, black slavery was a blot on the confidence of the American republic as the champion of the principle of liberal democracy. "Our republican robe is soiled, and trailed in the dust," Lincoln warned. "Let us repurify it. . . . Let us turn slavery from its claims of 'moral right' [and] return it to the position our fathers gave it; and there let it rest in peace."[10] Slavery, in fact, grated personally on Lincoln's self-made passion for work and social mobility, since it condemned one category of men to a lifetime of labor without the hope of improvement while turning another into a shiftless aristocracy that scorned honest labor as "slave work." "When one starts poor," Lincoln said in 1860, "free society is such that he knows he can better his condition; he knows that there is no fixed condition of labor, for his whole life." And Lincoln was his own best example. "I am not ashamed to confess that twenty-five years ago I was a hired laborer, mauling rails, at work on a flat-boat—just what might happen to any poor man's son."[11] (Years later, Frederick Douglass would attribute his own surprisingly nondiscriminatory and evenhanded welcome by Lincoln to "the similarity with which I had fought my way up, we both starting at the lowest round of the ladder").[12] But slavery, by its very nature, "fixed" the slave permanently to his shackles. "The condition of the negro slave in America," Lincoln wrote, "is now as fixed, and hopeless of change for the better, as that of the lost souls of the finally impenitent."[13] Slavery deprived the slave not only of the natural fruit of his labor but of all hope "that in due time the weights should be lifted from the shoulders of all men, and that all should have an equal chance."[14] By contrast, slave owners would only come to associate labor with enslavement and to prize informality, relaxation, and scorn for work. Slavery, Lincoln told Gillespie, is "the most glittering ostentatious & displaying property in the world. . . . Its ownership betokened not only the possession of wealth but indicated the gentleman of leisure who was above and scorned labour." On all of those counts, wrote Lincoln's congressional ally and biographer, Isaac Arnold, emancipation became Lincoln's "deepest, strongest desire of the soul," and from the time of his election, Lincoln "hoped and expected to be the *Liberator* of the slaves."[15]

What is true, however, is that Lincoln made no effort until 1854 to act with very much force on these convictions. Slavery had been legalized in the Southern states of the Union as part of the "federal consensus" that created the Union and the Constitution, and lawyer that he was, Lincoln shrank from making the sort of frontal challenge that might destroy slavery, the Union, and the Constitution together.[16] Even if he wanted to take direct action before the 1850s, there was the simple problem of knowing *what* direct action to take: slavery was the product of state, not federal, enactments, and a constitutional firewall prevented the federal government from intervening in what belonged exclusively to slave-state jurisdictions. But Lincoln did not believe that direct action was really needed anyway, simply because he was persuaded that slavery, pent-up as it was in the

Southern states by the Missouri Compromise of 1820, would gradually die out on its own. Nor, given the prevailing white supremacist thinking of his era, did Lincoln have much idea of what would happen if the slaves *could* be liberated. "If all earthly power were given me," Lincoln admitted, "I should not know what to do, as to the existing institution. . . . I think I would not hold one in slavery, at any rate; yet the point is not clear enough for me to denounce people upon." Not being entirely free of the racial shadow of white supremacist thinking himself, it was a question Lincoln preferred not to face: "Free them, and make them politically and socially, our equals?" he asked aloud. "My own feelings will not admit of this; and if mine would, we well know that those of the great mass of white people will not." He knew well enough to wonder "whether this feeling accords with justice and sound judgment," but in Illinois, which not only banned black slaves but free black immigration as well, justice was "not the sole question, if indeed, it is any part of it."[17]

Then came Stephen A. Douglas's Kansas-Nebraska Act in 1854, which opened the old Louisiana Purchase territories, from which slavery had once been excluded by the Missouri Compromise, to the introduction of slavery. At once, Lincoln realized that slavery was being given a new lease on life, and so he embarked on a campaign to reimpose limitations on its expansion—a campaign that eventually led him to his famous Senate race against Douglas in 1858 and to the presidency in 1860. At no point, significantly, did Lincoln campaign to *abolish* slavery; he was perfectly willing to work for its containment, but abolition posed all the old questions of who had the authority to do the abolishing, what would happen to the newly freed slaves, and what would they do once freed. (In fact, in 1857, the Supreme Court even made the anti-slavery campaign more difficult in the infamous *Dred Scott* decision, declaring not only that blacks could not be considered citizens but that neither Congress nor the executive branch had the authority to prevent the expansion of slavery into the territories.) Besides, Lincoln was never convinced that sudden, immediate abolition was a workable strategy for emancipation: it reeked too much of self-righteous moralism and was too reckless of unintended consequences. The best path Lincoln could imagine was a movement that involved "three main features—gradual—compensation—and [the] vote of the people"[18]—in other words, a timetable for emancipating slaves as they reached certain ages (this being the mechanism by which all the Northern states had freed their slaves decades before), a buyout to the owners to induce their cooperation and to provide sufficient liquidity for them to hire their newly freed slaves as free workers, and some form of action by the state legislatures to circumvent challenges to emancipation in the federal courts.

This, then, was the situation Lincoln confronted in 1861 as he took up the reins of office as president; and understanding that situation goes a long way toward explaining why Lincoln did not reach at once for slave emancipation when the Civil War broke out. In the larger sense, he did not have the power to do so—that power rested with the states, and that meant wooing the state legislatures through "soft," gradual emancipation and funded buyouts. But almost as dark a reason why Lincoln made no move toward emancipation, always hovering in the background, was the Supreme Court, which had handed down *Dred Scott*—and which might do something similar to any emancipation order Lincoln wrote. At the end of the day, emancipation would always end up as "a judicial question. How the courts would decide it, he did not know and could give no answer."[19]

But that does not mean Lincoln was content merely to do nothing about emancipation. If wooing the state legislatures was what it took, he would do the wooing. The outbreak of the Civil War might have put the slave-state legislatures of the Confederacy beyond his reach, but the four border slave states of Delaware, Missouri, Kentucky, and Maryland remained within the Union and within the orbit of presidential influence, while the District of Columbia was governed directly by Congress and required nothing beyond an act of Congress to make emancipation happen. As early as November 1861, Lincoln had drafted an emancipation plan for Delaware that offered to swap $719,200 "in the six per cent bonds of said United States" in return for the Delaware legislature's agreement that there "shall be neither slavery nor involuntary servitude" within the state.[20] He made the same offer more broadly to the congressional delegations of the other border states in March 1862, offering "to cooperate with any state which may adopt gradual abolishment of slavery, giving to such state pecuniary aid, to be used by such state in it's [*sic*] discretion, to compensate for the inconveniences, public and private, produced by such change of system."[21] And the following month, he signed into law a congressional measure ending slavery in the District of Columbia.

All of these plans had something in them to irritate the abolitionists: they did not immediately free the slaves, which looked to the abolitionists like a violation of justice in deference to the dictates of prudence; they gave money to slaveholders, which reminded the abolitionists of nothing so much as a reward for having robbed others; and they were content to wait until slaveholders (or at least their legislatures) were ready. "You will not inspire Old Abe," grumbled one abolitionist, Senator Zachariah Chandler, "with courage, decision, or enterprise, with a galvanic battery."[22] But from Lincoln's point of view, his "soft" emancipation schemes had a number of inarguable practical advantages.

Compensation might look like blood money, but if it persuaded slave owners to relinquish slavery, then the price would be far cheaper than paying for a civil war, which required literal blood money in far greater amounts. "In the mere financial, or pecuniary view, any member of Congress, with the census-tables and Treasury-reports before him, can readily see for himself how very soon the current expenditures of this war would purchase, at fair valuation, all the slaves in any named State," Lincoln argued. If the border slave states bit on "soft" emancipation, it would deflate Confederate enthusiasm and thus hasten an end to the war. "The leaders of the existing insurrection entertain the hope that . . . all the slave states North of such part will then say the 'Union, for which we have struggled, being already gone, we now choose to go with the Southern section,'" Lincoln explained. "To deprive them of this hope, substantially ends the rebellion; and the initiation of emancipation completely deprives them of it, as to all the states initiating it." Above all, "soft" emancipation, as a state enactment, avoided review by the Supreme Court. "Such a proposition, on the part of the general government, sets up no claim of a right, by federal authority, to interfere with slavery within state limits" and therefore leaves "the absolute control of the subject, in each case, to the state and it's [sic] people, immediately interested."[23]

Unhappily, these advantages had one fatal flaw, and that was Lincoln's assumption that the slaveholders' desire for a buyout would trump the racism that bound white slave owners emotionally, ideologically, and culturally to the slave system. Lincoln had always believed, wrote William H. Herndon to a friend, that self-interest "moved the man to every voluntary act of his life."[24] But racism in the border states proved much more powerful than self-interest. Congress had no difficulty passing a compensated emancipation scheme for the District of Columbia, where Congress was the legislature; but in Delaware and the other border states, truculent state legislators and slaveholders threw Lincoln's "soft" emancipation schemes right back in his face. After a "stormy debate" among the border-state congressmen, twenty of them replied that they would never cooperate with compensated emancipation and that Lincoln should "confine yourself to your constitutional authority."[25]

These ill tidings came crowding in on Lincoln in the spring of 1862, followed by even worse tidings from the battlefield. The year 1862 had started off optimistically for the Union armies, with Ulysses S. Grant seizing the key Confederate western outposts of Fort Henry and Fort Donelson, New Orleans falling to the U.S. Navy, and General George B. McClellan poised to launch his enormous Army of the Potomac in a grand land-and-sea combined operation against the Confederate capital at Richmond. The optimism was quickly obliterated, however: Grant suffered a catastrophic near-defeat at Shiloh in April, and thereafter Union momentum in the West evaporated; McClellan's great offensive crawled up the James River peninsula toward Richmond, then stalled, and finally fell back to Harrison's Landing. And to top off defeat with insult, when Lincoln came down to visit McClellan's army, McClellan treated the president to an ultimatum that warned him that any efforts on his part to "interfere with the relations of servitude" would "rapidly disintegrate our present Armies."[26]

This posed two immediate problems for Lincoln: First, entirely apart from whatever warning McClellan was trying to send Lincoln in his "Harrison's Landing Letter," the multiple failures of the Union armies that spring and summer might mean that the war could not be won by the Union government, and a negotiated peace might soon have to be contemplated. And if the Union government could not win, then it could never reestablish authority over the slave states, and that would kill all hope of ending slavery by state legislative action. Second, McClellan himself, who had quarreled frequently with Lincoln over military policy and who had no hesitation, as a Democrat, about criticizing Lincoln's political initiatives, might turn on Lincoln and attempt a political intervention. This was not as far-fetched as it sounds: McClellan and his officer corps had made a number of threatening noises about plans "to march upon the capital and disperse Congress as Cromwell did the Long Parliament" if Lincoln ever tried to emancipate the slaves.[27] The longer Lincoln sat and dallied, the more likely it was that an intervention might occur. Now was the time, if ever there was one, for a preemptive emancipation move by Lincoln.

Lincoln did have one last arrow in his quiver that might sanction such a move: the so-called war powers of the president. The Constitution provides that the president serve as commander-in-chief of the armed forces in time of war or insurrection, and certainly the Civil War counted as an insurrection as much as anything could. What was unclear, however, was just what functions might be attached to a civilian "commander-in-chief." George Washington had literally understood this provision to mean, at the time of the Whiskey Rebellion in 1795, that he would take the field as the military chief of the army. But Washington was a soldier by profession. Only two of his successors had been (Andrew Jackson and Zachary Taylor), and only a few others (Franklin Pierce, James Monroe, William Henry Harrison) had spent serious amateur time in the military; the rest, including Lincoln (who had never been more than a captain in the militia), were civilians whose worst decision would have been to take over active control of the armies. Nor did anyone have much understanding of what the legal niceties of being a "commander-in-chief" might involve. There had been only one significant federal court decision about the operation of martial law, and one attorney general, Caleb Cushing, helplessly admitted that "we are without law on the subject."[28] If no one was sure what martial law was, who could have any real inkling about the president's "war powers"?

Nevertheless, Lincoln's allies had been pressing him since the beginning of the war to use those "war powers" to "emancipate all persons held as slaves in any military district in a state of insurrection" with a war powers proclamation.[29] Lincoln, who anticipated more than enough legal complications around "soft" emancipation, did not need to add to them by creeping further out on the legal limb with a "hard" emancipation proclamation. He had already pulled back the bit on two Union generals—John Charles Frémont and David Hunter—who had tried to use martial law proclamations in their districts to emancipate slaves—and it made little sense to duplicate their recklessness. But by the summer of 1862, Lincoln's "soft" emancipation plans had gone onto the shelf (at least until new state legislative elections returned legislatures in Delaware, Missouri, Kentucky, and Maryland that were more willing to listen to the siren song of Lincoln's buyouts); and if the war ended in some form of negotiated peace, or if McClellan finally gathered the boldness to lead the Army of the Potomac in some form of military intervention, Lincoln might never get a chance to take those plans off the shelf again. "Our common country is in great peril," Lincoln warned the border state congressmen on July 12, "demanding the loftiest views, and boldest actions to bring it speedy relief."[30]

Ten days later, Lincoln took the "boldest actions" himself. He read to his cabinet a draft of a war powers proclamation threatening to free the Confederacy's slaves "as a fit and necessary military measure" on the strength of his standing as "Commander-in-Chief of the Army and Navy of the United States" by January 1 if the Confederates did not end their resistance. The cabinet was almost struck dumb, since Lincoln had kept this measure concealed from their attention for more than a month, perhaps as long as three months. The time, however, had been well spent, because the proclamation was as carefully crafted to operate within the bounds of the presidential war powers as Lincoln knew how. There were no lofty flights of Lincolnian rhetoric, and no eloquent appeals to liberty or justice, since eloquence alone would have accomplished little if the proclamation were brought under federal court scrutiny. His one hope for making emancipation pass judicial muster was a sober invocation of military necessity: that what he was doing was legally justified by the military contribution a slave emancipation would make toward winning the war and preserving the Constitution. Hence, the proclamation would have an escape clause (the Confederates could submit and cancel the rebellion—although, in that case, they would once again subject themselves to the smiling blandishments of Lincoln's compensated emancipation plans), and it would be limited only to those parts of the Confederacy that were actually in rebellion at the time of the proclamation's release (which meant, *not the border states* and not even the occupied districts of the South, since the first had never been at war with the government, and the second were no longer).

But even that was enough to make the hearts of his cabinet skip a beat. Secretary of State William Seward (who was himself no slouch on the subject of emancipation) warned that, from the perspective of foreign policy, issuing the proclamation while the Union armies were staggering in defeated circles would look like an act of desperation, maybe even an incitement to the slaves to rise up in a racial bloodbath against the masters. "It may be viewed as the last measure of an exhausted government, a cry for help," Seward objected, "the government stretching forth its hands to Ethiopia, instead of Ethiopia stretching forth her hands to the government."[31] Lincoln took the point and agreed to wait until the Union had won some significant military victory, so that the proclamation could look like it was adding strength to strength.

This was not a delaying tactic. Although Lincoln had only the most meager religious profile of his own, he had been struggling ever since the summer's cheerless defeats to discern the direction in which God was taking this war, and he was now seeking out a sign that would signal to him that God indeed favored an act of emancipation. When the Confederate army under Robert E. Lee crossed the Potomac to invade Maryland in September 1862, Lincoln upped the ante of his promise to Seward by "promising God that he would issue the paper if God would give us the victory over Lee's army."[32] The victory came, in large measure because a copy of Lee's campaign orders mysteriously fell into the hands of Union soldiers—a sign within the sign, so to speak—and allowed McClellan and the Army of the Potomac to pin Lee into a disastrous back-to-the-wall position at Antietam on September 17. McClellan, being George McClellan, allowed Lee to slip back across the Potomac into Virginia afterwards. But Antietam was still a victory, and Lincoln now proposed to keep his vow. Once the news was certain, on September 20, that Lee had withdrawn and the battle was over, Lincoln rewrote the proclamation, and on Monday, September 22, read and presented it to the cabinet as a preliminary to releasing it as a military order. As of January 1, all slaves held in "the States, and parts of states" that "shall then be in rebellion against the United States . . . shall be then, thenceforward, and forever free . . . of their servitude and not again held as slaves." And with a cool eye on the cooperation of generals like McClellan, Lincoln added that the Union military would "recognize and maintain . . . any efforts" the slaves "may make for their actual freedom"—which sounded ominously like a pledge to encourage slave insurrection—and would now begin recruiting black soldiers to fight in the Union armies.

Not surprisingly, the Confederates made no move toward surrendering. So, on January 1, 1863, after an exhausting morning presiding over the annual White House New Year's reception, Lincoln walked upstairs to his second-floor office, where he met Seward with the formal copy of the Emancipation Proclamation and signed it into law. "If my name ever goes into history it will be for this act, and my whole soul is in it," Lincoln said, and to emphasize that what the proclamation had decreed was indeed right, and not just legal,

Lincoln allowed himself one bow to the angels: "Upon this act, sincerely believed to be an act of justice, warranted by the Constitution, upon military necessity, I invoke the considerate judgment of mankind, and the gracious favor of Almighty God."[33]

Lincoln believed that "the name which is connected with this act will never be forgotten."[34] True, the Emancipation Proclamation might not render slaves in the Confederacy automatically free to wander off the plantation unhindered; but it did guarantee that once Union forces swarmed over those plantations, the slaves would cease to be slaves and would never be slaves again. By 1865, William Seward estimated that two hundred thousand runaways, fugitives, and "contrabands" had placed themselves under the umbrella of the proclamation on the broad upland road to freedom.[35] On those terms alone, the prince of the abolitionists, William Lloyd Garrison, lauded the proclamation as "a great historic event, sublime in its magnitude, momentous and beneficent in its far-reaching consequences," and Garrison congratulated Lincoln for "a mighty work for the freedom of millions."[36] Still, Lincoln never got over his anxiety that the courts might shred the proclamation and the whole idea of presidential "war powers" that underlay it. It was unlikely they would do so during the war; but once Lincoln proclaimed the wartime emergency over, all bets were off. "I think it is valid in law, and will be so held by the courts," Lincoln told a Union general in July 1863. But even if they didn't, "I think I shall not retract or repudiate it. Those who shall have tasted actual freedom I believe can never be slaves, or quasi slaves again."[37]

All the same, Lincoln was a man for whom prudence was the polestar of his conscious life, and it was prudence that dictated, in 1864, that he backstop the proclamation by urging Congress to adopt the Thirteenth Amendment to the Constitution, which would not just free slaves but would obliterate slavery as a legalized institution everywhere in the United States. As an amendment to the Constitution, emancipation would thus be placed forever beyond the reach of the courts; and as a legislative act, it would conform to the pattern of emancipation with which Lincoln had always felt most comfortable.[38] In the strictest *legal* sense, it was the Thirteenth Amendment that eliminated slavery, especially since the Emancipation Proclamation was superseded by the Thirteenth Amendment before the wartime emergency had ended and was never tried on constitutional grounds in the federal courts. But, in fact, the Thirteenth Amendment is really only a coda to the Emancipation Proclamation. Nor is it likely that Lincoln would have ever backed down from the proclamation, even in the face of the courts. (He warned Congress that he would resign first.) He was not going to break faith with the slaves he had freed—"I should be damned in time & in eternity for so doing"—and he was not going to lay aside a weapon that had caused so much fear and disruption within the Confederacy. "No human power can subdue this rebellion without using the Emancipation lever as I have done."[39]

Of course, the oddity we all deal with concerning the Emancipation Proclamation is that Lincoln *has* been damned, not for backing down from it, but for issuing it the way he did. All that this really demonstrates, however, is a lack of understanding of the real dilemma Lincoln faced. He could not have acted directly, except as a commander-in-chief promulgating a war powers proclamation, and even then he could not have acted universally. Likewise, he could not have written ethereal, lofty prose into the proclamation because it was a legal document whose every phrase would be scrutinized. The critics who score Lincoln for not having done "more" in the Emancipation Proclamation overlook how easy it would have been for him not to have issued it at all. The war could, conceivably, have been won without it; and he was under no obligation (at least, no earthly one) to have kept his "vow" to follow the Antietam battle with emancipation. What is extraordinary is that, with so many disincentives staring him in the face—the risks in law, in politics, and with his generals—he kept the vow and kept emancipation at the forefront of his policies. That is the standard by which Lincoln and his proclamation should be measured; and it is a standard that points to greatness, for the Emancipation Proclamation and for its author.

Notes

1. Ward Hill Lamon, quoted in Don E. Fehrenbacher and Virginia Fehrenbacher, eds., *Recollected Words of Abraham Lincoln* (Stanford, Calif.: Stanford University Press, 1996), 289. See also Frank B. Klement, "Lincoln, the Gettysburg Address, and Two Myths," in *The Gettysburg Soldiers' Cemetery and Lincoln's Address* (Shippensburg, Pa.: White Mane, 1993), 86.

2. Francis B. Carpenter, *Six Months at the White House with Abraham Lincoln: The Story of a Picture* (New York: Hurd & Houghton, 1866), 90.

3. Karl Marx in *Die Presse*, October 12, 1862, in *Europe Looks at the Civil War*, ed. B. B. Sideman and L. Friedman (New York: Collier, 1962), 160; Marx to Engels, October 20, 1862, in *The Civil War in the United States*, ed. Richard Enmale (New York: International Publishers, 1961), 258.

4. Lerone Bennett Jr., *Forced into Glory: Abraham Lincoln's White Dream* (Chicago: Johnson Publishing, 1999), 536.

5. *Times* (of London), October 7, 1862, quoted in *Abraham Lincoln: A Press Portrait*, ed. Herbert Mitgang (1971; repr., Athens: University of Georgia Press, 1989), 320.

6. Walter Kennedy, "Lincoln: The Un-Emancipator," in *Myths of American Slavery* (Gretna, La.: Pelican, 2003), 172.

7. Abraham Lincoln to Albert G. Hodges, April 4, 1864, in *Collected Works of Abraham Lincoln*, ed. Roy P. Basler, 9 vols. (New Brunswick, N.J.: Rutgers University Press, 1953–55), 7:281.

8. Joseph Gillespie to William Henry Herndon, January 31, 1866, in *Herndon's Informants: Letters, Interviews, and Statements about Abraham Lincoln*, ed. Douglas L. Wilson and Rodney O. Davis (Urbana: University of Illinois Press, 1998), 183.

9. Abraham Lincoln, Fragment on Slavery, July 1, 1854, in *Collected Works*, 2:222.

10. Abraham Lincoln, Speech at Peoria, Illinois, October 16, 1854, in ibid., 2:276.

11. Abraham Lincoln, Speech at New Haven, Connecticut, March 6, 1860, in ibid., 4:24.

12. Frederick Douglass, *Reminiscences of Abraham Lincoln by Distinguished Men of His Time*, ed. A. T. Rice (New York: North American Publishing, 1886), 193.

13. Abraham Lincoln to George Robertson, August 15, 1855, in *Collected Works*, 2:318.

14. Abraham Lincoln, Speech in Independence Hall, Philadelphia, February 22, 1861, in ibid., 4:240.

15. Isaac Arnold, *The History of Abraham Lincoln and the Overthrow of Slavery* (Chicago: Clarke, 1866), 300, 685–86.

16. Don E. Fehrenbacher, *The Slaveholding Republic: An Account of the United States Government's Relations to Slavery* (New York: Oxford University Press, 2001), 10.

17. Abraham Lincoln, Speech at Peoria, Illinois, October 16, 1854, in *Collected Works*, 2:256.

18. Abraham Lincoln to Horace Greeley (March 24, 1862), in ibid., 5:169.

19. Abraham Lincoln, in Alexander H. Stephens, *A Constitutional View of the Late War between the States: Its Causes, Character, Conduct and Results, Presented in a Series of Colloquies at Liberty Hall* (Philadelphia: National Publishing, 1868–70), 2:610–11.

20. Abraham Lincoln, Drafts of a Bill for Compensated Emancipation in Delaware, November 26, 1861, in *Collected Works*, 5:28.

21. Abraham Lincoln, Message to Congress, March 6, 1862, in ibid., 5:144–45.

22. Zachariah Chandler, quoted in Hans L. Trefousse, *The Radical Republicans: Lincoln's Vanguard for Racial Justice* (New York: Knopf, 1969), 180.

23. Abraham Lincoln, Message to Congress, March 6, 1862, in *Collected Works*, 5:144–45.

24. William H. Herndon to Jesse Weik (February 25, 1887), in, *The Hidden Lincoln: From the Letters and Papers of William H. Herndon*, ed. Emmanuel Hertz (New York: Viking, 1938), 179.

25. "The Border States and the President," *Washington Daily National Republican*, July 21, 1862.

26. George McClellan to Abraham Lincoln, July 7, 1862, in *The Civil War Papers of George B. McClellan: Selected Correspondence, 1860-1865*, ed. Stephen W. Sears (New York: Ticknor & Fields, 1989), 344–45.

27. George Julian, "Indemnification Bill," *Congressional Globe* (February 18, 1863), 37th Cong., 3rd sess., 1067.

28. Caleb Cushing, "Martial Law," in *Official Opinions of the Attorneys General of the United States* (Washington: R. Farnham, 1858), 8:371.

29. Thomas Eliot, "Conduct of the War," *Congressional Globe* (December 2, 1861), 37th Cong., 2nd sess., 5.

30. Abraham Lincoln, Appeal to Border State Representatives to Favor Compensated Emancipation, July 12, 1862, in *Collected Works,* 5:318.

31. Carpenter, *Six Months at the White House*, 22.

32. William O. Stoddard, *Inside the White House in War Times: Memoirs and Reports of Lincoln's Secretary*, ed. Michael Burlingame (Lincoln: University of Nebraska Press, 2000), 95.

33. Quoted by John W. Forney, in *Conversations with Lincoln*, ed. Charles M. Segal (New York: G. P. Putnam's Sons, 1961), 235.

34. Edward Everett Hale, memorandum of a conversation with Charles Sumner, April 26, 1862, in *Memories of a Hundred Years*, 2 vols. (New York: Macmillan, 1902), 2:189.

35. William C. Harris, "The Hampton Roads Peace Conference: A Final Test of Lincoln's Presidential Leadership," *Journal of the Abraham Lincoln Association* 21 (Winter 2000): 50.

36. William Lloyd Garrison, quoted in James M. McPherson, *The Struggle for Equality: Abolitionists and the Negro in the Civil War and Reconstruction* (Princeton: Princeton University Press, 1964), 121; Garrison to Lincoln, February 13, 1865, in *The Letters of William Lloyd Garrison: Let the Oppressed Go Free, 1861–1867*, ed. W. M. Merrell (Cambridge, Mass.: Harvard University Press, 1979), 5:258.

37. Abraham Lincoln to Stephen A. Hurlbut, July 31, 1863, in *Collected Works*, 6:358.

38. In fact, if Lincoln had had sufficient support in Congress in 1862 for such an amendment, he might have skipped the proclamation altogether; as it was, even in 1864, the proposed amendment died in Congress, and it was not until after the November 1864 elections reelected Lincoln and gave him an undeniable mandate that the Thirteenth Amendment was finally revived and passed. The Emancipation Proclamation was, in the summer of 1862 at least, the only way forward to emancipation.

39. Abraham Lincoln, interview with Alexander W. Randall and Joseph T. Mills, August 19, 1864, in *Collected Works*, 7:506.

6 Lincoln's Summer of Emancipation

Matthew Pinsker

*T*he question sounds simple. When did Abraham Lincoln write the Emancipation Proclamation? Yet the answer is complicated, depending not only on definitions (*which proclamation?*) but also on historical method. Some of the nation's finest historians disagree rather sharply over which account of Lincoln's mysterious drafting process offers the most credibility. On the apparently prosaic matter of exactly when and where Lincoln wrote the policy that he believed defined his legacy more than any other, there has never been a consensus verdict.

Here is what we do know. On Tuesday, July 22, 1862, Lincoln presented what is usually called the "First Draft" of his Emancipation Proclamation to his cabinet. This contained the core of his new policy, but only a handful of words from this private, 325-word "draft" actually appeared in the final public proclamation issued on January 1, 1863. Most of what we understand as constituting the text of the Emancipation Proclamation derived from a longer (about 1,050 words) public document, now called the "Preliminary Emancipation Proclamation," which the president first read to his cabinet and then released to the nation on Monday, September 22, 1862. Lincoln also held additional discussions about the proclamation with his cabinet for three days at the end of December. The result was an official document that, despite being just over 700 words in length and lacking any serious literary pretensions, was nonetheless one of the most combed-over and heavily revised public papers of the Lincoln presidency.[1]

Still, there is little doubt that Lincoln did the vast majority of the writing and revising on his own. He showed up at cabinet meetings with drafts prepared, and though he accepted some important advice about timing and phrasing, the essential decision and form of its expression was his alone. In particular, the origin of his emancipation decision in July appears to have been an acutely solitary moment. Thus, almost inevitably, some people claimed afterward that

they were present at the creation. Various insiders (or would-be insiders) recalled in the months and years after the Civil War that Lincoln had shared the
so-called First Draft with them first. Although such memories are notoriously
unreliable, historians have felt compelled by the absence of much contemporary
evidence to pick and choose from among these often dubious stories. The result
has been a case study in the perils of using recollected information. Yet perhaps
scholars have underestimated how much insight can be gleaned from a careful
review of the contemporary evidence, especially from midsummer of 1862.
After dispensing with the usual recollected suspects, this essay will attempt to
identify both a date and a place for the origins of Lincoln's emancipation policy,
based strictly on chronology, a close reading of the contemporary sources, and,
ultimately, on the absence of a certain type of testimony.

To begin properly, one must first recapture Lincoln's sense of place in the
early summer of 1862. For about a month prior to the presentation of the First
Draft at the pivotal July cabinet meeting, the president was living with his
family in a cottage on the grounds of the Soldiers' Home, a secluded military
retirement community about three and a half miles from the White House.
He spent most of those days, however, working inside the White House, the
"iron cage," as he called it, typically leaving only to walk over to the nearby
War Department telegraph office where he regularly obtained news from the
front. However, during the month preceding July 22, Lincoln also took two
trips outside of Washington. The first brought him via train to West Point,
New York, for a private conference with retired general Winfield Scott. The
second journey took him by sea to Harrison's Landing, Virginia, to meet
with his embattled commander, George B. McClellan. The president spent
three days on the Virginia peninsula. Not coincidentally, almost all of these
places—the Soldiers' Home, the White House, the telegraph office, even the
boat that carried the president's party to and from Virginia—have been identified in recollections as the birthplace of emancipation.[2]

In fairness, the brief, July 22 document could have been written almost
anywhere. It contained only three sentences. The first addressed a requirement
of a recently passed congressional statute titled "An act to suppress insurrection and to punish treason and rebellion, to seize and confiscate property of
rebels, and for other purposes," commonly known as the Second Confiscation
Act and signed into law by a reluctant president on July 17, 1862. According to
this new law, the president was supposed to issue a proclamation that would
establish a sixty-day period after which rebel property (including slaves) was
declared liable for seizure by the federal government. Since the new law also
promised that all slaves thus seized by Union forces would be "forever free,"
it appears that Lincoln (who worried about the constitutionality of this and
other provisions) then felt obligated to address the question of emancipation

on his own. The second sentence of the document thereby reconfirmed his support for compensated emancipation of the slaves in loyal Union territory and announced his intention "to again recommend the adoption of a practical measure" for the "gradual abolishment of slavery." The third sentence, however, was the truly revolutionary one. Lincoln ended by vowing that as "Commander-in-Chief of the Army and Navy of the United States," he would "order and declare" that any slaves still held in rebel territory after January 1, 1863, would be "forever" freed.[3]

Here was the moment when Lincoln first revealed his change of attitude concerning the *process* for emancipation—previously he had always insisted that the end of slavery had to be gradual, compensated, and voluntary. Now he was embracing a much different, two-track policy, carefully distinguishing between the type of emancipation appropriate for loyal regions and the procedure to be dictated in areas still rebelling against government authority. Moreover, by pledging to free slaves across an entire region ("within any state or states") where "the constitutional authority of the United States" was not "practically recognized, submitted to, and maintained," Lincoln was offering a decidedly more sweeping policy than the congressional confiscation scheme, which appeared to offer emancipation only on a case-by-case basis. This decisive shift in the president's long-standing views was arguably the most important moment in the entire process. As if to underscore this point, on the back of the document's second page, the president himself sometime later described the draft's convoluted three sentences as the "Emancipation Proclamation as first sketched and shown to the Cabinet in July 1862." That is why artist Francis Bicknell Carpenter chose this moment to celebrate in his famous 1864 painting, *The First Reading of the Emancipation Proclamation*.[4]

Yet, other than Lincoln's terse comment on the back of the document, he offered no direct written testimony as to exactly how and when he prepared the draft. Four competing recollections by various administration figures have subsequently defined the main options for historians seeking to describe the physical origins of that July 22 document. Three of these officials claimed that Lincoln either showed them versions of the draft or warned them it was coming before the so-called First Reading. A fourth figure admitted that he had known nothing about it beforehand but suggested that Lincoln confided the real story to him sometime in the following months. All of these versions contradict each other in some fashion. Vice President Hannibal Hamlin and Major Thomas Eckert of the War Department telegraph office both placed the origins of emancipation in June 1862, but in much different ways and at different locations. Pensions Commissioner Joseph H. Barrett identified the return voyage from Harrison's Landing in early July as the critical moment. By contrast, Secretary of the Navy Gideon Welles believed that the president wrote nothing at all about emancipation until he had first disclosed his plans to Welles and Secretary of State William Seward on Sunday, July 13, 1862—a few days after his return from Virginia. None of these various stories have escaped criticism, but all have appeared rather frequently in historical narratives about emancipation.

During the years after the Civil War, Vice President Hamlin, a prominent Maine politician and committed antislavery advocate, repeatedly claimed that some weeks before the pivotal cabinet meeting (from which he had been excluded), the president had shared a draft of the proclamation with him privately. Hamlin's story, which had at least a few different iterations, usually involved a dramatic scene set at the president's summer cottage (ultimately dated by Hamlin's grandson as occurring on June 18, 1862), culminating with Lincoln pulling a document from a drawer in his personal writing desk that turned out to be "the first draft of a military proclamation freeing four millions of slaves." Hamlin recalled that Lincoln even offered to make changes in the proclamation based upon his recommendations.[5]

Major Eckert's tale was somewhat less impressive in its stagecraft than Hamlin's but nonetheless has proved equally enduring. Decades after the war, the officer recalled that sometime in late June, during the anxious days surrounding the bloody Seven Days' Battles, the president began writing his initial proclamation in the telegraph office as he nervously awaited more news from the Virginia peninsula.[6] Eckert's emancipator was certainly less decisive than Hamlin's. The officer remembered that a contemplative Lincoln "would put down a line or two, and then sit quiet for a few minutes" before haltingly scribbling some more phrases. Eckert claimed that the entire process took weeks to complete.[7]

These two accounts by Hamlin and Eckert have divided some of the nation's finest historians. John Hope Franklin's well-regarded 1963 study, *The Emancipation Proclamation*, manages to quote from each of these recollections at length without questioning either source or even acknowledging their apparent incompatibility as descriptions.[8] David Herbert Donald also mentions both accounts in his definitive 1995 biography, *Lincoln*, but clearly favors the telegraph office tale. The historian dismisses the Hamlin story as "rather too circumstantial," yet offers no comparable critique of Eckert's recollection, from which he quotes several lines with apparent approval.[9] By contrast, Mark E. Neely Jr. highlights the telegraph office story as particularly "dubious" in his chapter titled "Emancipation" in *The Last Best Hope of Earth* and views the "generally unquestioned anecdote" as a case study in how "myths about Lincoln grow."[10] Allen Guelzo's authoritative study, *Lincoln's Emancipation Proclamation: The End of Slavery in America*, tends to agree with Neely about Eckert's account. Guelzo considers the proposition that the president would have preferred writing "in the noisy clatter of the War Department telegraph office" to be something that "stretches credulity." Unlike Neely, however, who ignores the issue, Guelzo also addresses and raises questions about Hamlin's self-aggrandizing memories, though the author treats the vice president's account more seriously than most. He devotes more than a page of his book to dissecting the evolution of Hamlin's story, ultimately offering him some grudging credit for being "persistent" in the face of skeptics.[11]

But persistence should matter little when memories are so directly contradicted by evidence from the period. The only contemporary exchange between Hamlin and Lincoln on the subject of emancipation, a private letter by the vice president written in September 1862, contains absolutely no reference to their presumably pivotal encounter at the Soldiers' Home but instead offers a telling acknowledgment that Hamlin was not even sure that "this note," congratulating Lincoln on the public announcement of his new policy, "will ever meet your eye."[12] Even more revealing, to accept Eckert's telegraph office account requires believing that Lincoln spent weeks from the end of June 1862 writing a three-sentence, 325-word document that began by referring to a law passed on July 17.

In addition, the premise of both recollections appears almost demonstrably false. Lincoln was surely not drafting emancipation proclamations in June or even through early July in 1862. He was hinting that he might, but that was something he had been doing for months. "The Union must be preserved, and hence all indispensable means must be employed," Lincoln had warned in his 1861 annual message, even as he announced that he would be doing nothing about slavery "in haste."[13] When he revoked General David Hunter's field order freeing slaves in Georgia, Florida, and South Carolina on May 19, 1862, the president again rejected the necessity for an emancipation decree but also indicated that the idea had occurred to him. He wrote that "whether it be competent for me, as Commander-in-Chief of the Army and Navy, to declare the Slaves of any state or states, free" was a decision that "I reserve to myself." By holding onto his options in such ostentatious fashion, Lincoln was obviously trying to send a signal, mainly to the political leaders of Union slave states. He earnestly wanted them to adopt plans for gradual emancipation. "You can not," he wrote on May 19, "be blind to the signs of the times." Few shrewd observers were. By the end of May, for example, Secretary of War Edwin M. Stanton was privately predicting that "a decree of Emancipation would be issued within two months."[14]

Yet hints, warnings, and predictions are not the same as action. More than a month after revoking the Hunter order, Lincoln still appeared convinced that a military decree at that time was unnecessary and perhaps even dangerous. On June 20 (two days after he supposedly shared his draft proclamation with Vice President Hamlin), Lincoln told a delegation of Quakers that "If a decree of emancipation could abolish Slavery, John Brown would have done the work effectually. Such a decree surely could not be more binding upon the South than the Constitution, and that cannot be enforced in that part of the country now. Would a proclamation of freedom be any more effective?"[15] Admittedly, throughout his presidency, Lincoln employed the tactic of playing devil's advocate—of testing his audiences by assuming positions opposed to his own. Yet, if he was truly acting with the Quaker delegation in June 1862, then he was doing so without much strategy behind it. Consider the caginess of the more famous letter to editor Horace Greeley on August 22, 1862: "My paramount object in this struggle *is* to save the Union, and is *not* either to save or to destroy slavery. If I could save the Union without freeing *any* slave I would do it, and if I could save it by freeing *all* the slaves I would do it; and if I could save it by freeing some and leaving others alone I would also do that."[16] Lincoln's strategy in the Greeley letter, however subtle at the time, is clear in retrospect. The president had already decided to emancipate rebel slaves by August 1862, so framing the issue as one of national necessity ("save the Union") was undeniably effective in preparing for the next step forward. There is no such clarity in viewing the May 19 or June 20 statements as examples of political positioning.

Other contemporary evidence makes even clearer that President Lincoln continued to resist the prospect of issuing an emancipation decree through early July. On Tuesday morning, July 1, 1862, Senator Orville Hickman Browning of Illinois discussed the subject with Lincoln at his office in the White House. Browning, who had been appointed to the U.S. Senate after the death of Lincoln's rival, Stephen A. Douglas, in June 1861, had known Lincoln for years. In Illinois, their relationship had been mainly professional, though as a bachelor, Lincoln had felt close enough to rely upon Browning's gregarious wife, Eliza, for occasional romantic advice. Still, in recent months (particularly after the death of twelve-year-old Willie Lincoln in February), the families had grown far closer. Only the night before, the president and his wife had entertained the Brownings and another couple at their new summer cottage at the Soldiers' Home.[17] So it was without any particular sense of surprise that Browning noted in his diary on July 1 that the president had summoned him to the White House that morning to "read a paper embodying his views of the objects of the war, and the proper mode of conducting it in its relations to slavery," one that Lincoln told him he had "sketched hastily with the intention of laying it before the Cabinet."[18]

Though Browning's description makes this paper sound like a good candidate for the famous first draft, the paper that Lincoln read to him on the morning of July 1 contained a series of propositions that fell far short of any emancipation decree. The president made clear, according to Browning's diary, that while "No negroes necessarily taken and escaping during the war are ever to be returned to slavery," he was also determined to stipulate that "No inducements are to be held out to them to come into our lines," since the overwhelming number of escapees (or "contrabands," as they were called) were "becoming an embarrassment to the government." On the subject of enlisting the former slaves as soldiers, Lincoln was adamantly opposed, at least in Browning's careful phrasing, "At present." He was also firm in his view that "Congress has no power over slavery in the states." This was especially significant because Lincoln knew that Browning had been fighting the more radical provisions regarding emancipation within the Second Confiscation Bill, which was then under intense debate. Browning would actually lobby the president to veto the measure because of these provisions (which he considered unconstitutional), once it passed the Congress in mid-July. On the subject of slavery, Lincoln was, as usual, maddeningly cautious, warning that "so much of it as remains after the war is over will be in precisely the same condition that it was before the war began."[19]

The physical text of this July 1 memorandum has never been found, yet it is not hyperbole to assert that Browning's diary entry offers as reliable a summary of Lincoln's position during this period as any other source currently available to historians. Here is private, contemporary evidence from a true presidential intimate who was expert enough to understand and convey all of the nuances of Lincoln's attitudes. Thus, it was especially significant that Browning, who strongly opposed an emancipation decree, felt confident in writing about Lincoln on July 1, "His views coincided entirely with my own." Even if there was some degree of projection in that judgment, there is still more than enough in this entry to repudiate the gist of the recollections by Hannibal Hamlin, Thomas Eckert, or anyone else who claims that Lincoln was preparing draft proclamations for black freedom prior to this moment.

At the very least, it is difficult to understand why scholars have not employed the Browning diary entry more prominently in their narratives of the emancipation decision. John Hope Franklin doesn't mention it at all in his 1963 monograph. Mark Neely also excludes the incident from his chapter on the subject. David Donald quotes a line from the entry, but does so without making clear in the main body of his text when (or in what form) the exchange with Browning had occurred. On the other hand, Allen Guelzo provides the July 1 date in his brief description of what Lincoln told Browning that morning, but does so while cataloguing various memoirs and other remembered claims concerning the First Draft. He makes no effort to distinguish a direct contemporary account from other recollected and often secondhand stories.[20]

Browning's diary also proves useful for documenting the uncertainty that enveloped Washington in early July—knowledge of which is essential for understanding Lincoln's continued hesitation to act in regard to slavery. It is easy to forget that the failure of the Union forces during the pivotal "Seven Days' Battles" was not made entirely clear in Washington for several more days after the bloody fight. On July 2, Browning described how contradictory messages from McClellan had left the president "deeply anxious"—anxious, but not depressed. There was an awareness of the terrible human price both sides had paid, but its meaning was not yet certain. On the morning of July 4, Browning reported that the president had shared dispatches with him showing that, although the fighting around Richmond had been "terrible," the "advantages" had been "decidedly with us."[21] For Lincoln, this mixed news was cause for more intelligence gathering, not grounds for despair. According to aide John G. Nicolay, the president spent most of the rest of the day at the War Department, awaiting further dispatches.[22] Certainly the effort did strain Lincoln, who told a delegation of veterans later that, "I am indeed surrounded, as is the whole country, by very trying circumstances." Lincoln then encountered a wagon train of recently wounded soldiers while riding back to the Soldiers' Home that evening. A newspaper reporter captured his curious reaction, noting that the president "rode beside them for a considerable distance, conversing freely with the men, and seeming anxious to secure all the information possible with regard to the real condition of affairs on the Peninsula." The next evening, the president shared additional dispatches with Browning that asserted the "spirit of the Army" was still "excellent" and indicated the results of the fighting had been "much more satisfactory to us than was previously supposed."[23]

The confusing aftermath of the Seven Days' Battles is significant in the narrative of emancipation because it explains why Lincoln surely had not yet come to any new conclusions about the state of the war. Instead, he wired McClellan "a thousand thanks" on July 5 and vowed that "we shall hive the enemy yet."[24] He was obviously not sitting in the telegraph office, as Eckert later claimed, preparing a major shift in policy that was rooted in his army's failures. Yes, he was "deeply anxious," in Browning's words, but not yet decisive about anything. Later that summer, Senator Charles Sumner from Massachusetts recalled to English abolitionist John Bright that he had urged Lincoln on July 4 to mark the nation's independence with an emancipation proclamation. He claimed that Lincoln had replied, "I would do it if I were not afraid that half the officers would fling down their arms and three more states would rise."[25] Sumner's recollection suggests the likely truth: Lincoln was still contemplating, not yet emancipating, in early July.

For Lincoln, the only serious option by the end of that first week was to gather more information. He decided to go to the Virginia peninsula himself.

The president's party left on Monday, July 7, and did not return to Washington until Thursday, July 10, 1862. During this remarkable and unprecedented visit to the front, the president met with General McClellan, who read him a letter on Tuesday, July 8 (exactly a week after the president's revealing session with Browning) that made clear the general's own views about the proper "objects of the war" in relation to slavery. "Neither confiscation of property, political executions of persons, territorial organization of States, or forcible abolition of slavery," McClellan wrote firmly, "should be contemplated for a moment."[26]

According to Joseph Barrett, a former newspaperman who had also served as one of Lincoln's official campaign biographers before becoming commissioner of pensions, it was "under these circumstances" that emancipation was born. Without detailing at first how exactly he knew these details, Barrett reported in the 1865 edition of his biography that "while on board the steamboat, returning from Harrison's Landing . . . Mr. Lincoln wrote the first draft of his Emancipation Proclamation."[27] Modern scholars have generally ignored Barrett on this point. His own peers, however, took him far more seriously. In his memoir, painter Francis Carpenter offered an enthusiastic endorsement for Barrett's original claim, despite admitting that he had never heard such an account from Lincoln himself. He recalled instead that while he was preparing for his painting *First Reading*, Lincoln had merely told him that it had been about "midsummer, 1862," when he finally decided that "we had reached the end of our rope" and "must change our tactics, or lose the game!"[28] Secretary of the Navy Gideon Welles agreed in his recollection that Lincoln had indeed been composing on board the ship on July 10, but described the effort as a "carefully written speech," which the president then read a couple of days later to congressional representatives from the Union slave states, urging them once again to adopt his gradual emancipation measure.[29]

How any of these men imagined that Lincoln could write legibly on board the U.S.S. *Ariel* is not entirely clear. Nor is there much explanation for why he would feel compelled to spend his few rare hours at sea writing instead of absorbing the fresh air. Even more persuasive, White House aide John Nicolay claimed at the time in a private letter that Lincoln "came home" from the peninsula "in better spirits than he went in."[30] Barrett did try to elaborate on his recollection in a 1904, two-volume edition of his biography, but he only succeeded in confusing the issue. He finally acknowledged that he had heard the story directly from President Lincoln but then made the mistake of suggesting the shipboard document was the "rough draft of his September proclamation." Perhaps not coincidentally, Carpenter had made the identical error in his 1866 memoir. After endorsing Barrett's story, the painter had proceeded to describe how the original draft was written on "four half sheets of official foolscap" that later had ended up in Albany, New York. But the document he was describing was the draft released on September 22 and not the one shared with the cabinet on July 22.[31]

More important, despite Barrett's assertion to the contrary, the only words we have directly from Lincoln himself on this subject contradict these claims. In a letter written in 1864 to newspaper editor Albert Hodges, the president described the reasons why he had come to the emancipation decision. He emphasized how the failure of the voluntary abolition policy had compelled him to adopt the concept of a military decree. "When, in March, and May, and July 1862, I made earnest, and successive appeals to the border states to favor compensated emancipation," he wrote, "I believed the indispensable necessity for military emancipation, and arming the blacks would come, unless averted by that measure." "They declined the proposition," he noted, "and I was, in my best judgment, driven to the alternative of either surrendering the Union, and with it, the Constitution, or of laying strong hand upon the colored element." He added, "I chose the latter."[32] This presidential version of events directly challenges the idea that the Harrison's Landing meeting with McClellan was pivotal because Lincoln's final, disappointing encounter with the border state representatives did not take place until after his return from the peninsula, on Saturday, July 12.

The only recollection that actually fits with Lincoln's own account is one from Secretary Welles. On Sunday, July 13, according to Welles, the president asked him to come along on the ride out to the northwest section of the district where a funeral for the recently deceased infant son of Edwin Stanton was taking place. According to one version of the story, the president was also joined by Secretary Seward and his daughter-in-law, Anna Seward. Welles claimed that on this journey, Lincoln "first mentioned to Mr. Seward and myself the subject of emancipating the slaves by proclamation." Welles wrote that Lincoln had told them that this was "the first occasion when he had mentioned the subject to any one."[33]

This account from Welles is probably the single most frequently cited source in the various historical narratives of the initial emancipation decision. Franklin, Neely, Donald, and Guelzo all quote Welles in describing the events of July 13.[34] Yet, what is often described as a diary entry has some problems in its provenance. Despite its inclusion within the "diary," this account is recollected and was not recorded contemporaneously. Welles added it sometime later, as a kind of undated preface to the diary that he did not begin keeping in earnest until the middle of August. It is even possible that Welles did not write this particular material until the early 1870s, when he was preparing a magazine article on the subject. The details also change with each version of the story. One version places the conversation on the ride out to the funeral; another, on the return. One notes the presence of Anna Seward; another identifies only Seward and Welles. In one version, Seward speaks; in another, he appears almost mute. But most important, the gist of the recollection—that Lincoln had already decided upon military emancipation by Sunday morning—again seems to be contradicted by contemporary evidence. On the same day that the president was allegedly telling Welles that "it was a military necessity absolutely essential for the salvation of the Union, that we must free the slaves or be ourselves subdued," he was also sending George McClellan a brusque note challenging the general's low estimates of his effective fighting force. Lincoln believed that the Army of the Potomac had forty-five thousand more men available on the peninsula than McClellan was reporting. "If I am right," Lincoln wrote on Sunday, "and you had these men with you, you could go into Richmond in the next three days."[35] That doesn't quite sound like a president on the verge of feeling subdued.

More significant, there is no corroboration for Welles's story from William Seward. The secretary of state, who died in 1872, left no direct commentary about his role in the affair. On the other hand, Senator Browning noted in his diary that he spent the afternoon of July 13 in private conversation with Seward, who offered no hint that anything unusual was afoot. That is not unexpected (the president had asked for discretion, according to Welles), but it is revealing that Browning reports that the two men talked mainly about the congressional debate over confiscation. This was still the number one issue weighing on everyone's mind. After weeks of stalemate, the joint House-Senate conference committee had finally emerged on Friday afternoon with a bill. This was major news—the type that would have dominated many carriage ride conversations around Washington in the subsequent days. If Lincoln had addressed Seward and Welles about the topic of emancipation, it was almost certainly in the context of his concerns over the new confiscation legislation.

Good evidence for this conclusion comes from Welles himself. In one of his actual diary entries for that year, recorded on September 22, 1862, the naval secretary described how he had always believed that invoking the "war power" was the only legal process for emancipation (short of a constitutional amendment), claiming that "This was the view which I took when the President first presented the subject to Seward and myself last summer as we were returning from the funeral of Stanton's child." The key here is what exactly Welles meant by "the subject" that Lincoln had "first presented" over the summer. Since the secretary was writing on the day of the cabinet discussion about the Preliminary Emancipation Proclamation, it has been easy to confuse the precise nature of this early version of his recollected claim. For this reason, the few sentences that immediately precede it are especially revealing: "The question of power, authority, in the Government to set free the slaves was not much discussed at this meeting [on September 22], but had been canvassed by the President in private conversation with the members individually. Some thought legislation advisable before the step was taken, but Congress was clothed with no authority on this subject, nor is the Executive, except under the war power,—military necessity, martial law, when there can be no legislation. This was the view which I took . . ."[36]

In other words, "the subject" that Lincoln had introduced during the carriage ride was a "question of power" regarding emancipation that concerned "the Government" and not just the president. When Welles referenced his argument during the July conversation ("This was the view which I took") in the September 22 diary entry, he was emphasizing his judgment that "Congress was clothed with no authority on this subject" as much as his position on a presidential decree. Seen from this perspective, the July 13 carriage ride thus appears far more likely to have been focused on soliciting reactions to the emerging congressional confiscation policy than on the dramatic unveiling of any new presidential initiative.

The fact that Welles would later deny such an interpretation doesn't make it any less powerful. Written only a few months after the events, the recollection embedded in the September 22 diary entry contains a greater ring of truth than the secretary's other subsequent (and presumably enhanced) memories. In September 1862, Welles offered no self-aggrandizing claim about how Lincoln had confided in him and Seward and no others. Nor was there any attempt to re-create the details of the conversation. Instead, Welles wrote in 1862 simply that Seward had been "not at all communicative" in July—a reaction far more understandable if the subject was the legality of congressional confiscation rather than the far more provocative topic of presidential emancipation. Combined with the evidence from Browning's diary entry and Lincoln's own writings on the day of the alleged conversation, it seems reasonable to conclude that Welles subsequently inflated the importance of his July exchange with Lincoln.

Yet, regardless of exactly what was discussed on July 13, Welles never claimed that he saw a draft of a proclamation. So the question remains, when did Lincoln begin writing? In the 1864 Hodges letter, Lincoln stated that he did not see the "indispensable necessity" of military emancipation until after the border state representatives had "declined the proposition" for compensated emancipation.[37] The president had met with these leaders on Friday, but he did not receive their official rejection until Monday. That same day, July 14, the president also received his first copy of the Second Confiscation Bill, delivered to the White House by Orville Browning. The combination of these two events triggered an urgent reaction from the White House. Now pressed on all sides, Lincoln insisted on time for reflection and writing. "At the President[']s this morning," reports Browning's diary for Tuesday, July 15. "He was in his

Library writing, with directions to deny him to everybody."[38] This might very well have been the moment of emancipation's birth; however, the purpose of this intense activity seemed far more centered on the draft of a veto message for the confiscation law.

When Senator Browning delivered the copy of the confiscation bill on Monday and urged its rejection, the president had promised that he would give the matter "his profound consideration." The bill contained fourteen sections that strengthened existing punishments for the crime of treason and authorized the president to employ a wide range of new tools to crush the rebellion, including the wholesale seizure of rebel property and slaves with only *in rem* court proceedings (which allowed for hearings without the owners being present). The statute also protected all fugitive slaves and declared captured rebel slaves to be "forever free," authorizing the president to employ them in the military, to "organize or use them in such manner as he may judge best," or to colonize the ex-slaves "in some tropical country beyond the limits of the United States." Many of the bill's seizure provisions were not effective immediately, but instead were triggered only sixty days after the president had issued a "public warning and proclamation."[39] Lincoln worried that this bill was both unworkable and unconstitutional.

At first, the president tried to convince the Republican leadership on Capitol Hill to extend their session (which was due to expire the next day) so that they could address his concerns. When they appeared to refuse, he was then provoked into a rare display of temper. "I am sorry Senators could not so far trust me," Lincoln wrote on Tuesday, "as to believe I had some real cause for wishing them to remain."[40] This must have been the moment when the president directed his White House aides to shut the doors to the library to allow him to prepare what would become a vigorously argued statement of about 1,250 words that detailed his constitutional objections to the proposed statute. Once again, the best evidence of Lincoln's state of mind comes from the Browning diary, because, despite all of the instructions to the contrary, the Illinois senator managed to push his way into the presidential library on Tuesday and provided the only eyewitness account of the embattled executive. Browning reported that he found his old friend looking "weary, care-worn and troubled" in the midst of his showdown with Congress. The two men shook hands while Browning expressed concern for Lincoln's health. "He held me by the hand," the senator wrote, "pressed it, and said in a very tender and touching tone—'Browning, I must die sometime.'"[41]

By Tuesday evening, however, the president's position seemed a little stronger. Senate Republicans, led by the powerful William Pitt Fessenden of Maine, secured at least part of Lincoln's requested delay, extending the session until Thursday afternoon. They also arranged by Wednesday evening, over fierce objections from some congressional radicals, for an unprecedented joint resolution that attempted to explain away at least some of the perceived constitutional violations contained within the confiscation law. This was enough for the increasingly overwrought president, who decided to sign the legislation after all.[42]

Thursday, July 17, 1862, was thus a pivotal day. Lincoln spent the morning holed up in an office at the Capitol building, signing the end-of-session bills. With his signature on the Second Confiscation Act, the president also sent along the drafted veto message, in what was widely perceived as a fit of petulance, but which from a modern perspective looks suspiciously like a presidential signing statement. Capitol Hill was full of rumors about the president's contradictory behavior. George Julian, an Indiana Republican, later recalled that the president was privately "arraigned as a deliberate betrayer of freedmen and poor whites."[43] Many Republican legislators were angry because they suspected Lincoln of planning to undermine a statute they had debated for months. They were certainly correct about the president's discontent with their confiscation policy, but few had any idea that he was on the verge of undoing their work by exceeding it.

On Thursday evening, the president returned to his cottage at the Soldiers' Home, happy to find his wife and youngest son back in Washington after more than a week's absence in New York. On Friday and Saturday, he began to catch up on correspondence and to conduct exit interviews with various legislators who were preparing to leave town. An important delegation of senators arrived on Saturday to meet with both the president and the cabinet, urging them to take advantage of the new tools provided by the confiscation law. In what must have come across as both patronizing and unnecessary, the senators insisted that the administration reenergize its prosecution of the flagging war effort.[44] Thus, the absence of any commitments on the president's Sunday schedule must have come as a great relief.

By Monday morning, Lincoln was certainly ready to strike back. He directed his aides to call the cabinet officers to a special meeting at ten o'clock that morning, an occurrence that Secretary of the Treasury Salmon P. Chase sardonically described in his diary as "a novelty." The president then began to outline a series of orders that he had drafted for commanders in the field, quite obviously in response to critics on both Capitol Hill and from across the North. In his diary account, Chase described the president as being "profoundly concerned at the present aspect of affairs" and "determined to take some definitive steps in respect to military action and slavery."[45] Yet the practical effect of the orders—to authorize seizing Confederate property in the field, to employ slaves as laborers, to require an accounting of all these actions, and to provide for the colonization of the ex-slaves—was mainly to execute most of the requirements of the recently passed confiscation law. The men discussed the measures for some time on Monday without reaching any definitive conclusions.

The regular Tuesday cabinet meeting continued their discussion and actually began with a review of Lincoln's fourth draft order providing for colonization of ex-slaves "in some tropical country." According to Chase's diary, the members unanimously agreed that this proposal should be "dropped." They then proceeded to endorse the other three remaining orders from Monday's discussion, though there was some debate about the propriety of arming slaves who might be enlisted into the military. "The President was unwilling to adopt this measure," reported Chase, "but proposed to issue a Proclamation, on the basis of the Confiscation Bill, calling upon the States to return to their allegiance—warning the rebels the provisions of the Act would have full force at the expiration of sixty days—adding, on his own part, a declaration of his intention to renew, at the next session of Congress, his recommendation of compensation to States adopting the gradual abolishment of slavery—and proclaiming the emancipation of all slaves within States remaining in insurrection on the first of January, 1863."[46] What the Chase diary makes clear is that Lincoln had prepared his emancipation proclamation at the same time and for the same reason as he had organized his military orders—*on the basis of the confiscation bill*. The measures discussed on Monday and Tuesday represented a unified response to this latest congressional intrusion into the conduct of the war.

The measures of this unified response were almost surely written together. The text of the military orders appears in a supplement to Lincoln's *Collected Works*. They were undated by the president but have since been identified by editors as being written at the Tuesday cabinet meeting.[47] Yet Chase indicated that Lincoln had shown up at the special Monday session with material already prepared. During the previous week, there was only one date totally clear on Lincoln's calendar and void of any other writings: Sunday, July 20, 1862. Was this the date for the origins of emancipation? No proof exists, but in retrospect it makes perfect sense. Abraham Lincoln must have spent most of that Sunday afternoon writing both the military orders and the draft public proclamation in the second-floor library at the White House. That was the spot where Browning reported that Lincoln had written the veto message, and it was the location for the special cabinet meeting on Monday. Here is where the president had easy access to his books and old statutes, and it is also where he could obtain some additional seclusion from the crowds that often gathered around his office. He had done his thinking and intelligence gathering over several weeks and in a number of places—at his office, in the War Department, on the grounds of the Soldiers' Home, during trips outside of Washington, and even while engaged in carriage rides within the district—but it seems eminently reasonable to conclude that his actual emancipation writing was accomplished on a Sunday afternoon in mid-July within the confines of the White House library.

Unfortunately, for once the Browning diary is not helpful; but there is an intriguing contemporary letter from White House aide John Hay that provides powerful support for this hypothesis. Hay, then twenty-three years old, wrote an affectionate, chatty note to a young lady on Sunday, July 20, that seemed to dangle confidential information as a tool for an ongoing flirtation. The president, Hay wrote, "will not conserve slavery much longer." He added, with blithe assurance, "When next he speaks in relation to this defiant and ungrateful villainy it will be with no uncertain sound." There is no Hay diary entry for this day, but his Sunday letter practically shouts out knowledge of Lincoln at work on a proclamation. "If I have sometimes been impatient of his delay," Hay wrote to his correspondent, Mary Jay, the daughter of a prominent New York abolitionist, "I am so no longer."[48]

The fact that the First Draft of the Emancipation Proclamation actually begins with a sentence required by the Second Confiscation Act suggests very strongly that the document was written sometime between the date of the law's passage (Thursday, July 17) and the discussion of the draft itself (Tuesday, July 22). In retrospect, it is rather remarkable that reference to the July 17 law has not raised more fundamental doubt about the earlier dating of the First Draft by the various recollected claimants. How could such a short document, so clearly written in response to the new law, have been composed at any time prior to its passage? Moreover, Salmon Chase's contemporary descriptions of the two successive cabinet meetings, on Monday, July 21, and Tuesday, July 22, should make it equally obvious that the draft was not announced as some solitary thunderbolt, but rather was presented as part of a series of related orders crafted in direct response to the requirements of the statute. Finally, a careful study of the president's schedule in July, coupled with the heavy-handed hints of his young aide, seems to lead quite naturally to Sunday, July 20, 1862, as the pivotal creative date.

Yet, if all of this deduction is so obvious and natural, then why has no prominent historian offered this hypothesis before? The answer lies partly with the realization that dating emancipation is not such a prosaic matter after all, but instead goes to the heart of a critical interpretative question: Why did Lincoln embrace emancipation? Historical differences over the answer to this question help explain why scholars have clung so tenaciously to their recollected sources.

John Hope Franklin's 1963 anniversary study of the Emancipation Proclamation was celebratory in nature. In the shadow of a new era of civil rights challenges, he went to great lengths to demonstrate that Lincoln was a will-ing and eager emancipator. He wrote confidently (and perhaps wishfully) that the "best evidence" suggested that the president had decided on military emancipation "in the late spring of 1862."[49] When documenting this claim, Franklin employed a number of recollections from Hamlin, Eckert, and others, all testifying to Lincoln's sincere support for black freedom. David Donald proved far more circumspect in his use of recollected evidence, but the story of Lincoln scrawling out his proclamation in the telegraph office fit neatly with his thesis about the essential passivity of Lincoln's nature. Even at the moment of greatest decision, Donald's Lincoln appeared to be cautious, almost hesitant. In his concise, 1993 monograph, Mark Neely was less interested in the immediate narrative of Lincoln's decision making and more concerned about explaining the president's embrace of emancipation as part of his evolution as commander-in-chief. He was also quite skeptical about the contemporary evidence. "Immediate contemporary sources for the origins of the proclama-tion are unfortunately very limited," Neely wrote tersely.[50] Allen Guelzo, on the other hand, found more material to consider, but he also had more space to devote to these narrative questions and more interest in resolving them. Thus, he has offered the most thorough review of the various contemporary and recollected claims, but apparently relying on the "prudence" that he found so admirable in his subject (the "last Enlightenment politician," in his words), Guelzo merely concluded in his work that it was "unclear" when Lincoln began composing his First Draft.[51]

Perhaps it still is. The Browning diary entries, the various contemporary remarks by the president, the connections to the Second Confiscation Act, the quiet Sunday, the Chase diary entry and his letter to Richard Parsons (see note 45), the Hay letter, the military orders, the text of the First Draft itself—these facts do not constitute indisputable evidence that an act of writ-ing occurred at a particular time and place. Yet, it should be equally clear that the recollections historians have generally relied upon before now to support their claims are not without their own serious question marks. Sunday, July 20, 1862, might not emerge as the consensus choice for emancipation's date of origin, but it quite obviously deserves consideration. And if that means reevaluating the connection between confiscation and emancipation, then perhaps that would also be a welcome outcome. Historians almost never ignore congressional confiscation policy when discussing Lincoln's actions, but they have downplayed its impact because presidential emancipation so thoroughly superseded the other policy in the months that followed.[52] A careful review of contemporary evidence suggests that this has been a mistake. While con-gressional confiscation was certainly not the cause of Lincoln's emancipation policy, it was quite clearly the trigger. To put it more provocatively, it seems that political necessity mattered almost as much as military necessity in the actual drafting of emancipation. The recollections that historians have relied upon have papered over this inconvenient fact. Thus, looking beyond July 1862 has obscured a fuller understanding of Lincoln's actual summer of emancipation. Ultimately, this might be the most startling conclusion of all. Despite a significant amount of evidence and generations of penetrating scholarship, we are clearly still struggling in ways both large and small to define the greatest decision of our greatest president.

Notes

1. Emancipation Proclamation—First Draft, July 22, 1862, in *The Collected Works of Abraham Lincoln*, ed. Roy P. Basler, 9 vols. (New Brunswick, N.J.: Rutgers University Press, 1953–55), 5:336–38; Preliminary Emancipation Proclamation, September 22, 1862, in ibid., 5:433–36; final Emancipation Proclamation, January 1, 1863, in ibid., 6:28–31.

2. For a fuller account of this critical month and a more complete description of the places that Lincoln occupied or visited, see Matthew Pinsker, *Lincoln's Sanctuary: Abraham Lincoln and the Soldiers' Home* (New York: Oxford University Press, 2003). The president's reference to the "iron cage" is on 51.

3. To view a copy of the original First Draft, see Abraham Lincoln, Preliminary Draft of Emancipation Proclamation, Tuesday, July 22, 1862, Abraham Lincoln Papers at the Library of Congress, Series 1, General Correspondence, 1833–1916, online at http://memory. loc.gov/ammem/alhtml/malhome.html.

4. *Collected Works*, 5:336–37. For a good description of the origins of Carpenter's famous painting, which hangs near the Senate's west stairway in the Capitol, see Mark E. Neely Jr., introduction, *The Inner Life of Abraham Lincoln: Six Months at the White House*, by Francis B. Carpenter (1866; repr., Lincoln: University of Nebraska Press, 1995), v–xviii.

5. Charles E. Hamlin, *The Life and Times of Hannibal Hamlin*, 2 vols., (1899; repr., Port Washington, N.Y.: Kennikat, 1971), 2:428–29. For a good discussion of Hamlin's evolving tale, see Allen C. Guelzo, *Lincoln's Emancipation Proclamation: The End of Slavery in America* (New York: Simon & Schuster, 2004), 141–42.

6. Eckert actually claimed that Lincoln first began writing the draft following "his arrival one morning in June, 1862, shortly after McClellan's 'Seven Days' Fight.'" The problem is that the Seven Days' Battles began on June 25 and ended on July 1, 1862. The most sensible possibility, assuming that story has any truth at all, is that Eckert meant to write, "shortly after McClellan's 'Seven Days' Fight' commenced." See David Homer Bates, *Lincoln in the Telegraph Office: Recollections of the United States Military Telegraph Corps during the Civil War* (1907; repr., Lincoln: University of Nebraska Press, 1995), 138.

7. Some historians have mistakenly identified Eckert's story as coming from David Homer Bates, who was the author of the 1907 recollection, *Lincoln in the Telegraph Office*, where this account from Major Eckert first appeared. Bates was a cipher operator under Eckert's command and apparently received a letter from his former boss recounting what had happened during the summer of 1862 as he was preparing his memoir for publication. Thus, Bates put the entire passage about Lincoln's drafting emancipation in quotation marks and carefully prefaced it by writing, "Some of the incidents connected with the writing of that immortal document have now been recorded by Eckert, as follows." See ibid., 138–41.

8. John Hope Franklin, *The Emancipation Proclamation* (New York: Doubleday, 1963), 35–37.

9. David Herbert Donald, *Lincoln* (New York: Simon & Schuster, 1995), 363–64, 654n.

10. Mark E. Neely Jr., *The Last Best Hope of Earth: Abraham Lincoln and the Promise of America* (Cambridge, Mass.: Harvard University Press, 1993), 108–9.

11. Guelzo, *Lincoln's Emancipation Proclamation*, 140–44.

12. Hannibal Hamlin to Abraham Lincoln, September 25, 1862, Abraham Lincoln Papers at the Library of Congress, online at http://memory.loc.gov/ammem/alhtml/malhome.html.

13. *Collected Works*, 5:49.

14. Ibid., 5:223; Stanton quoted in Guelzo, *Lincoln's Emancipation Proclamation*, 140.

15. *Collected Works*, 5:278.

16. Ibid., 5:388.

17. Pinsker, *Lincoln's Sanctuary,* 29.

18. Theodore Calvin Pease and James G. Randall, eds., *The Diary of Orville Hickman Browning: 1850–1864*, 2 vols. (Springfield: Illinois State Historical Library, 1925), 1:555.

19. Ibid.

20. Donald, *Lincoln*; 365; Guelzo, *Lincoln's Emancipation Proclamation*, 142.

21. Pease and Randall, *Diary of Browning*, 1:556.

22. Michael Burlingame, ed., *With Lincoln in the White House: Letters, Memoranda, and Other Writings of John G. Nicolay, 1860–1865* (Carbondale: Southern Illinois University Press, 2000), 84.

23. *Collected Works*, 5:306; reporter's description, quoted in Pinsker, *Lincoln's Sanctuary*, 37; Pease and Randall, *Diary of Browning*, 1:557.

24. *Collected Works*, 5:307.

25. Quoted in Don E. Fehrenbacher and Virginia Fehrenbacher, eds., *Recollected Words of Abraham Lincoln* (Stanford, Calif.: Stanford University Press, 1996), 434.

26. Quoted in Stephen W. Sears, *George B. McClellan: The Young Napoleon* (New York: Ticknor & Fields, 1988), 227.

27. Joseph H. Barrett, *Life of Abraham Lincoln* (New York: Moore, Wilstach & Baldwin, 1865), 823.

28. Carpenter, *Inner Life*, 86–87. Note that Allen Guelzo is one of the few modern scholars who references Barrett's claim, but he believes the information originally came from Francis Carpenter. Yet Carpenter acknowledged in one edition of his memoir that he never heard Lincoln himself place emancipation's origins on the return from Harrison's Landing but instead had relied upon Barrett for this "circumstance," which he suggested, "from the known relations of the author," was "undoubtedly true" (Guelzo, *Lincoln's Emancipation Proclamation*, 144–45).

29. Gideon Welles, "The History of Emancipation," *Galaxy,* December 1872, 842, available online via "Making of America," Cornell University Library, http://cdl.library.cornell.edu/cgi-bin/moa/moa-cgi?notisid=ACB8727-0014-113.

30. Burlingame, *With Lincoln in the White House*, 85.

31. Joseph H. Barrett, *Abraham Lincoln and His Presidency*, 2 vols. (Cincinnati: Robert Clarke, 1904), 2:112; Carpenter, *Inner Life*, 86–87.

32. *Collected Works*, 7:282.

33. John T. Morse, ed., *Diary of Gideon Welles: Secretary of the Navy under Lincoln and Johnson; Volume 1, 1861–March 30, 1864* (Boston: Houghton, Mifflin, 1911), 70. See also Welles, "History of Emancipation," 838–52.

34. Franklin, *Emancipation Proclamation*, 37–38; Neely, *Last Best Hope of Earth,* 107–8; Donald, *Lincoln*, 362; Guelzo, *Lincoln's Emancipation Proclamation*, 145. Out of these historians, Guelzo is probably the sharpest in his criticism of Welles, whose account he labels as a "slight dissent." Guelzo also points out that the naval secretary was "notoriously shaky about dating events" (*Lincoln's Emancipation Proclamation*, 145).

35. *Collected Works*, 5:322.

36. Morse, *Diary of Gideon Welles*, 144.

37. *Collected Works*, 7:282.

38. Pease and Randall, *Diary of Browning*, 1:559.

39. The text of the Second Confiscation Act is available online at the Freedmen and Southern Society Project of the University of Maryland, http://www.history.umd.edu/Freedmen/conact2.htm.

40. *Collected Works*, 5:326.

41. Pease and Randall, *Diary of Browning*, 1:559–60.

42. "The President and the Confiscation Bill," *New York Times*, July 18, 1862. See also Donald, *Lincoln*, 364–65.

43. George W. Julian, "Lincoln and the Proclamation of Emancipation," in *Reminiscences of Abraham Lincoln by Distinguished Men of His Time*, ed. Allen Thorndike Rice (1885; revised ed., New York: Harper & Brothers, 1909), 237–38.

44. See Pinsker, *Lincoln's Sanctuary,* 44–45; and entry for July 19, 1862, in *Lincoln Day by Day: A Chronology, 1809–1865*, ed. Earl Schenck Miers (1960; repr., Dayton, Ohio: Morningside, 1991), 3:28.

45. David Donald, ed., *Inside Lincoln's Cabinet: The Civil War Diaries of Salmon P. Chase* (New York: Longmans, Green, 1954), 95. Chase described the same scene in slightly different terms in a letter dated July 20, 1862 (but not completed until after July 22). "The Slavery question perplexes the President almost as much as ever and yet I think he is about to emerge from the obscurities where he has been groping into somewhat clearer light," he wrote to Richard C. Parsons. "Today he has had his Secretaries in Consultation & has read us several orders which he is thinking of promulgating." In the letter, the secretary also referred to the First Draft as the "proclamation warning the rebels of the confiscations denounced by Congress and declaring his purpose to enfranchise the slaves of all rebels (unless they return to their allegiance in Sixty days) in all the Gulf States." See Chase to Parsons, Sunday, July 20, 1862, in *The Salmon P. Chase Papers: Volume 3, Correspondence, 1858 to March, 1863*, ed. John Niven (Kent, Ohio: Kent State University Press, 1993), 231.

46. Donald, *Inside Lincoln's Cabinet*, 99.

47. Lincoln to Edwin M. Stanton, [July 22, 1862], in *The Collected Works of Abraham Lincoln: First Supplement, 1832–1865*, ed. Roy P. Basler (1974; repr., New Brunswick, N.J.: Rutgers University Press, 1990), 141–42.

48. John Hay to Mary Jay, Washington, Sunday, July 20, 1862, in *At Lincoln's Side: John Hay's Civil War Correspondence and Selected Writings*, ed. Michael Burlingame (Carbondale: Southern Illinois University Press, 2000), 23.

49. Franklin, *Emancipation Proclamation*, 34.

50. Neely, *Last Best Hope of Earth*, 201.

51. Guelzo, *Lincoln's Emancipation Proclamation*, 3, 140. Guelzo does not mention the Hay letter of July 20, 1862.

52. See a thoughtful essay on this subject by Herman Belz titled "Protection of Personal Liberty in Republican Emancipation Legislation," in his *Abraham Lincoln, Constitutional-*

ism, and Equal Rights in the Civil War Era (New York: Fordham University Press, 1998), 101–18. For another perspective that sharply criticizes the scholarly indifference to congressional confiscation policy, though in a much less thoughtful and persuasive manner, see Lerone Bennett Jr., *Forced into Glory: Abraham Lincoln's White Dream* (Chicago: Johnson Publishing, 2000).

7 The Role of the Press
Hans L. Trefousse

*T*he importance of the press, *the* medium during the nineteenth century, is well known. Popular knowledge of major events was disseminated by the newspapers throughout the country, and although they often copied from one another and reported matters in similar language, when friendly to Lincoln and stressing his progressive actions, their contribution to his reputation for giving freedom to African Americans, supporting the antislavery cause, granting emancipation, and promoting the Thirteenth Amendment, is evident.

Of course, different papers expressed differing policies. Extreme abolitionist journals, such as the *Liberator, the National Anti-Slavery Standard*, and Karl Heinzen's *Der Pionier,* tended at times to be critical of Lincoln's allegedly too careful approach and what they considered his tardiness. Democratic journals like the *New York World* were highly critical, and that Southern organs attacked him incessantly stands to reason. But others, as will be seen, were more friendly.[1]

The friendly press highlighted Lincoln's antislavery activities before his nomination and election to the presidency. When in 1856 he received 110 votes at the Republican convention at Philadelphia, the papers naturally did not fail to mention it, but the *New York Evening Post* reported that he "was a good fellow, a fierce friend of freedom, and an old line whig." And then came the Illinois senatorial contest in 1858. Although the state legislatures then elected United States senators, at Springfield in June Lincoln was nominated as the sole candidate of the state, and he delivered his famous "House divided against itself" speech, predicting that the nation would eventually be all slave or all free. The *New York Times* called it "elegant," while the *Chicago Daily Tribune* referred to it as a "logical and masterly argument."[2]

The subsequent campaign against the famous Illinois Democratic senator Stephen A. Douglas received elaborate coverage, with a stress on Lincoln's pleas for freedom and emancipation. As the *Chicago Press and Tribune* pointed out, he appealed to the Declaration of Independence with its stress on liberty and equality. Concerning a reply to Douglas at Springfield on July 20, the paper considered "the speech of Mr. Lincoln . . . an able vindication of Republicanism" (meaning opposition to slavery). The ensuing six debates with Douglas received special attention. When on August 17 the two met at Ottawa, the same paper praised his "excellent" answer to Douglas. "He lifted the curtain that hid the conspiracies and conspirators from view, and laid bare before the gaze of ten thousand auditors the work in which the little Catiline [a reference to Lucius Sergius Catalina, the Roman conspirator] was engaged, showed up who were his confreres and associated in the plot to overthrow the Constitution, nationalize slavery, and convert our Union in a negro-breeding despotism." After the Freeport debate on the twenty-seventh, in which Lincoln showed the inconsistency of Douglas's idea of "popular sovereignty" with the *Dred Scott* decision, Justice Roger B. Taney's refusal of the right of popular choice about slavery in the territories, even the often critical *New York Evening Post* wrote, "Mr. Lincoln closed the debate in a calm review of Douglas' speech, charging him with perversion of truth and disingenuous argument. He dwelt briefly on the creed of the Republican Party [the prohibition of slavery in the territories] and urged it upon his audience as the only policy calculated to give peace to the country and to put it again on the right track." The *New York Daily Tribune*, equally impressed, commented, "he said . . . the present [fugitive slave] law is objectionable in several important particulars and ought to be modified . . . [and] as to the abolition of slavery in the District of Columbia, he should be glad to see it done, and believes Congress has the constitutional power to do it." The succeeding debates gave rise to further praise, pointing out Lincoln's steadfast opposition to the expansion of slavery.[3]

After the Cooper Union speech in New York in February 1860, during which Lincoln first came to the favorable attention of the East, and which Harold Holzer has called "the speech that made Abraham Lincoln president," the *New York Daily Tribune* was enthusiastic about his condemnation of slavery and his demand that its spread be arrested, with the *Evening Post* echoing this opinion.[4]

The 1860 presidential campaign naturally brought forth innumerable praises for the candidate from Illinois. As early as February, the *Chicago Press and Tribune* emphasized his devotion to freedom. "He has that radicalism which a keen insight into the meaning of the anti-slavery conflict, is sure to give." Continuing its praise, it called him "Right on the question of slavery, on the Homestead question, on all the issues which divide the parties." Upon the actual nomination, the *New York Evening Post,* though noting that many had been in favor of William H. Seward, the senator from New York and former governor, rejoiced "that a candidate is fixed upon who has so many recommendations as Abraham Lincoln, whose character embraces so many excellent qualities, and whose personal history gives him so strong a hold on the good will of the people." The *Courier and Enquirer* praised him as "No expediency candidate but one who early embraced the Republican causes"; and the *New York Tribune* thought his position as a Republican rendered him satisfactory to the most zealous member of the party, while the moderation of his character commended him to the opposing group. "Republicans, you have now selected your candidate for the campaign of 1860," stated the *Chicago Press and Tribune*. "Abraham Lincoln of Illinois leads the column of the Friends of Freedom."[5]

During the campaign, the *National Anti-Slavery Standard*, which was generally critical of Lincoln for not doing enough to end slavery, after complaining that the "amount of anti-slavery" in the Republican platform "is certainly small enough," nevertheless expressed its hope that "Mr. Lincoln will not fall below what it requires." The *Chicago Press and Tribune,* speaking of the troubles in Missouri, where Unionists had deposed the secessionist governor, pointed out in July that "Mr. Lincoln has been a valiant soldier from the day of the first invasion of Missouri to the present time. He saw from the first, not only the object of the repeal of the Missouri Compromise [the potential opening of Kansas and Nebraska to slavery], but the craving aim of the villains who used the power which this repeal gave them to oppress and butcher a free and peaceful people." Pointing out his opposition to the attempt to deny the people of Kansas a fair vote on the proslavery Lecompton Constitution for the territory, the paper went on to state, "we take great pleasure in giving wide publicity to the fact that he has been an Anti-Lecompton man from the beginning, that his money and his personal services have been at the disposal of the cause of freedom and a good government for Kansas" The *New York Spectator*, referring to foreign doubts about the United States in the wake of efforts by the South to show that the entire country was devoted to slavery, predicted that Lincoln's election would change that tune, because, "our agents abroad will speak the language of liberty instead of slavery."[6]

Challenged by Stephen A. Douglas, John C. Breckinridge, and John Bell, Lincoln managed to defeat his opponents, though he only received 39 percent of the popular vote. After the election, the *Chicago Press and Tribune* wrote, "The Republic renews its ancient glories. The great ideas which led to the Revolution—which first found utterances in the Declaration of Independence, and which were afterward embodied in political form in the Federal Constitution, will live in the hearts of the American people. . . . There is hope yet for freedom, for honesty, for purity. . . . It is enough to say that the triumph is a glorious one—that Abraham Lincoln is President-elect of this great Republic. And let all the people say Amen!"[7]

After the election, the South proceeded to secede and form the Confederacy. Various forms of compromise were suggested to save the Union, particularly the one by Senator John J. Crittenden of Kentucky, proposing to extend the old dividing line of 36°30′ of the Missouri Compromise all the way to the Pacific. Lincoln's refusal to compromise brought forth new encomiums, again stressing his devotion to the antislavery cause. The *Chicago Daily Tribune* quoted him: "I will suffer death before I will consent . . . to any compromise." And in praise of his devotion to freedom, it cited the *Illinois Journal*'s comment: "WE know that he stands firmly and squarely on the ground assumed in letter of acceptance—the basis of which was the authoritative declaration of the party in convention at Chicago—and that the South has no terrors to drive him, Commerce no blandishment to coax him, Concession no wiles to drive him from it." Clearly, he felt that the proposed compromise involved a weakening of the party's antislavery principles.[8]

After the outbreak of war, the Republican press, even the critical antislavery papers, such as the *New York Tribune*, sustained the commander in chief. The day after the Confederates attacked Fort Sumter on April 12, 1861, Lincoln issued a proclamation calling for seventy-five thousand troops in defense of the republic. According to the *New York Courier and Enquirer*, "To the simple, dignified, calm but firm Proclamation of the President of the United States [calling for troops], the loyal States of this Union will respond in the name of God, Amen!" In December, the president issued his first annual address, and in it, he endorsed the First Confiscation Act, which included the confiscation of slaves used against the Union. Declaring this the most important part of the message, the *Chicago Daily Tribune* praised the speech for including it. In March of 1862, when he published a call for the compensated emancipation of slaves in the border states, newspapers widely lauded his purpose. "The wisdom of the measure proposed by Mr. Lincoln in his message to Congress . . . impresses us more and more . . . ," wrote the *New York Tribune*. "The first era of the supremacy of the rights of man in this country dates from the Declaration of Independence; the second began on the 6th of March, 1862, with the Emancipation Message of President Lincoln." Meanwhile, the *Chicago Daily Tribune* commented that "the great idea in the message is, that the nation should be purged of the curse of slavery, and the safety, unity and perpetuity of the Union can only be ensured by the extension of the principle of freedom to all its parts." Even the usually dubious *Liberator* was glad that the president now had "the constitutional right, power and opportunity to produce liberty throughout all the land to all the inhabitants thereof." And the *New York Spectator* claimed that the president's message had been "received in all parts of the country with a degree of favor that may be said to almost ensure the happiest results."[9]

The Preliminary Emancipation Proclamation of September 22, 1862, in which Lincoln declared he would free all slaves in areas still in rebellion after January 1, 1863, naturally brought forth widespread journalistic comment, not all favorable, but much of it laudatory. The hostile *Washington Daily National Intelligencer* provided a mild example of the former: "With our well known and oft repeated views respecting the inutility of such proclamations, it can hardly be necessary for us to say that, where we expect no good, we shall be only too happy to find that no harm had been done by the present declaration of the Chief Executive." And the often hostile *New York Herald* thought the proclamation had been forced upon the nation by the abolitionists and the secessionists of the South, and that it would suddenly emancipate three or four million human beings and throw them "in the fullness of their helplessness and ignorance upon their own resources and the wisdom of the white race to properly regulate and care for them in their new condition of life."[10]

The friendly papers were enthusiastic. The *New York Evening Post* declared, "We will not discuss the question whether Mr. Lincoln's proclamation of freedom to the African race in the rebel states might not have been more op-portunely issued at the time of the passage of the confiscation and Emancipa-tion Act of July last. We put aside the question whether the interval between the date of the proclamation and the time fixed for carrying its provisions into effect be the wisest part of the proceeding. It satisfied us that the step had at last been taken. The twenty-second of September in this year will hereafter be a day to be commemorated with peculiar honor, a day illustrious in the annals not only of our own country, but of the world, the day to which the present Chief Magistrate of the United States will recur hereafter, as the most glorious of his life." The *Philadelphia Inquirer* agreed: "The wisdom of the step taken—we refer at present to that clause in the document which declares free the slaves of the Rebel States after the first of January—is unquestionable, its necessity indisputable." The *Cincinnati Daily Commercial* refuted the charges of the president's opponents and asserted that no friend of the country had a right to be displeased at this policy. The *Chicago Daily Tribune* was certain that "President Lincoln set his hand and affixed the great seal of the nation to the grandest proclamation ever issued by man." The *National Anti-Slavery Standard*, while not satisfied with the limited nature of Lincoln's document, nevertheless admitted that "we rejoice with unspeakable joy that he has at last openly committed himself to a measure, which, if carried out in good faith . . . must ensure the utter and speedy destruction of the slave system, and give us a country free from the damning reproach of making merchandise of the children of God." The *New York Times* called it "the great event of the day" and could not see why Democrats were attacking the proclamation, given that it was a purely military document. The *Washington Daily Morning Chronicle* considered it purely vindicated by the November elections, in which, though the Democrats gained seats, the Republicans and their border state allies still retained control of the House of Representatives.[11]

That December, the annual message of 1862 brought forth still more praise for the president. Reaffirming his emancipation message, he also proposed a constitutional amendment offering compensation for all slaveholders who would free their slaves prior to January 1, 1900. "Thank God he adheres to the pledge of his emancipation proclamation of the 22d of September," opined Washington's *Daily Morning Chronicle*; and the *New York Daily Spectator*, commenting upon his proposed amendment for freedom in the border slave states by 1900, pointed out that "in his argument in favor of these proposed amendments the President very properly assumes that slavery is an evil and that it is the cause of rebellion, and the source and strength of its continuance," an argument with which the *Cincinnati Daily Commercial* agreed. The critical *Liberator,* while conceding to him the desire to see slavery some day or other banished from the country, nevertheless thought it a folly to buy up Southern treason in lots to suit purchasers and ending the rebellion by a shrewd regard for pecuniary considerations.[12]

January 1, 1863, was the day on which the Emancipation Proclamation was to go into effect. The *Chicago Daily Tribune* marked the occasion:

> On this, the first day of the year of grace, eighteen hundred sixty-three, when Abraham Lincoln, raised up, as we believe, for this very purpose, gives freedom to three millions of slaves in the rebel States, let us take an example from history, that we may see how the hand of God delivered his people in the past, and how we have reason to hope His justice and wisdom will be vindicated in the future history of our nation. . . . Then let us thank God for Abraham Lincoln; and pray that through him the nine other plagues may be averted; and that as the proclamation of freedom rings through the land the angel of mercy may proclaim, "Glory to God in the highest; on earth peace and good will toward men."

The *Daily Morning Chronicle* in Washington was equally enthusiastic:

> True to his warning and his promise, President Lincoln has today, by virtue of his office as Commander-in-Chief of the Army and Navy of the United States, promised freedom to all persons of African descent held as slave labor in such States and parts of States as are now in rebellion against the Government. . . . And for this New Year's gift, the man who has wrought the work . . . Abraham Lincoln, is entitled to the everlasting gratitude of a despised race enfranchised, the plaudits of a country saved, and an inscription of undying fame in the impartial records of history.[13]

The *New York Evening Post* was not far behind in its praise. It noted: "True to his warnings and his promises, the Commander-in-Chief has issued promptly, on the first day of the New Year, his proclamation of freedom to the slaves of the rebels in arms." Radical as this action might be, the paper thought the president should have taken this step long before. "But," it conceded, "we hail his acceptance of the true policy none the less fervently because it comes so late." The *New York Times*, though often critical, declared that "President Lincoln's proclamation . . . marks an era in the history not only of this war, but of this country and the world. It is not necessary to assume that it will set free immediately the enslaved blacks of the South, in order to ascribe to it the greatest and most permanent importance." Even the often faultfinding *Liberator* was enthusiastic. "The Proclamation," read its headline. "Three Million of Slaves set free: 'Glory, Hallelujah!'" Nine days later, it glorified the proclamation again. "We cannot stop without one word of rejoicing at the approach of the hour of deliverance and exaltation of America," it wrote, quoting a clergyman in Rome: "The proclamation is as life from the dead." The *New York Spectator* asserted, "We can-not think that any truly loyal citizen will, on reflection, interpose any objection to this decree." Yet the hostile *New York Leader* expressed that it regretted to learn the president shared the designs of his radical advisers.[14]

Of course, there was much criticism of the freedom proclamation. Should it not have had a more moral tone? Would it not interfere with latent Unionism in the South? Again, the press came to Lincoln's aid. Pointing out that enlistments of Unionists in the seceded states had not ceased since the proclamation was issued and were, indeed, more brisk than before, the *National Anti-Slavery Standard* dismissed the charge of ill effects upon the South. And if some British papers characterized the document as feeble and halting, the *Daily Morning Chronicle* in Washington reported that the Emancipation Proclamation had done much to improve the public sentiment of the Old World, as liberty now stood out in bold contrast to slavery.[15]

In May 1863, Lincoln's devotion to freedom was tested with the arrest of Clement L. Vallandigham, the country's leading Copperhead, as alleged pro-Confederates were called. Arrested because of his violation of General Ambrose E. Burnside's order prohibiting speeches sympathizing with the South, he was condemned to imprisonment, only to be sent into exile to the South by the president. As the *Daily Morning Chronicle* put it, "The President . . . has approved the findings of the court-martial in Vallandigham's case, but he ordered him forthwith sent beyond our lines. General satisfaction is expressed at the result, which so happily meets the difficulties of the case—avoiding the possibility of making him a martyr, and yet effectively destroying his power of evil." When in May a committee of Democrats in Albany protested against his actions, the president wrote a spirited defense of his actions, including his belief in the permanency of the guarantee of freedom of speech, which the *National Anti-Slavery Standard* promptly praised. "Whatever may be thought of the expediency and propriety of the head of the Nation descending to expostulation and argument with impudent enemies, we think there can be no two opinions, among honest men, as to the force and conclusiveness with which he establishes his points."[16]

That August, Lincoln wrote a letter to a Union mass meeting in Springfield, Illinois, that was widely reported. According to the *National Anti-Slavery Standard*, "The Nation breathes freer than it did ten days ago. . . . We all know what pressures have been brought to bear on the President to compel him to equivocate, at least, as to this Emancipation policy. . . . The relief which the clear and unmistakable words of the President have occasioned is the greater from the uneasiness that went before. . . . The letter is a fitting commentary on the text of the Discourse on Freedom, proclaimed last New Year's day." The *Chicago Daily Tribune* put it more forcefully:

> He will stand by the Proclamation! We have never doubted Abraham Lincoln.
> . . . Least of all, have we ever had any doubt of the firmness of his anti-slavery convictions, nor of his perfect sincerity in imposing them, so far as he could justly do so, upon the policy that his administration has pursued. . . . It has been feared that even he looked upon his Proclamation as a temporary expedient, born of the necessities of the situation, to be adhered to or retracted as a short-sighted and time serving policy dictated; and that when the moment for attempting to compromise might come, he would put it aside as he would an order to move an army, or send a squadron to sea. . . . The Springfield letter dispels all doubts and silences all crackers.[17]

In mentioning the president's popularity, the press tended to emphasize his Emancipation Proclamation. "He is today the most popular man in the United States . . . ," asserted the *Chicago Daily Tribune* on November 3, 1863. "The people believe in him because of his Emancipation Proclamation and his willingness to stand by and maintain it." Some two weeks later, on the nineteenth, he delivered his famous Gettysburg Address, with its emphasis on the cause of freedom. Many of the newspapers were enthusiastic. Comparing it with Edward Everett's much longer speech, the *Springfield Republican* said, "Surprisingly fine as Mr. Everett's oration was in the Gettysburg consecration, the rhetorical honors [of] the occasion were won by Mr. Lincoln. His little speech is a perfect gem; deep in feeling, compact in thought and expression, and tasteful and elegant in every word and comma." The *Daily Morning Chronicle* predicted that the speech, though short, would receive the attention of thousands who would read it; and *Harper's Weekly* thought that Lincoln's words were from the heart to the heart and could not be read without kindling emotion. If the hostile *Chicago Times* called it in bad taste, even the Democratic *New York World* had to admit that it was calculated to arouse deep feeling.[18]

The president's annual message in December 1863, with its proclamation of amnesty, contained a further pledge never to retract the Emancipation Proclamation and a promise never to return to slavery anyone freed by that document. "That sentence shed daylight through the whole matter," commented the *Chicago Daily Tribune*. "That Proclamation, followed up and made effective, wipes the Confederacy proper, as it was a year ago, clean of slavery. As to the Border States, which the President exempts, those are taking care of themselves. Every one of them will abolish it."[19]

In Washington, the *Daily Morning Chronicle* continued its strong support of Lincoln's moves toward freedom. Delighted at the presence of blacks at his New Year's reception, it commented, "we rejoice that we have a President who is a democrat in fact as well as by nature." And it believed he was in line with popular opinion. "He executes the will of the people . . . ," it asserted. "His growth in political knowledge, his steady movement toward emancipation, are but the growth and movement of the national mind."[20]

In view of the possibility that the Emancipation Proclamation might be held unconstitutional by the Supreme Court, it became clear to many Republicans that only a constitutional amendment could overcome this difficulty and assure the permanency of emancipation. Eighteen sixty-four was an election year in which the matter might be, and indeed, was about to be, decided. As early as January 12, the *Brooklyn Daily Union* prominently featured the report that Senator John B. Henderson had introduced two resolutions for amendments to the Constitution, one outlawing slavery, and the other, simplifying the amendment process, while relying on the president's emancipation and amnesty proclamations. Then, on February 11, the *Daily Morning Chronicle* reported that Senator Charles Sumner had also introduced an amendment prohibiting bondage. It read, "Everywhere within the limits of the United States, and of each State or Territory thereof, all persons are equal before the law, so that no person can hold another as slave." Four days later, it reported that the Senate Judiciary Committee had changed it to its present form: "Neither slavery nor involuntary servitude, except as a punishment for crime whereof the party shall have been duly convicted, shall exist within the United States, or any place subject to their jurisdiction." Passed by the Senate on April 8, it was rejected by the House in June, but was part of the platform adopted by the Republicans, who now called themselves the National Union Party, at their convention in Baltimore. Thus, it became an issue in the reelection of the president, who was renominated there on June 7.[21]

The president's renomination as *the* antislavery candidate had been promoted by the press for some time. Refuting the idea that the convention planned for June should be postponed, the *Chicago Daily Tribune* on February 13 stated that, "so far as Mr. Lincoln is concerned, it is not necessary. We believe him to be the first choice of a vast majority of the Union men of the United States." In a comparison of Jefferson Davis with Abraham Lincoln, the *Brooklyn Daily Union* on March 26 found the latter by far the better man and concluded that he would probably be renominated. The *Chicago Daily Tribune* fully agreed. As it wrote on March 30, "It is notorious that the army almost *en masse* desire the re-election of President Lincoln. Officers and men prefer him to any other candidate; they have faith in him, they believe him to be their warm friend and that he does all for them in his power. They know him to be as true to the cause of liberty as Jefferson, and to National unity as Jackson." On May 27, the *Daily Morning Chronicle* commented, "Next to the summary defeat of the rebel armies, the deadliest blow that could be inflicted on the rebellion is the knowledge that the 'despot' who 'lords' it in the White House, who issued the Emancipation Proclamation, and has enlisted negro soldiers, is supported by the zealous and universal approbation of the American people."[22]

The actual renomination of the president on the antislavery Union platform naturally occasioned all sorts of favorable comments. Noted the *Brooklyn Daily Union*:

> It was the unquestioned will of the American people that Mr. Lincoln should be again nominated for the Presidency, and it was their unequivocal right, by means of their regularly delegated representatives, to indicate that will. . . . The Convention has made that work one to which every patriot can give his whole heart. For it has placed Messrs. Lincoln and Johnson on a platform of principles by which every lover of his country and of liberty can stand to the last. . . . The platform is absolutely strong. . . . It aims a direct and irresistible blow at slavery and demands its extirpation by the only complete, thorough, and unquestionable method.

The *New York Times* not only praised the nomination but also stressed its agreement with the call for a constitutional amendment in the platform. The *New York Evening Post* agreed, and the *Daily Morning Chronicle* likewise expressed its total approval of the renomination and the platform's demand for the amendment.[23]

On December 6, Lincoln delivered his annual address for 1864. Reasserting his determination to enforce the Emancipation Proclamation, he also advocated the passage of the constitutional amendment by the House of Representatives, two ideas immediately hailed by friendly press. The *New York Evening Post* wrote:

As often as the public have had reason to exclaim, "God bless Abraham Lincoln," they will utter the benediction with a new zest on reading his late message. . . . . His words are few and plain, but unambiguous; no one can mistake their meaning. He recommends Congress in the first place, to pass an act for an amendment of the constitution prohibiting slavery, which only failed of the requisite two-thirds vote by a few votes. He recommends it because the measure is just and politic in itself, and because the people, at the recent election, may be said to have given a distinct and emphatic approval of it; but asserts, whatever Congress may do, he will never recede a single step from the position he has taken in regard to the subject.

The *Liberator* rejoiced that Lincoln was urging "prompt action with reference to the amendment of the Constitution." The *Cincinnati Daily Commercial* likewise praised his advocacy of the amendment. "This measure," it wrote, "will be, undoubtedly, the most important, in its general character, before Congress and the nation, during the next year, and it receives additional importance and prominence from the recommendation of the Executive." Other papers agreed.[24]

Congress debated the actual measure in January 1865. "The vote on the Constitutional amendment abolishing slavery . . . will be very close . . . In the event of its failure the President is determined to call an extra session of Congress immediately after adjournment," wrote the *New York Times*. And when the House passed the resolution on January 31, several papers immediately connected it with the administration's victory in the November election. On the following day, a serenade welcomed the president at the White House, and as the papers pointed out, he immediately said that this honor to him was due to the passage of the amendment. He had even signed it, though this was unnecessary in the case of an amendment.[25]

The president's Second Inaugural Address, which has been called his greatest speech, was certainly hailed by the press. In comparison with its predecessor in 1861, which stressed the maintenance of the Union, observed the *New York Tribune*, the new one "points boldly to Slavery, its implacable assailant, and says [referring to the Book of Esther], 'This Haman shall hang on the gallows erected for Mordecai.'" Concerning slavery, the *Liberator* asserted that "It will inspire fresh confidence in the integrity and firmness of the President in touching that hateful system, deepen the popular feeling as the duty and necessity of utterly abolishing it in the present struggle." Other newspaper comments were similar.[26]

Thus, at the very end of Lincoln's career, in covering the second inaugural, the press forcefully demonstrated one last time how important its influence was in support of the president and his devotion to freedom and the anti-slavery cause.

Notes

1. *Liberator*, March 14, 1862; *National Anti-Slavery Standard*, October 27, 1860; *New York World*, June 6, 1863; *Der Pionier*, October 1, 1862; Hans L. Trefousse, *First among Equals: Abraham Lincoln's Reputation during His Administration* (New York: Fordham University Press, 2005), 4–5; Robert S. Harper, *Lincoln and the Press* (New York: McGraw Hill, 1951), 56–58, 66–69; Harry J. Maihafer, *War of Words: Abraham Lincoln and the Civil War Press* (Washington: Brassey's, 2001), 24–25.

2. *New York Times*, June 21, 1858; *New York Evening Post*, June 19, 1856; *Chicago Daily Tribune*, June 19, 1858; Harper, *Lincoln and the Press*, 20.

3. *Chicago Press and Tribune*, July 12, 16, 20, August 23, September 21, October 9, 15, 18, 1858; *New York Evening Post*, September 2, 1858; *New York Daily Tribune*, September 1, 1858.

4. Harold Holzer, *Lincoln at Cooper Union: The Speech That Made Abraham Lincoln President* (New York: Simon & Schuster, 2004), 156–58.

5. *Chicago Press and Tribune*, February 16, May 19, 1860; *New York Evening Post*, May 19, 1860; *Courier and Enquirer* quoted in ibid.; *New York Tribune*, May 19, 1860.

6. *National Anti-Slavery Standard*, October 27, 1860; *Chicago Press and Tribune*, July 31, 1860; *New York Spectator*, October 4, 1860.

7. *Chicago Press and Tribune*, November 7, 1860.

8. David Herbert Donald, *Lincoln* (New York: Simon & Schuster, 1995), 268; *Chicago Daily Tribune*, February 5, 1861.

9. *The Collected Works of Abraham Lincoln*, ed. Roy P. Basler, 9 vols. (New Brunswick, N.J.: Rutgers University Press, 1953–55), 4:331–32; *New York Tribune*, April 15, 16, 1861, March 8, 1862; *New York Courier and Enquirer*, cited in *New York Tribune*, March 15, 1862; *Chicago Daily Tribune*, December 4, 1861, March 8, 1862; *Liberator*, March 14, 1862; *New York Spectator*, March 13, 1862.

10. *Washington Daily National Intelligencer*, September 23, 1862; *New York Herald*, September 23, 1862.

11. *New York Evening Post*, September 23, 1862; *Philadelphia Inquirer*, September 23, 1862; *Cincinnati Daily Commercial*, September 25, 1862; *Chicago Daily Tribune*, September 23, 1862; *New York Times*, September 23, November 12, 1862; *National Anti-Slavery Standard*, September 27, 1862; *Washington Daily Morning Chronicle*, November 7, 1862.

12. *Collected Works*, 5:513–27; *Washington Daily Morning Chronicle*, December 2, 1862; *New York Daily Spectator*, December 4, 1862; *Cincinnati Daily Commercial*, December 4, 1862; *Liberator*, December 5, 1862.

13. *Chicago Daily Tribune*, January 1, 1863; *Washington Daily Morning Chronicle*, January 2, 1863.

14. *New York Evening Post*, January 2, 1863; *New York Times*, January 2, 1863; *Liberator*, January 2, 9, 1863; *New York Spectator*, January 5, 1863; *New York Leader*, January 3, 1863.

15. *National Anti-Slavery Standard*, February 28, 1863; *Washington Daily Morning Chronicle*, January 28, 1863.

16. Benjamin P. Thomas, *Abraham Lincoln* (New York: Alfred A. Knopf, 1952), 379–81; *Washington Daily Morning Chronicle*, May 22, 1863; Donald, *Lincoln*, 441-42; *Collected Works*, 6:260–69; *National Anti-Slavery Standard*, June 27, 1863.

17. *Collected Works*, 6:406–10; *National Anti-Slavery Standard*, September 12, 1863; *Chicago Daily Tribune*, September 3, 1863.

18. *Chicago Daily Tribune*, November 3, 1863; *Springfield Republican*, November 21, 1863; *Washington Daily Morning Chronicle*, November 21, 1863; *Harper's Weekly*, December 5, 1863; *Chicago Times*, quoted in *Brooklyn Daily Union*, December 1, 1863; *New York World*, November 27, 1863.

19. *Chicago Daily Tribune*, December 14, 1863.

20. *Washington Daily Morning Chronicle*, January 2, 6, 1864. The January 2 article is quoted in Benjamin Quarles, *The Negro in the Civil War* (Boston: Little, Brown, 1946), 233.

21. *Brooklyn Daily Union*, January 12, 1864; *Washington Daily Morning Chronicle*, February 11, 15, 1864; James McPherson, *Battle Cry of Freedom: The Civil War Era* (New York: Oxford University Press, 1988), 706, 716.

22. *Chicago Daily Tribune*, February 13, March 30, 1864; *Brooklyn Daily Union*, March 26, 1864; *Washington Daily Morning Chronicle*, May 27, 1864.

23. *Brooklyn Daily Union*, June 9, 1864; *New York Times*, June 9, 10, 1864; *New York Evening Post*, June 9, 1864; *Washington Daily Morning Chronicle*, June 9, 11, 1864.

24. *Collected Works*, 8:136–53; *New York Evening Post*, December 7, 1864; *Liberator*, December 9, 1864; *Cincinnati Daily Commercial*, December 7, 1864; *Philadelphia Inquirer*, December 7, 1864; *New York Tribune*, December 7, 1864.

25. *New York Times*, January 8, 1865; *Brooklyn Daily Union*, February 1, 2, 1865; *Philadelphia Inquirer*, February 1, 1865; Stephen B. Oates, *With Malice toward None: The Life of Abraham Lincoln* (New York: Harper & Row, 1977), 405; *Collected Works*, 8:253–54.

26. Ronald C. White, *Lincoln's Greatest Speech: The Second Inaugural* (New York: Simon & Schuster, 2002); *Collected Works*, 8:332–33; *New York Tribune*, March 6, 1865; *Liberator*, March 10, 1865; *Brooklyn Daily Union*, March 6, 1865; *Washington Daily Morning Chronicle*, March 6, 1865; *New York Times*, March 6, 1865.

8 Marching to Freedom: The U.S. Colored Troops

John F. Marszalek

*P*resident Abraham Lincoln had guided the nation through a harsh and bloody civil war caused by the nation's inability to solve the problem of slavery. In 1863, he had issued a historic antislavery document, the Emancipation Proclamation, but its validity after the war's conclusion was uncertain. There was need for something more definitive, and the result was the Thirteenth Amendment, passed in January 1865, ratified during that year, and made official in December. It ended any doubts about slavery and eliminated it throughout the nation.

With the passage of this amendment, victorious Unionists breathed a collective sigh of relief, and even many uncompromising abolitionists believed that the nation's major problem of race relations had finally been solved.[1] With the benefit of hindsight, however, historians know that while this amendment eliminated slavery, it never dealt with the underlying attitudes supporting the enslavement of black people.

The winding road to emancipation is the story of a nation's racism and a civil war resulting from it, the evolution of Abraham Lincoln's mind-set, and the actions of black slaves and free people themselves. There was little agreement on the path to be taken or the speed of the trip, but eventually everyone seemed to agree that black men wearing Union uniforms would play a major role in bringing about emancipation. It was indeed over the mangled or dead bodies of the black soldiers in the United States Colored Troops (USCT) that emancipation, freedom, and equality were debated.

The black men themselves best understood their central role in this process when the Emancipation Proclamation was promulgated in the middle of the war and their participation in the military was insured. One of the black units they formed, the First Arkansas Colored Regiment, expressed their thoughts

to the tune of "John Brown's Body," later the "Battle Hymn of the Republic."
Several verses of this song demonstrated the black soldiers' understanding of
the connection between their soldiering and emancipation:

> We heard the Proclamation, master hush it as he will.
> The bird he sing it to us, hoppin' on the cotton hill.
> And the possum up the gum tree, he couldn't keep it still,
> As he went climbing on. (Chorus)
> They said, "now colored brethren, you shall be forever free
> From the first of January, eighteen hundred, sixty-three
> We heard it in the river going rushing to the sea.
> As it went sounding on. (Chorus)
> Father Abraham has spoken and the message has been sent.
> The prison doors he opened, and out the pris'ners went,
> To join the sable army of the "African Descent,"
> As we go marching on. (Chorus)[2]

The very idea of a black man in uniform seemed outrageous to most white
Americans in both the North and the South in 1861. Conveniently, they ignored the black soldiers who had fought in places like Bunker Hill and under
Andrew Jackson in New Orleans, viewing such individuals as the exceptions
rather than the rule. Whether in the slave states or in the free, in the South or
in the North, white people viewed blacks as inferior. In 1857, the U.S. Supreme
Court had ruled in the *Dred Scott* decision that the Founding Fathers had not
included blacks when they wrote the Constitution. Blacks had no rights that
"whites were bound to respect"; they were not citizens of the United States.
Because Americans considered soldiering as one of the highest marks of citizenship, blacks were not to have that privilege.

It was not far into the Civil War, however, when black participation in the
military began to appear possible, even necessary. There was no plan; the idea
evolved over time and from necessity rather than out of any heartfelt desire
to benefit a downtrodden race. As in American wars before and after, it came
down to a conflict between society's fear of a black man in arms and the need
for his services. The need eventually won out, but the fear created discrimination and hesitancy throughout the process.[3]

Blacks could hardly become soldiers in the Civil War as long as most of them
remained slaves. In Virginia, where the first battles of the war took place, black
people took quick action to gain their own freedom; they fled to Union army
camps, causing a dilemma for military commanders. Should these officers return
the fugitives to their owners under the still existing Fugitive Slave Law of 1850,
or should they maintain them in slavery or freedom inside Union lines? Slaveholders insisted on their rights to their property, and Federal officers usually

agreed. As late as the fall of 1861, slave masters received military authority to search for their runaways behind Union lines, and some Federal officers such as Brigadier General William T. Sherman in Kentucky were still returning fugitives. Brigadier General Thomas West Sherman, commander of a Union expedition to South Carolina, explicitly promised white Southerners there that he would not interfere with their "social and local institutions." In Missouri, Major General Henry W. Halleck ordered his subordinates to refuse escaped slaves any admission to army camps, arguing that they were spies.[4]

One military man regarded black fugitives more positively. In Virginia, Major General Benjamin F. Butler refused the demand of a Confederate officer for the return of three runaway slaves. Butler called these individuals "contraband" of war and said that he intended to use them as laborers for his army's needs. The term *contraband* caught on quickly because it kept slaves from their Southern masters without acknowledging their freedom. On July 9, 1861, the House of Representatives passed a resolution stating that it was not the duty of Federal troops to return fugitives to their owners; but to make sure that there was no misunderstanding, Congress also passed the Crittenden Resolution of July 22 and July 25, insisting that the war was being fought to preserve the Union, not to end slavery. Yet, since the nation was at war, victory was the desired end, and political leaders vaguely realized that the slaves had a role to play in the conflict. On August 6, Congress passed the First Confiscation Act, authorizing the appropriation of all property used in furtherance of the rebellion. Such property included slaves. In a matter of months, contrabands had gained the possibility of freedom—because of the needs of war.[5]

The movement toward emancipation did not stop there. On August 30, 1861, an emboldened Major General John C. Frémont proclaimed military government in Missouri and specifically told slave masters in that border state that "their slaves, if any they had, are hereby declared free men." This statement created a crisis for President Abraham Lincoln, who personally opposed slavery but was worried that loyal border slave states like Missouri, Maryland, and particularly Kentucky would reject the Union and join the Confederacy if slavery there was threatened. Lincoln was also unhappy that a military man dared make such a major policy decision without his authorization. Frémont's statement of martial law was acceptable, but "in relation to the confiscation of property and the liberation of slaves," Lincoln found Frémont's proclamation "objectionable in its non-conformity to the Act of Congress, passed the 6th of last August, upon the same subject."[6]

The action of Lincoln's secretary of war, Simon Cameron, disturbed the president even more. In his late 1861 War Department annual report, Cameron suggested the use of black soldiers in the Union army. Lincoln was convinced that the public was not ready to accept such a revolutionary idea and that it would create dissension that would hinder the war effort. He refused to allow the suggestion to stand in his annual message to Congress.[7]

Lincoln soon removed both Frémont and Cameron, but their departures did not suppress the idea of blacks in uniform. Throughout the nation, blacks offered their services to the embattled nation. Two untutored black men in Cleveland, Ohio, for example, asked for "the poor priverlige of fighting," confident "that a reigement of collard men can be raised in this State." Two weeks later, an Oberlin black man told the secretary of war about an already organized unit: "we are partly drilled and would wish to enter active service amediately," he said. Two white New York abolitionists similarly offered to raise a black regiment. There was no outpouring of national support for such black service, however. Federal and state governments rejected all requests and offers. The nation could still not imagine anything as radical as blacks in Union blue.[8]

Except for his negative reactions to Frémont and Cameron, President Lincoln said little about emancipation or black soldiers. He worried about taking any action in these early days of the war that would imperil the effort to preserve the Union. The Civil War had begun over the disagreement about slavery's future in the territories, but Lincoln knew that there was no great popular desire to end the institution where it already existed in the South. In his First Inaugural Address, he had promised to obey all national laws, and these included constitutional protection for slavery. His personal wish was for the institution's demise, but as president, he had to act carefully. He worried that any precipitous actions could be disastrous.[9]

The president thus nudged emancipation along cautiously, trying to bring the public along on the divisive issue without losing support for the war. The nation certainly realized the possibility of emancipation, and the issue was "vehemently discussed" among officers and enlisted men in the army. Their contact with contrabands made the matter particularly relevant to them. Lincoln began his campaign for freedom slowly by suggesting gradual compensated emancipation and repatriation (colonization) of freed slaves. He also considered achieving emancipation on a state-by-state basis. For border state Delaware, Lincoln drafted several proposed bills. The idea went nowhere, but this activity demonstrated Lincoln's desire for black freedom at the right time and under the right conditions.[10]

In March 1862, Lincoln made his views public in proposing a resolution to Congress: "Resolved that the United States ought to co-operate with any state which may adopt gradual abolishment of slavery, giving to each state pecuniary aid, to be used by such state in its discretion to compensate for the inconvenience, public and private, produced by such a change of system." This proposal, he wrote, "would be merely initiatory" but was being "recommended in the hope that it would soon lead to important practical results." When the *New York Times* and other New York newspapers supported the idea, and then Congress passed the resolution on April 10, Lincoln was encouraged. Congress's elimination of slavery in the District of Columbia on April 11, 1862, under a compensated emancipation plan, was another positive sign.[11]

To Lincoln's disappointment, matters spun out of his control. In the Military Department of the South headquartered at Hilton Head, South Carolina, Major General David Hunter issued a proclamation of emancipation on May 9, 1862, saying that "Slavery and martial law in a free country are altogether incompatible; the persons in these three States, Georgia, Florida, and South Carolina, heretofore held as slaves, are therefore declared forever free." With a military man once more challenging his authority, Lincoln acted swiftly. On May 19, he declared Hunter's action void, reminding the nation of the congressionally passed compensated emancipation resolution of April 10. It "now stands [as] an authentic, definite, and solemn proposal of the nation," he said.[12]

Lincoln could have stopped there, but he did not. Foreshadowing his Preliminary Emancipation Proclamation of September 1862, he made a prophetic statement: "I further make known that, whether it be competent for me, as Commander-in-Chief of the Army and Navy, to declare the slaves of any State or States free and whether at any time, or in any case, it shall become a necessity indispensable to the maintenance of the Government to exercise such supposed power, are questions which, under my responsibility, I reserve to myself, and which I cannot feel justified in leaving to the decision of commanders in the field." In short, Lincoln believed that, in the case of military necessity, he, as commander-in-chief, had the power to move against slavery, however and whenever he wished. Clearly, the justification for the Emancipation Proclamation was settled in his mind.

Meanwhile, antislavery proponents both inside and outside of Congress also forced matters along. On June 19, 1862, the House and the Senate outlawed slavery in the territories; and a month later, on July 17, two major laws appeared. First, the Second Confiscation Act empowered federal courts to free slaves utilized in the fight against the Union and gave the president authority to use blacks in any way he saw fit to defeat the rebellion. Second, the Militia Act authorized the use of blacks in the military as laborers "or [in] any military or naval service for which they may be found competent." Lincoln was unconvinced about the feasibility of using blacks in other than a military labor capacity, but he signed both bills nonetheless.[13]

Lincoln took the opportunity to state his position when a religious group presented him with a resolution condemning slavery. "If there be any diversity in our views, [it is] as to how we may best get rid of it [slavery] already amongst us." Utilizing one of his stories, the president explained: "Were an individual asked whether he would wish to have a wen on his neck, he could not hesitate as to the reply [and would say no]; but were it asked whether a man who has such a wen should at once be relieved of it by the application of the surgeon's knife, there might be diversity of opinion, perhaps the man might bleed to death, as the result of such an operation." Lincoln still worried that the sudden excising of slavery from the body politic might result in the demise of the Union. He continued to wait for a better moment to act, although his readiness to do so was clear.[14]

In the meantime, Lincoln put out further, seemingly confusing, signals. On August 4, 1862, he told a delegation of midwesterners who came to offer two Indiana black regiments that "he was not prepared to go the length of enlisting Negroes as soldiers" because of his concern "that to arm the Negroes would turn 50,000 bayonets from the loyal Border States against us that were for us." In a meeting with black leaders on August 14, 1862, he urged them to support colonization as the solution to the problems of slavery and racial prejudice. When leading antislavery editor Horace Greeley, reflecting the existence of uncompromising abolitionist pressure, expressed unhappiness with Lincoln's slavery policy, the president responded that his main task as chief executive was to save the Union and "*not* either to save or to destroy slavery. . . . What I do about slavery and the colored race, I do because I believe it helps to save the Union; and what I forbear, I forbear because I do *not* believe it would help to save the Union." In response to a pro-emancipation memorial from Chicago churchgoers, Lincoln, on September 13, 1862, could see nothing positive about issuing a statement emancipating the slaves. "Would my *word* free the slaves, when I cannot even enforce the Constitution in the rebel states? . . . Understand, I raise no objection against it on legal or constitutional grounds; for, as commander-in-chief of the army and navy, in time of war, I suppose I have the right to take any measure which may best subdue the enemy. Nor do I urge objections of a moral nature." Lincoln thus seemed to be opposing publicly what he had already decided privately to do: issue the Emancipation Proclamation. Yet, he once again insisted on his right as commander-in-chief to act against slavery. "Whatever shall appear to be God's will I will do," he concluded.[15]

Lincoln also continued to struggle to keep control of the emerging black soldier issue, which was clearly tied to the emancipation debate. On August 23, 1862, his secretary of war, Edwin Stanton, told fiery Kansas abolitionist senator James H. Lane, who was enlisting blacks in Kansas, that only the president had such authority. To prove it, Stanton authorized Brigadier General Rufus Saxton, just two days later, to raise five thousand black troops in South Carolina, the first time the Lincoln administration authorized the arming of blacks.[16]

Lincoln issued the Preliminary Emancipation Proclamation on September

22, 1862, five days after the Union victory at Antietam, freeing slaves in those areas that were still in rebellion against the United States on the first day of the new year. He said nothing about black soldiers, but in the final proclamation of January 1, 1863, he included a paragraph authorizing the use of black troops. On the eve of its release, George E. Stephens, a black reporter for the weekly *Anglo African*, recognized that this statement would "necessitate a general arming of the freedmen."[17]

In reality, the Second Confiscation Act, the Militia Act, and Stanton's order to Saxton had already opened the door for blacks in uniform. Even before Lincoln issued the proclamation, there existed the First Kansas Colored Infantry (later one of two 79th U.S. Colored Troops, or USCT), the First South Carolina Infantry (African Descent) (later the 33rd USCT), and the First, Second, and Third Infantry, Corps D'Afrique (later the 73rd, 74th, and 75th USCT). Lane's First Kansas Regiment had already fought at Island Mound, Missouri, in late October 1862 and had suffered the first black battlefield casualty of the war. On December 9, a white Pennsylvania congressman had introduced a House bill to raise one hundred black regiments, and on December 18, Secretary of the Navy Gideon Welles had authorized a wide use of blacks in the navy. Emancipation and military service were thus emerging as the two parts of an integrated movement toward black freedom. According to its white commander, Colonel T. W. Higginson, the First South Carolina Regiment on February 1, 1863, "carried the regimental flag and the president's [Emancipation] Proclamation far into the interior of Georgia and Florida."[18]

Limited as the proclamation was on paper, it was proving to be wide in its actual implementation, and many Unionist supporters feared, with much insight, that the Civil War was becoming a war of black liberation, not a conflict over state sovereignty alone. Confederates were particularly outraged and viewed Lincoln as a fomenter of servile insurrection. To demonstrate his disdain, the Confederate president, Jefferson Davis, issued a general order calling for the enslavement of captured black soldiers and, for good measure, made public his own proclamation on January 5, 1863, stating that, as of February 22, all free blacks in the South would be enslaved.[19]

Confederates saw black soldiers in particular as proof of Union determination to incite a racial bloodbath, while many Unionists, both in the army and outside it, found it difficult to reconcile themselves to the idea of blacks fighting in what they saw as a white man's war. Southerners were convinced that blacks would make ineffective fighters, a view that many Northerners shared. In fact, little enthusiasm existed, in the North or the South, for black Union soldiers, except among Northern abolitionists and black men themselves.[20]

Black males interpreted military service as a way to demonstrate that they were men worthy of citizenship and equal rights, not inferior underlings suited only for slavery. They had offered their services from the earliest days of the war, had even begged to be given a chance, but were always told that they were neither wanted nor needed. Now the situation had changed. The Union army needed more soldiers to fill the ranks depleted from combat and disease, and therefore the concept of blacks in uniform made more sense now than it had during the heady early days of the conflict.

White leadership in the recruiting of black soldiers began with the state of Massachusetts and its governor, John Andrew. Although some historians have argued that Andrew's zeal for enlisting blacks stemmed from his desire to maintain skilled white workers for his state's booming industries, in fact he was a strong supporter of both the use of black soldiers and the men themselves.[21]

When Andrew began his efforts, some black leaders, notably Frederick Douglass, were already recruiting. On March 3, 1863, Douglass, whose own sons fought with the famous 54th Massachusetts Regiment, issued his ringing call: "Men of Color, to Arms! . . . Who would be free themselves must strike the blow. Better even to die free than to live slaves. . . . The iron gate of our prison stands half open. One gallant rush from the North will fling it wide open, while four millions of our brothers and sisters shall march out into Liberty! . . . [T]his is our golden opportunity—let us accept it—and forever wipe out the dark reproaches unsparingly hurled against us by our enemies." To gain emancipation and freedom for all blacks, black men would have to fight, another black leader insisted.[22]

Stanton and his War Department shared Douglass's desire for black troops. On March 24, 1863, they authorized Brigadier General Daniel Ullmann to recruit in Louisiana, bolstered by an introductory letter from Abraham Lincoln to Commanding General Nathaniel Banks. On March 25, 1863, Secretary of War Stanton sent Adjutant General Lorenzo Thomas to the Mississippi River valley to recruit there. Lincoln also encouraged Military Governor Andrew Johnson in Tennessee to raise a black unit, insisting on March 29 that "the bare sight of fifty thousand armed and drilled black soldiers on the banks of the Mississippi, would end the rebellion at once."[23]

There was, thus, movement at all levels to establish more black fighting units. Henry W. Halleck, commanding general of the Federal army, told Ulysses S. Grant, commander of the Union armies in the Western theater, that he and his men had to accept that it was national policy to use black soldiers. "That policy is, to withdraw from the use of the enemy all the slaves you can, and to employ those so withdrawn, to the best possible advantage against the enemy." To coordinate the recruiting and organization of black units and to establish boards to examine whites who wished to serve as their officers, the War Department in March 1863 established a Bureau of Colored Troops in the Adjutant General's office.[24]

Civil and military leaders made false promises to Frederick Douglass and Governor Andrew about the equality of treatment blacks could expect in the army. In fact, black soldiers faced disdain and discrimination. The army segregated them into separate units under white officers. The few black officers in service were quickly eliminated. Black troops endured the worst fatigue duty possible, much beyond what white soldiers faced. When in contact with white units, they suffered unrelenting prejudice. Some of their white officers treated them in a harsh manner reminiscent of slavery, but sometimes the officers and men developed close bonds with each other. Medical care was shockingly inadequate for the black soldiers, and they received the worst weapons and equipment. Even their families suffered; slaveholders in the loyal border states made life difficult for the wives and children of black soldiers.[25]

On the other side of the battle line, Confederates became outraged at the mere sight of black soldiers and refused to give them prisoner-of-war status and eligibility for exchange; they insisted that black soldiers were fit only for enslavement and their white officers, for execution. When wounded in battle and found by Confederate soldiers, men of the U.S. Colored Troops faced gross mistreatment from the captors both inside and outside of hospitals. Confederates regularly murdered them. Fort Pillow, Tennessee, April 12, 1864, was a Confederate massacre of the greatest infamy, but there were other examples of similar treatment, such as at Poison Springs, Arkansas, on April 18, 1864.[26]

Adding insult to all this injury, the government ruled that black soldiers were not to be accorded the same pay that white soldiers received. White privates earned $13 a month plus $3 for clothing, while black soldiers, even the noncommissioned officers, received only $10 a month, less $3 for the cost of their uniforms. This gross injustice particularly riled the black men because their families depended on them for financial support. Numerous black soldiers refused to accept any pay that was less than what white soldiers received. Upset that his promises of equal treatment had proven wrong, Governor Andrew offered to have the state of Massachusetts make up the difference. But the soldiers refused the offer. Equal pay signified not only much needed income but also respectability.[27]

Frequently, soldiers protesting pay inequity faced punishment for their intransigence, and at least one man, Sergeant William Walker of the Third South Carolina, suffered execution for having his men stack arms rather than continue soldiering for unequal pay. On June 15, 1864, Congress finally passed a law establishing equal pay and, at least on paper, equality of equipment and medical care. But discrimination did not go away, and black soldiers continued to suffer.[28]

Following the Emancipation Proclamation, Lincoln defended the use of black troops at every opportunity. He realized the Confederate determination to keep blacks out of the Federal military, so he told Union commanders to work hard to include them. "The enemy will make extra efforts to destroy them; and we should do the same to preserve and increase them," he said. As reported in the *New York Tribune* on June 1, 1863, Lincoln declared that "he would gladly receive into the service not ten thousand but ten times ten thousand colored troops [and] expressed his determination to protect all who enlisted and said that he looked to them for essential service in finishing the war." He even ordered retaliation against the Confederates for any mistreatment of black soldiers, but this General Orders No. 252 was never really implemented.[29]

In a letter to James C. Conkling (August 26, 1863), which was read aloud at a "mass-meeting of unconditional Union men," Lincoln forthrightly confronted anti-emancipation conservatives in his own hometown who were unwilling to "fight to free Negroes." Lincoln pointed out strongly that "some of them seem willing to fight to free you." He continued: "Negroes, like other [people,] act upon motives. Why should they do anything for us, if we will do nothing for them? If they stake their lives for us, they must be prompted by the strongest motive—even the promise of freedom. And the promise being made it must be kept." This was the strongest endorsement Lincoln ever made of black recruitment and courage—and the bitterest indictment he ever uttered of white resistance to African American enlistment. When peace came, the president warned, "There will be some black men who can remember that, with silent tongue, and clenched teeth, and steady eye, and well-poised bayonet, they have helped mankind on this great consummation; while, I fear, there will be some white ones, unable to forget that, with malignant heart, and deceitful speech, they have strove to hinder it."[30]

Despite such handicaps, the U.S. Colored Troops displayed tenacity and valor in combat. They did not see as much fighting as they might have because of prejudicial fatigue and guard duties to which they were subjected. Yet, when black soldiers did go into battle, they performed heroically, realizing that they carried the hopes of an entire race on their shoulders and that their enemy had no compunction about murdering them on the spot should they fall into his hands. One black soldier, in an angry letter to the secretary of war, put it bluntly: "If I thought that I was not fighting for my freedom and freedom of the Colored race, I would throw my armes in Naraganset bay and live on roots in Greenland." Another reflected a more common attitude when he told his wife, "I am a soldier now and I shall use my utmost endeavor to strike at the rebellion and the heart of this system that so long has kept us in chains."[31]

The most famous battle involving black soldiers occurred at Fort Wagner, near Charleston, South Carolina, on July 18, 1863. Led by white abolitionist officer Colonel Robert Gould Shaw, the 54th Massachusetts charged along a narrow beach into the face of a heavily gunned entrenchment, suffering enormous casualties, including Shaw, but pressing forward nonetheless. Black soldiers showed similar gallantry at Milliken's Bend, Olustee, and a variety of other battles and skirmishes. Their performance at Port Hudson in May 1863 was another example of their valor and impressed observing whites. "They are mostly contrabands," a white officer said, "and I must say I entertained some fears as to their pluck. But I have now none. . . . These men did not swerve, or show cowardice. I have been in several engagements, and I never before beheld such coolness and daring. Their gallantry entitles them to a special praise. And I already observe, the sneers of others are being tempered into eulogy."[32]

Black performance in battle thus opened white eyes. Yet, many further expressions of discrimination occurred. Major General Ambrose Burnside, for example, opposed the recruitment of blacks in the Midwest and Kentucky because the "enrollment of these negroes is what the loyal people fear will do the harm." Besides, the army needed blacks for labor, not soldiering, he said. Major General William T. Sherman similarly opposed black recruitment, despite a personal letter from Lincoln asking for his cooperation. He told a white recruiter less than two weeks after Lincoln's intercession that "The Negro is in a transition state and is not the equal of the white man," who, according to Sherman, should do the fighting.[33]

Abraham Lincoln disagreed vehemently with such attitudes, telling several visiting politicians in mid-August 1864 that the nation desperately needed black soldiers. If they were no longer part of the Union military, "we would be compelled to abandon the war in 3 weeks," he said. "My enemies say I am now carrying on this war for the sole purpose of abolition," he continued. "It is & will be carried on so long as I am President for the sole purpose of restoring the Union. But no human power can subdue this rebellion without using the Emancipation lever as I have done." Emancipation, black soldiers, and victory were all intertwined, an enormous change from his attitude and that of white society earlier in the war.[34]

Though blacks continued escaping slavery by fleeing to Union armies and many black males became part of the military, the question remained: What would the status of blacks be once the conflict was over? The Emancipation Proclamation had not freed every slave everywhere, and it was only valid during the war. What would be the position of black people in the postwar world?

Throughout the conflict, Lincoln tried to prevent future problems by encouraging compensated emancipation in the states. Building on the April 1862 compensated emancipation law for Washington, D.C., he directly supported this idea in Missouri, Louisiana, Arkansas, Tennessee, and Maryland. On February 24, 1864, he happily signed into federal law the proposal to compensate loyal owners for the loss of slaves who were drafted into the army, since such service gained them their freedom. Although he consistently supported *"gradual over immediate* emancipation" because he "had thought the *gradual* would produce less confusion, and destitution, and therefore would be more satisfactory," if the people of Maryland preferred immediate action, "I have no objection to their judgment prevailing." Lincoln wanted slavery ended. "I wish all men to be free. . . . I wish to see, in process of disappearing that only thing [slavery] which ever could bring this nation to civil war." The president of the United States, long a personal opponent of slavery, had concluded, as the nation's chief executive, that slavery had to end for the war effort to be victorious and for no future conflict to occur.[35]

In his December 1, 1862, annual message to Congress, Lincoln had urged the passage of a thirteenth amendment to the Constitution, one calling for state-controlled, gradual, and compensated emancipation with voluntary colonization, the entire process to last until 1900. He had slowly moved away from this position in response to slave owners' intransigence, black people's pressure, and white abolitionists' protests. Meeting in convention as the National Union Party in 1864, the Republicans included in their platform a resolution calling for more direct action. It stated that the party was "in favor . . . of such an amendment to the Constitution, to be made by the people in conformity with its provisions, as shall terminate and forever prohibit the existence of slavery within the limits or the jurisdiction of the United States." Lincoln had pushed for the inclusion of such a statement in the platform, so he accepted it enthusiastically. He called such an amendment "a fitting and necessary conclusion to the final success of the Union cause." The Senate passed it, but the House of Representatives fell short of the two-thirds necessary for passage.[36]

The nation's interest in the 1864 presidential campaign, pitting Lincoln against George B. McClellan, overshadowed interest in the amendment. News from the battlefields was alternately discouraging—and then encouraging—as Grant fought bloody battles against Robert E. Lee, and Sherman captured Atlanta and then marched to the sea. Black troops continued to play their important role in the fighting, suffering terribly at the Crater in Virginia on July 30, 1864, and assuming an important role in the Union victory at Nashville on December 15–16, 1864.[37] Lincoln won reelection in November 1864, and congressional action on a proposed constitutional amendment ending slavery in the United States began in earnest with debate on January 6, 1865. By the end of the month, Congress had passed the amendment, and although he did not have to sign it, Lincoln did so anyway.

Responding to a crowd that came to the White House to serenade him, the president provided his interpretation of the progress of emancipation during his presidency, tying it, as always, to the Union. He called for the reunification of the nation "so as to remove all causes of disturbance in the future" and stated, therefore, "it was necessary that the original disturbing cause should, if possible, be rooted out." Everyone would agree, Lincoln said, "that he had never shrunk from doing all that he could to eradicate Slavery by issuing an emancipation proclamation." The crowd applauded profusely. But, he added, the "proclamation falls short of what the amendment will be when fully consummated." The newly reelected president had worried that "the question might be raised whether the proclamation was legally valid." After all, it might be said, "It only aided those who came into our lines and that it was inoperative as to those who did not give themselves up, or that it would have no effect upon the children of the slaves born hereafter." The Thirteenth Amendment, Lincoln said, "winds the whole thing up. . . . [I]t was the fitting if not indispensable adjunct to the consummation of the great game we are playing." The Thirteenth Amendment, he said, was "a King's cure for all the evils."[38]

Illinois ratified the Thirteenth Amendment on February 1, followed by Rhode Island and Michigan on February 2. Within a few days, Maryland, New York, and West Virginia ratified the amendment, followed on February 8 by Massachusetts and Pennsylvania. The ratification process continued over the course of 1865, the nation inexorably moving toward total emancipation.

Certainly, the role of black soldiers in winning the war had helped bring about this constitutional amendment. Throughout the war, 178,975 blacks served in the U.S. Colored Troops, which represented about 10 percent of the approximately 2 million men who served in the Union military. They formed 145 infantry regiments, 7 cavalry regiments, 12 heavy artillery regiments, 1 light artillery battery, and 1 engineer regiment. Black soldiers participated in 41 large engagements and 449 lesser ones and were awarded sixteen Medals of Honor. The first U.S. Army units to enter Richmond were the 22nd, 36th, 38th, and 118th USCT regiments, demonstrating dramatically their major role in the victorious war effort.[39]

Without Lincoln, however, there would have been no emancipation or black soldiers. The president's deliberate approach had worked. Frederick Douglass, the great black abolitionist and orator, explained it best in 1876 during a major speech: "From the genuine abolition ground, Mr. Lincoln seemed tardy, cold, dull, and indifferent, but measuring him by the sentiment of his country, a sentiment he was bound as a statesman to consult, he was swift, zealous, radical, and determined."[40]

The ability of blacks to serve in the American military and their excellent performance while in uniform should have ensured their citizenship, or so many hoped. Thomas Long, a black soldier in the First South Carolina Regiment, certainly thought so: "If we hadn't become sojers, all might have gone back as was before, our freedom might have slipped through de two houses of Congress and president Linkum's four years might have passed by & notin been done for we. But no tings can never go back, because we have showed our energy & our courage & our naturally manhood."[41]

It was not to be so, and a wide variety of events demonstrated repeatedly in the years after the Civil War that slavery was gone but racism remained. In February 1865, for example, after reading about discrimination against blacks on Philadelphia streetcars, a black soldier commented, "I do not mean to grumble, but merely to show how inconsistent it is to require us to battle for privileges which we are not allowed to enjoy."[42] In truth, prejudice and discrimination against blacks in arms or in civilian life had existed during the war and intensified afterward. The Thirteenth Amendment did not prove to be a "King's cure" for race relations in the reconstituted nation. Americans later added to the Constitution the Fourteenth Amendment ensuring black citizenship and the Fifteenth Amendment to protect black voting, but the former slaves, now citizens, continued to suffer. The reunification of the nation after the Civil War was realized through an agreement among white Americans to keep blacks in a subordinate position, constitutional amendments or not.

One dramatic demonstration that the Thirteenth Amendment's elimination of slavery did not end racial discrimination, or even ensure continued black participation in the military, occurred in the postwar years. In April 1880, Johnson C. Whittaker, formerly a South Carolina slave, was the sole black cadet attending the United States Military Academy. Late one night, three masked men assaulted him and promised to return to kill him if he did not leave. A military court of inquiry and a court-martial both declared him guilty of self-mutilation to avoid an examination two months hence. When the army's judge advocate general threw out the court-martial decision on procedural and factual grounds in December 1881, the secretary of war, in March 1882, expelled Whittaker anyway, for allegedly failing a June 1880 oral examination. This decision demonstrated the tenuous place black people held in the military in particular and in the nation in general. The identity of the war secretary made the incident even more tragic. He was Robert T. Lincoln, the deceased president's sole surviving child. The "cure" had not worked, even on the "King's" son.[43]

Notes

1. See, for example, the *Liberator*, December 22, 1865.

2. Charles H. Wesley and Patricia W. Romero, eds. *Negro Americans in the Civil War: From Slavery to Citizenship*, International Library of Negro Life and History (New York: Association for the Study of Negro Life and History, 1967), 160.

3. John F. Marszalek, "The Black Man in Military History," *Negro History Bulletin* 36 (October 1973): 122–25.

4. Benjamin Quarles, *The Negro in the Civil War*, rev. ed. (Boston: Little, Brown, 1969), 58; George E. Stephens to Mr. Editor, October 17, 1861, in *A Voice of Thunder:*

The Civil War Letters of George E. Stephens, ed. Donald Yacovone (Urbana: University of Illinois Press, 1997), 134; William T. Sherman to Alexander McCook, November 8, 1861, and T. W. Sherman, "Proclamation to the People of South Carolina," November 8, 1861, in *Blacks in the Military: Essential Documents*, ed. Bernard C. Nalty and Morris J. MacGregor (Wilmington, Del.: Scholarly Resources, 1981), 22, 23; John F. Marszalek, *Commander of All Lincoln's Armies: A Life of General Henry W. Halleck* (Cambridge, Mass.: Harvard University Press, 2004), 111–12.

5. Quarles, *Negro in the Civil War*, 58–60; *House Journal*, 37th Cong., 2nd sess., July 9, 22, 1861, 56, 123; *Senate Journal*, 37th Cong., 2nd sess., July 25, 1861, 92; *Stats at Large of USA* 12 (1859–63): 319.

6. John C. Frémont, "Proclamation," August 30, 1861, and Lincoln to Frémont, September 11, 1861, in Wesley and Romero, *Negro Americans in the Civil War*, 30, 32.

7. Dudley Taylor Cornish, *The Sable Arm: Negro Troops in the Union Army, 1861–1865* (1956; repr., New York: Norton, 1966), 22–23.

8. W. T. Boyd and J. T. Alston to Simon Cameron, November 15, 1861, William A. Jones to Simon Cameron, November 27, 1861, and G. W. Clark to Simon Cameron, November 30, 1861, in *Freedom: A Documentary History of Emancipation, 1861–1867*, ed. Ira Berlin, Joseph P. Reidy, and Leslie S. Rowland, 2nd ser., *The Black Military Experience* (New York: Cambridge University Press, 1982), 80–82; Quarles, *Negro in the Civil* War, 29–30.

9. Lincoln, First Inaugural Address—Final Text, March 4, 1861, in *The Collected Works of Abraham Lincoln,* ed. Roy P. Basler, 9 vols. (New Brunswick, N.J.: Rutgers University Press, 1953–55), 4:262–71.

10. George E. Stephens to Mr. Editor, November 30, 1861, in Yacovone, *Voice of Thunder*, 148; Annual Message to Congress, December 3, 1861, in *Collected Works*, 5:48; Drafts of a Bill for Compensated Emancipation in Delaware, November 26(?), 1861, in ibid., 5:29–31.

11. Message to Congress, March 6, 1862, and Lincoln to Henry J. Raymond, March 9, 1862, in *Collected Works*, 5:144–46, 152–53; *Stats at Large of USA* 12 (1859–63): 376–78.

12. David D. Hunter, General Orders No. 11, Headquarters, Department of the South, May 9, 1862, and Lincoln, Proclamation, May 19, 1862, in Wesley and Romero, *Negro Americans in the Civil War*, 33–34.

13. *Stats at Large of USA* 12 (1859–63): 432, 589–92, 597–600; Message to the Senate and House of Representatives, July 17, 1862, in *Collected Works*, 5:328–31.

14. Remarks to Committee of Reformed Presbyterian Synod, July 17, 1862, in *Collected Works*, 5:327.

15. Remarks to Deputation of Western Gentlemen, August 4, 1862, in *Collected Works*, 5:356–57; Quarles, *Negro in the Civil War,* 147–48; Lincoln to Horace Greeley, August 22, 1862, in *Collected Works*, 5:388–89; Reply to Emancipation Memorial Presented by Chicago Christians of All Denominations, September 13, 1862, in ibid., 5:419–25.

16. Edwin M. Stanton to J. H. Lane, August 23, 1862, in *War of the Rebellion: Official Records of Union and Confederate Armies* (Washington, D.C.: Government Printing Office, 1880–1902), 3rd ser., 2:45; Stanton to Rufus Saxton, August 25, 1862, in ibid., 1st ser., 14:377–78.

17. Proclamation by the President of the United States, September 22, 1862, in Wesley and Romero, *Negro Americans in the Civil War*, 45; George E. Stephens to Mr. Editor, December 31, 1862, in Yacovone, *Voice of Thunder*, 219.

18. Preliminary Draft of Final Emancipation Proclamation, [December 30, 1862], in *Collected Works*, 6:23–26; Quarles, *Negro in the Civil War,* 114–15; H.R. *593*, 37th Cong., 3rd sess., December 8, 1862; Gideon Welles, Circular regarding Enlistment of Contrabands,

December 18, 1862, in Nalty and MacGregor, *Blacks in the Military*, 35; Budge Weidman, "Preserving the Legacy of the United States Colored Troops," *Prologue* 29, no. 2 (1997): 90; T. W. Higginson, Report, February 1, 1863, in Nalty and MacGregor, *Blacks in the Military*, 28–29.

19. Allen C. Guelzo, *Lincoln's Emancipation Proclamation: The End of Slavery in America* (New York: Simon and Schuster, 2004); General Orders No. 111, War Department, December 24, 1862, in *War of the Rebellion*, 2nd ser., 5:797; Quarles, *Negro in the Civil War*, 180.

20. Ira Berlin, Joseph Reidy, and Leslie Rowland, eds., *Freedom's Soldiers: The Black Military Experience in the Civil War* (New York: Cambridge University Press, 1998), 7.

21. Richard H. Abbott, "Massachusetts and the Recruitment of Southern Negroes, 1863–1865," *Civil War History* 14 (September 1868): 197–210.

22. Frederick Douglass, "Men of Color, to Arms!" in Wesley and Romero, *Negro Americans in the Civil War*, 71.

23. Assistant Adjutant General Thomas M. Vincent to Brigadier General Daniel Ullmann, March 24 1863, in Nalty and MacGregor, *Blacks in the Military*, 26; Lincoln to Nathaniel P. Banks, March 29, 1863, in *Collected Works*, 6:154–55; Michael T. Meier, "Lorenzo Thomas and the Recruitment of Blacks," in *Black Soldiers in Blue: African American Troops in the Civil War Era*, ed. John David Smith (Chapel Hill: University of North Carolina Press, 2002), 249–75; Lincoln to Andrew Johnson, March 26, 1863, in *Collected Works*, 6:149–50.

24. Henry W. Halleck to U. S. Grant, March 31, 1863, in Berlin, Reidy, and Rowland, *Freedom*, 143–44; General Orders Nos. 143 and 144, Adjutant General's Office, May 22, 1863, in *Index of the General Orders, Adjutant General's Office* (Washington, D.C.: Government Printing Office, 1863).

25. Adolph J. Gla and nine others to Nathaniel Banks, April 7, 1863, in Berlin, Reidy, and Rowland, *Freedom's Soldiers,* 92–94; "Sergeant," 54th Massachusetts Infantry, to the *Liberator*, August 26, 1864, in *A Grand Army of Black Men: Letters from African-American Soldiers in the Union Army, 1861–1865*, ed. Edwin S. Redkey (New York: Cambridge University Press, 1992), 210–11; James C. Beecher to Brigade Commander, September 13, 1863, in Berlin, Reidy, and Rowland, *Freedom's Soldiers*, 112–13, 137–39; Joseph T. Glatthaar, *Forged in Battle: The Civil War Alliance of Black Soldiers and White Officers* (New York: Free Press, 1990); Lorenzo Thomas to Assistant Surgeon General, January 16, 1865, in Berlin, Reidy, and Rowland, *Freedom,* 645–46; Joseph Miller, November 26, 1864, in ibid., 138–39.

26. J. M. Williams to T. R. Livingston, May 21, 1863, E. Kirby Smith to R. Taylor, June 13, 1863, and David Hunter to Jefferson Davis, April 23, 1863, in Berlin, Reidy, and Rowland, *Freedom,* 574–75, 578–79, 573–74. See also Andrew Ward, *River Run Red: The Fort Pillow Massacre in the American Civil War* (New York: Viking/Penguin, 2005); John Cimprich, *Fort Pillow: A Civil War Massacre and Public Memory* (Baton Rouge: Louisiana State University Press, 2005); Gregory J. W. Urwin, ed. *Black Flag over Dixie: Racial Atrocities and Reprisals in the Civil War* (Carbondale: Southern Illinois University Press, 2004).

27. Glatthaar, *Forged in Battle*, 169–76.

28. Jack Fincher, "The Hard Fight Was Getting into the Fight at All," *Smithsonian Magazine*, October 1990, 52; An Act of 15 June 1864, in Nalty and MacGregor, *Blacks in the Military*, 31; Stephens to Mr. Editor, August 1, 1864, in Yacovone, *Voice of Thunder*, 319–22.

29. Lincoln to David Hunter, April 1, 1863, and Remarks to New York Committee, May 30, 1863, as reported in *New York Tribune*, June 1, 1863, in *Collected Works*, 6:158, 239; General Orders No. 252, War Department, July 31, 1863, in Berlin, Reidy, and Rowland, *Freedom*, 583.

30. Lincoln to James C. Conkling. August 26, 1863, in *Collected Works*, 6:406–10.

31. William Linden Lyons to Edwin Stanton, February 2, 1864; Samuel Cabble to wife, undated, Records of the Adjutant General's Office, 1780s–1917, RG 94, National Archives and Records Administration, Washington.

32. Elias D. Strunke to Daniel Ullmann, May 29, 1863, in Berlin, Reidy, and Rowland, *Freedom*, 528–30.

33. Ambrose E. Burnside to Lincoln, June 27, 1863, and Lincoln to William T. Sherman, July 18, 1864, in *Collected Works*, 6:299–300, 7:449–50; Sherman to John A. Spooner, July 30, 1864, in Berlin, Reidy, and Rowland, *Freedom*, 110–11.

34. Lincoln, interview with Alexander W. Randall and Joseph T. Mills, August 19, 1864, in *Collected Works*, 7:506–8.

35. An Act of 24 February 1864, in Nalty and MacGregor, *Blacks in the Military*, 31; Lincoln to John A. J. Creswell, March 7, 1864, and Lincoln to Henry W. Hoffman, October 10, 1864, in *Collected Works*, 7:226–27, 8:41–42.

36. Annual Message to Congress, December 1, 1862, and Reply to committee notifying Lincoln of his renomination, June 9, 1864, in *Collected Works*, 5:528–37, 7:380–83.

37. Garland H. White to *Christian Recorder*, August 8, 1864, in Redkey, *Grand Army of Black Men*, 110–13; James Lee McDonough, *Nashville: The Western Confederacy's Final Gamble* (Knoxville: University of Tennessee Press, 2004), 163–68, 265–66.

38. Response to a Serenade, February 1, 1865, in *Collected Works*, 8:254–55. An excellent study of the Thirteenth Amendment is Michael Vorenberg, *Final Freedom: The Civil War, the Abolition of Slavery, and the Thirteenth Amendment* (New York: Cambridge University Press, 2001).

39. A convenient compilation of basic information on the USCT is Gregory J. W. Urwin, "United States Colored Troops," in *Encyclopedia of the American Civil War*, ed. David S. Heidler and Jeanne T. Heidler (New York: W. W. Norton, 2000). See also R. J. M. Blackett, ed., *Thomas Morris Chester: Black Civil War Correspondent* (Baton Rouge: Louisiana State University Press, 1989), 303.

40. *Oration of Frederick Douglass on the Occasion of the Unveiling of the Freedmen's Monument in Memory of Abraham Lincoln in Lincoln Park, Washington, D.C., April 14, 1876* (Washington, D.C.: Gibson Brothers, 1876).

41. Quoted in Jack D. Foner, *Blacks and the Military in American History* (New York: Praeger, 1974), 51.

42. Henry Carpenter Hoyle to *Christian Recorder*, February 18, 1865, in Redkey, *Grand Army of Black Men*, 219.

43. See John F. Marszalek, *Court Martial: A Black Man in America* (New York: Charles Scribner's Sons, 1972). Paperback edition retitled *Assault at West Point* (New York: Collier, 1994); see also the television network Showtime movie under the same name (1994).

9 Lincoln and the Rhetoric of Freedom

Ronald C. White Jr.

> [T]his amendment is a King's cure for all the evils.—Abraham
> Lincoln, Response to a serenade, February 1, 1865

*J*ubilant crowds surged towards the White House on the evening of February 1, 1865, one day after the passage of the Thirteenth Amendment. Residents and visitors to Washington converged along the driveway that led to the north portico of the White House. They were coming to offer their thanks to President Abraham Lincoln for his leadership in the successful effort to pass the new amendment that outlawed slavery forever. Earlier that day, Lincoln had signed the Thirteenth Amendment in a poignant ceremony.

Many of Lincoln's friends were surprised that he signed the amendment because they believed his participation was not required by the Constitution. Many of Lincoln's critics used his signing as the occasion to complain about growing presidential power. In response to the serenade, Lincoln spoke with overflowing emotion to a cheering crowd. He may have spoken extemporaneously on this occasion; however, as president, he had increasingly declined to do so because of too many past missteps. His remarks were reported in accounts by correspondents for the *New York Tribune, New York Herald,* and *New York Times.* Their versions of his words did not completely agree with each other. No text in Lincoln's hand has been found.

Toward the end of his brief remarks, Lincoln offered those famous words that became the seal of his belief about the meaning of the amendment: "But this amendment is a King's cure for all the evils."[1] The crowd burst into applause.

But what did Lincoln mean? As I will show, Lincoln's words point backward and forward to his developing rhetoric of freedom. He rose to political prominence as a public speaker in a culture oriented around the spoken word that rewarded those who learned its ways. Lincoln refined his rhetorical skills not only at political rallies but also in numerous courthouses throughout Illinois. Stephen A. Douglas, on the eve of his debates with Lincoln in the summer of 1858, acknowledged that Lincoln was "the strong man of his party—full of wit, facts, dates, and the best stump-speaker, with droll-ways and dry jokes, in the west."[2]

During his presidency, Lincoln's rhetoric grew and changed, exhibiting new dimensions both in content and style. Lincoln was a speaker more than a writer. In our day, we have forgotten the difference between the art of writing and that of speaking. Lincoln's secretaries, John G. Nicolay and John M. Hay, declared, "Nothing would have more amazed him while he lived than to hear himself called a man of letters."[3]

Today's politicians are often tied to Teleprompters, reading a speech instead of speaking it. They speak not so much to the audience in front of them but to the audiences on the nightly news or the morning newspapers. Lincoln, used to stump speaking and debating in Illinois, spoke to real audiences.

For example, in August 1863, Lincoln was invited to speak in Springfield to a massive Republican rally on September 3. He finally decided he could not accept the invitation because he could not leave Washington. He decided to send his speech to be read by his good friend James C. Conkling. *The Collected Works of Lincoln*, edited by Roy P. Basler, calls this document the "Letter to James C. Conkling," but it was in truth Lincoln's speech to the Springfield rally.

William O. Stoddard, one of Lincoln's private secretaries, was present when Lincoln worked on the speech at the oak cabinet table in Lincoln's office in the White House. Lincoln asked Stoddard whether he might try out some of the speech on him. Stoddard, in one of his memoirs, has left an observation on Lincoln as speaker. "He is more an orator than a writer, and he is quickly warmed up to the place where his voice rises and his long right arm goes out, and he speaks to you somewhat as if you were a hundred thousand people of an audience, and as if he believes that fifty thousand of you do not at all agree with him. He will convince the half of you, if he can, before he has done with it."[4]

Today, when we have become accustomed to a phalanx of presidential speech writers, we are prompted to ask: Were Lincoln's speeches Lincoln's speeches? The answer is yes. Lincoln's pattern was to work alone over a long period of time on his major speeches. Throughout his presidential years, he was carrying on internal conversations with himself about ideas and future speeches. As an aid in this effort, he was in the habit of writing notes to himself on small slips of paper, which he filed either in his top hat or the bottom drawer of his desk.

A notable exception was Lincoln's First Inaugural Address. Lincoln asked four persons for their advice. He surely was surprised when William H. Seward, his new secretary of state, made forty-nine suggestions. Lincoln adopted twenty-seven of Seward's revisions. Most important, Lincoln accepted Seward's ideas for a new, final paragraph. But Lincoln took Seward's words and transformed them into his own eloquent prose poetry.[5]

Lincoln wrote for the ear, while today most persons write for the eye. He used strong, one-syllable, Saxon words. Out of the 701 words in the Second Inaugural Address, 505 are one syllable. Lincoln consistently employed rhetorical devices—grammatical parallelism, repetition, alliteration, antithesis—that helped his audiences hear and remember what they heard. Lincoln's words were first meant to be heard and then read. He spoke slowly. His cadence, which he learned from the King James Bible and Shakespeare, made his words seem like prose poetry. Of course, he expected that people would read his words in the next day's newspapers.

To better understand Lincoln as a speaker, I suggest taking the time to hear the different selection of his words in this chapter. Speak them aloud. Do so slowly, as Lincoln would have done. If you do so, you will be able to better appreciate Lincoln's rhetoric of freedom.

Central in Lincoln's eloquent rhetoric was his long love affair with freedom. In the course of thirty-three years of political aspirations, elections, disappointments, and fulfillment, Lincoln returned again and again to probe the nature of freedom, to parse its constituent parts, and to celebrate both its past and its future meanings. Lincoln always emphasized that the meaning of freedom was never static. Even though he revered the Founders, he believed that freedom had not simply been once and for all delivered. Each generation needed to redefine freedom for its own time.

In different moments of his life and political career, he singled out whom and what were the enemies of freedom. The challenge of slavery and the crisis of the Civil War forced Lincoln in his time to think deeply and speak boldly about freedom in a variety of his presidential speeches. Even as Lincoln's rhetoric grew and changed during his four plus years as president, so did his understanding and communication of the meaning of freedom.

What were some of the significant signposts of his developing rhetoric of freedom? Understanding some of the key episodes in this journey will help us better appreciate his response to the serenading crowd at the White House on February 1, 1865.

As Lincoln was settling into his new hometown of Springfield in the spring and summer of 1837, he was invited to speak to the Young Men's Lyceum. Lincoln, at age twenty-eight, rose to the occasion with grand and sometimes rambling oratory on January 27, 1838. He titled his speech "The Perpetuation of Our Political Institutions." Lincoln offered his best thoughts and rhetoric on the past, present, and future of America's experiment in republican government. Speaking in a rhetorical "we," he spoke from the vantage point of "lovers of freedom" and "every lover of liberty."[6]

Lincoln began by both praising the Founders and evoking their heritage handed down to his generation.

> We find ourselves under the government of a system of political institutions, conducing more essentially to the ends of civil and religious liberty, than any of which the history of former times tells us. We, when mounting the stage of existence, found ourselves the legal inheritors of these fundamental blessings. We toiled not in the acquirement or establishment of them—they are a legacy bequeathed to us, by a once hardy, brave, and patriotic, but now lamented and departed race of ancestors.[7]

Lincoln, in this early speech, drew the circle of freedom to include both civil and religious liberty.

If a major subject was all praise to the Founders, a contrapuntal theme was the role of Lincoln and his generation just now coming into their maturity. "Their's [sic] was the task (and nobly they preformed it) to possess themselves, and through themselves us, of this goodly land; and to uprear upon its hills and its valleys, a political edifice of liberty and equal rights."[8]

His generation's task was much more limited, compared with that of the Founders. Tucked away inside Lincoln's soaring language, we hear a plaintive sadness. Lincoln, speaking fifty years after the election of George Washington as the first president of the new nation, believed that nearly all of the great work of nation building had already been accomplished. Rather than builders, Lincoln and his generation were given the subsidiary role of transmitters. "'Tis ours only to transmit these, the former, unprofaned by the foot of the invader; the latter, undecayed by the lapse of time, and untorn by [usurpation]—to the latest generation that fate shall permit the world to know."

Lincoln recognized that there remained the task of defending these hard-won liberties. The immediate problem that he addressed was an outbreak of mob violence that had pervaded the country, from New England to Louisiana, from slaveholding to nonslaveholding states. How should America respond to this growing "mobocratic" spirit? Lincoln exhorted his audience, "Let reverence for the laws, be breathed by every American mother, to the lisping babe, that prattles on her lap—let it be written in Primers, spelling books, and in Almanacs;—let it be preached from the pulpit, proclaimed in legislative halls, and enforced in courts of justice." Lincoln believed that reverence for laws, which he hoped would become "the *political religion* of the nation," was a starting point in 1838 in preserving freedom."[9]

When Lincoln reentered politics after the passage of the Kansas-Nebraska Act in 1854, his rhetoric about freedom focused on the one issue on which the Founders had taken a pass: slavery. Lincoln did not speak of slavery in his Young Men's Lyceum Lecture of 1838, but nearly every speech he delivered in the 1850s dealt with America's "peculiar institution" head on. He spoke with a new clarity and passion about freedom and its opposite, slavery. Lincoln spoke in the 1850s with a tone of moral indignation.

At Peoria, on October 16, 1854, Lincoln declared, "Our republican robe is soiled, and trailed in the dust. Let us repurify it." He urged his audience forward by asking them to go backwards—all the way back to the Declaration of Independence. "Let us re-adopt the Declaration of Independence, and with it, the practices, and policy, which harmonize with it. Let north and south—let all Americans—let all lovers of liberty everywhere—join in the great and good work."[10]

In increasingly divisive times, Lincoln's rhetoric was often distinguished by his use of inclusive language in his appeal. At Peoria, his rhetoric achieved power by again and again using repetition, following the pattern he found in the Psalms, many of which he had committed to memory:

north and south   all Americans
in the great   and good

When Lincoln returned to the political battles dividing America, his rhetoric was directed not simply to America but to the world. Derided as a provincial from a Western state not long removed from the frontier, he had a larger vision of the problems and the possibilities than almost any of his opponents. "If we do this, we shall not only have saved the Union; but we shall have saved it, so as to make, and to keep it, forever worthy of the saving. We shall have so saved it, that the succeeding millions of free happy people, the world over, shall rise up, and call us blessed, to the latest generation."[11]

Although Lincoln admired the classical oratory of Henry Clay, Daniel Webster, John C. Calhoun, and Edward Everett, he also felt free to depart from it. Becoming a young adult at the high tide of the Second Great Awakening, Lincoln employed rhetoric that sometimes partook of the language and style of revivalists and ministers, who adopted the more popular, vernacular language of the day as they mastered the techniques of mass communication in the growing marketplace of the political economy.

Four times in one sentence, Lincoln used the verb *save* as the predicate for the subject *Union*. Lincoln delighted in repetition. We have come to appreciate repetition as a hallmark of African American preaching and political address. Martin Luther King Jr.'s rhetoric of freedom, as heard in his "I have a dream" speech of 1963, is an example of the power of repetition. As a rhetorical device, Lincoln used repetition to build his words into a mighty crescendo of meaning.

Finally, his audience heard Lincoln's use of biblical language—"shall rise up, and call us blessed" (Malachi 3:12)—as the culmination of his oratory of the political act of saving the Union.

"Never has such a paper been delivered to the National Legislature under auspices so grave, and rarely, if ever, has one been awaited with equal solicitude by the people of the country." The *Washington National Intelligencer* understood immediately the import of Abraham Lincoln's annual message to Congress on December 1, 1862.[12] This, his second annual message, came at the end of a difficult summer and fall of military setbacks, interrupted only in September by a significant but controversial victory at Antietam. It was also delivered after disastrous fall elections for Republicans in both state and national races. Lincoln composed his Second Annual Message to Congress exactly one month before he was scheduled to sign the controversial Emancipation Proclamation, on January 1, 1863.

Lincoln's annual messages rose above the limits of the event. Until Lincoln, annual messages had not been known for their literary or rhetorical style. Before the press conferences of the next century, Lincoln used his annual messages as an opportunity to speak through Congress to the American people. Of all of his regular and special messages to Congress in his four years as president, the annual message of 1862 rose to the zenith of his presidential eloquence. "As our case is new, so we must think anew, and act anew."[13]

For the first year and a half of the war, the burden of Lincoln's rhetoric had been to show that he was acting with fidelity to the great ideals of the past, especially as they were enshrined in the Declaration of Independence and the Constitution. At the same time, he argued that the Confederate States of America were presenting a novel and illegitimate understanding of the principles and sacred texts of the nation's past.

By the summer and fall of 1862, Lincoln began to change the definition of the aims of the war. His decision to press for emancipation, a judgment he had mulled over by himself for months, and which he presented to his cabinet on July 22 and again on September 22, was a prime example of his willingness to "think anew, and act anew." Now, on December 1, 1862, Lincoln declared, "Fellow-citizens, *we* cannot escape history. We of this Congress and this administration, will be remembered in spite of ourselves. No personal significance, or insignificance, can spare one or another of us."

Lincoln had evoked symbols of the past in his inaugural address in making his appeal for preserving the Union. In his 1862 annual message to Congress, he changed his appeal. "The fiery trial through which we pass, will light us down, in honor or dishonor, to the latest generation." It will be *the latest generation*, the distant future that will judge the actions of Lincoln and his contemporaries.

In Lincoln's final sentences, he offered a complex, rhythmic balance of ideas about freedom:

> In *giving* freedom to the *slave*,
>   we *assure* freedom to the *free*—
> honorable alike in what we give,
>   and what we preserve.

Lincoln then moved from this almost musically balanced pair of ideas,

> We shall nobly save,
>   or meanly lose

to his decisive conclusion, spoken in six final, simple, but powerful monosyllable words:

> the last best, hope of earth.[14]

The annual message of December 1, 1862, was Lincoln's finest message to Congress. His words transcended the limitations of the event. He expressed the prospect for freedom and democracy in words that deserve to be known alongside the Gettysburg Address and the Second Inaugural Address.

Some cabinet members were surprised when Lincoln accepted the invitation to travel to Gettysburg to speak on November 19, 1863. They knew that he was in the habit of turning down almost all invitations to speak outside Washington. The president was not even asked to give the main oration—that honor fell to Edward Everett. David Wills, the successful Gettysburg attorney who was in charge of the dedication of the first national military cemetery, wrote to the president about his limited assignment: to "set apart these grounds to their Sacred use by a few appropriate remarks."[15]

On that November day, after Edward Everett had spoken for two hours and seven minutes, Lincoln rose, adjusted his spectacles, and took out of his left breast pocket his dedicatory remarks. Behind the expansive crowd, Lincoln could see row after row of soldiers' graves. He began: "Four score and seven years ago our fathers brought forth, on this continent, a new nation, conceived in Liberty, and dedicated to the proposition that all men are created equal."[16] Lincoln started in the past, putting the dedication at Gettysburg in the larger perspective of American history. His first words—"Four score and seven years ago"—were a biblical allusion that accented permanence based on lines from Psalm 90: "The days of our years are threescore years and ten; And if by reason of strength they be fourscore years."[17]

At Gettysburg, he not only drew on biblical words but employed a biblical cadence expressed in the rhythms of the King James Version so familiar to him and that he thought appropriate for the gravity of the day.

In the same breath, Lincoln underscored the nation's beginnings: "on this continent, a new nation." Whenever Lincoln invoked the rhetoric of liberty, he made choices of how and what he would emphasize about freedom. By asking his audience to calculate back eighty-seven years, he reminded them that the nation's starting point was not the Constitution but the Declaration of Independence. His opening words highlighted historical continuity and encouraged the listener to enter into the intellectual and spiritual content and tone of his address.

The trajectory of his crucial first sentence was to underscore the timeless American truth that "all men are created equal." A word in this first sentence that protruded for some of his audience was *proposition*. Senator Charles Sumner did not like the word. English poet Matthew Arnold was supposed to have objected to this long Latinate word interrupting Lincoln's Saxon prose poem.[18]

If Lincoln began his address by appealing to the Declaration of Independence, his utilization of the word *proposition* alluded to a different sort of truth than Jefferson's "truths," which were "self-evident." Lincoln decided to emphasize at Gettysburg that the United States was an experiment still in process. In using the word *proposition,* he was appealing to reasoned argument as he did in his inaugural address on March 4, 1861. Yet, at Gettysburg, this was a different Lincoln from the new president who had spoken in March and July 1861. He had come to understand the fragility of the Union. In the structural design of this brief speech, the word *proposition* functioned as a turning point in which Lincoln changed the arc of his rhetoric from past ideas to present realities.

> The world will little note, nor long remember what we say here, but it cannot forget what they did here. It is for us the living, rather, to be dedicated here to the unfinished work which they who fought here have thus far so nobly advanced. It is rather for us to be here dedicated to the great task remaining before us—that from these honored dead we take increased devotion to that cause for which they gave the last full measure of devotion—that we here highly resolve that these dead shall not have died in vain—that this nation, under God, shall have a new birth of freedom—and that government of the people, by the people, for the people, shall not perish from the earth.

In the last three sentences of an address of ten sentences, Lincoln shifted the focus of his ideas a final time. In the architecture of his brief address, he had called back the past, honored what the soldiers did in the near present, and now spoke in the future tense about the responsibility of the hearers. Lincoln concluded his address with a long, complex sentence of eighty-two words.

In his closing paragraph, Lincoln once again made use of repetition: "to be dedicated," "to be here dedicated"; "we take increased devotion," "the last full measure of devotion." Lincoln, who always took great care in choosing his words, used *dedicate* and *devotion,* two religious words that conjured up the call to commitment present in the revival services of the Second Great Awakening and in the New York Avenue Presbyterian and other Protestant churches he attended in Washington during the war.

The words *a new birth of freedom* were layered with both political and religious meanings. The metaphor first suggests a comparison with the old. In the "new birth" that slowly emerged in Lincoln's thinking at Gettysburg, he no longer defended an old Union but proclaimed a new one. The old Union was pervaded by slavery. The new Union would fulfill the promise of freedom, the crucial step into the future that the Founders had failed to undertake. The "new birth" in Christian preaching contrasted the old physical birth with a new spiritual one.

The idea of a new birth was a paradox in both politics and religion. Lincoln had come to see the Civil War as a ritual of purification. To achieve the new freedom, the old Union had to die. To enter into the new birth, the old person had to die. In death, there was a preparation for a new union and a new humanity.

At this point in the speech, Lincoln made his only extemporaneous addition to his speaking text. He added the words *under God.* His speaking text read, "that this nation shall have a new birth of freedom." We do not know what prompted Lincoln to add these two words. His addition produced an awkward construction that changed the rhythm of his sentence.

Unlike extemporaneous words he had used in some earlier speeches, after the Gettysburg Address Lincoln made no apology for the interjection of "under God." And he decided to include these words in all three subsequent copies he prepared at later dates.

In his annual message to Congress of the previous December, Lincoln had said, "As our case is new, so we must think anew, and act anew." Almost one year later at Gettysburg, he was ready to speak of "the new birth of freedom."

The invitation was tendered by the American Sanitary Commission to speak in Baltimore, in Maryland, a border state, in April 1864. The memory of Baltimore was still fresh after more than three years. Baltimore represented one of the lowest moments in Lincoln's life. It was through Baltimore that he had sneaked, disguised, the night of February 22, 1861, on the way to his inauguration. It was from Baltimore that the plug uglies had come to disrupt his inaugural proceedings on March 4, 1861. It was in Baltimore that the first Northern troops, coming to Washington in the dark days immediately after the fall of Fort Sumter in April 1861, were attacked.

It was the nature of the invitation that may have caused him to come to Baltimore. The Sanitary Commission had emerged as one of the largest voluntary organizations of the war, working with the health and hygiene of the troops, supplementing what the government was able to do. Lincoln was grateful for its efforts, and his way of saying thanks was to accept an invitation to speak at its fund-raising fair in Baltimore.

His speech was brief but memorable.

> The world has never had a good definition of the word liberty, and the American people, just now, are much in want of one. We all declare for Liberty; but in using the same *word* we do not all mean the same *thing*. With some the word liberty may mean for each man to do as he pleases with himself, and the product of his labor; while with others the same word may mean for some men to do as they please with other men, and the product of other men's labor. Here are two, not only different, but incompatable [*sic*] things, called by the same name—liberty. And it follows that each of the things is, by the respective parties, called by two different and incompatable [*sic*] names—liberty and tyranny.[19]

At Baltimore, Lincoln worked with the word *liberty* from different angles of vision. He started out by stating the need for definition. He asserted that everyone used the word, but people were using very different definitions of it. Lincoln, whose legal practice helped reinforce his rhetorical attention to definitions, carefully delineated two distinct understandings of liberty. Both concern the products of labor. The crux of the difference was revealed in the phrases "the product of his labor" and "the product of other men's labor."

What made Lincoln's point so compelling was not simply the truth of his contention but the way the truth was stated. His use of one of his favorite rhetorical devices, grammatical parallelism, certainly evoked an "aha" of recognition in Lincoln's audience.

We notice also how Lincoln's words build into a crescendo of meaning. The somewhat benign observation at the beginning—that we all speak of liberty but mean different things by the word—culminated in Lincoln's dramatic assertion that the two definitions really were the difference between "liberty and tyranny."

At this point in his address, Lincoln changed the angle of vision by invoking a different kind of definition. He employed a fable that he learned from *Aesop's Fables* as a boy in Indiana.

The shepherd drives the wolf from the sheep's throat, for which the sheep thanks the shepherd as a *liberator*, while the wolf denounces him for the same act as the destroyer of liberty, especially as the sheep was a black one. Plainly the sheep and the wolf are not agreed upon a definition of the word liberty; and precisely the same difference prevails to-day among us human creatures, even in the North, and all professing to love liberty. Hence we behold the processes by which thousands are daily passing from under the yoke of bondage, hailed by some as the advance of liberty, and bewailed by others as the destruction of liberty.[20]

Lincoln used this fable to illustrate the contradictions in definitions. It was clear to all that the North was the *liberator*. Those who had been freed, the African American slaves, were depicted as offering their thanks. The destroyer of the sheep was the South. Lincoln made his point clear by describing one of the sheep as a *black one*. Lincoln understood that the point in the original fable was that the tyrant will always find a pretext for his tyranny.

If the Emancipation Proclamation had been intended as a body blow to slavery, right away questions were raised about its scope and permanence. Some argued that it was only a wartime measure by a commander-in-chief. Might it be outlawed by a future Congress? Would it be declared unconstitutional by the courts? The story of the passage of the amendment is told elsewhere in the pages of this book.

As Lincoln spoke on February 1, 1865, he understood that the threads of the Emancipation Proclamation, woven together in the passionate rhetoric of his speech to the Springfield rally, had become an unbreakable cord in the Thirteenth Amendment.

What did Lincoln mean by his suggestive words, that the amendment was *a King's cure*? At a first hearing, it might seem an odd, Old World analogy to use at such a high moment in a democracy in the New World. Who is the king? Is Lincoln pointing to a benevolence that comes from above? The word *cure* is the language of a physician. Yes, slavery had been a disease that had infected the body politic of the nation. At Gettysburg, Lincoln had invoked language of ritual purification. Now, after the passage of the Thirteenth Amendment, to *cure* is also to purify the body.

Lincoln's employment of *all the evils* brings us back to his rhetoric of freedom. At first glance, it might seem that the Thirteenth Amendment is about only one evil—slavery. But the depth of Lincoln's speaking about slavery, so often lost on his opponents, was his increasing proclivity to speak of *all the evils* involved in slavery. Lincoln's developing rhetoric of freedom ranged across political, economic, and religious freedoms. He increasingly spoke out against slavery because it went against the doctrine of equality in the Declaration of Independence, denied the right of people to participate in a system of free labor, and deprived black men and women their birthright as sons and daughters of God.

Lincoln's words on February 1 also pointed forward to March 4, 1865. His speeches were always intertwined. How are we to understand Lincoln's readiness in the Second Inaugural to shine so much light on the darkness of slavery? I believe that standing behind the composition of Lincoln's muscular words about the evils of slavery was his immediate memory of the recent wrestling in the halls of Congress over a constitutional amendment that would abolish slavery forever. He took the opportunity to expand on the sentiments he spoke about extemporaneously on February 1 in the prose poetry of his Second Inaugural Address.

In a brief 701 words, Lincoln decided to devote the bulk of his central paragraph to slavery. First, he spoke of slavery as the cause of the war. "These slaves constituted a peculiar and powerful interest. All knew that this interest was, somehow, the cause of the war." Second, he spoke of responsibility for slavery.

> If we shall suppose that American Slavery is one of those offences, which, in the providence of God, must needs come, but which, having continued through His appointed time, He now wills to remove, and that He gives to both North and South, this terrible war, as the woe due to those by whom the offence came, shall we discern therein any departure from those divine attributes which the believers in a Living God always ascribe to Him? [21]

Lincoln's audience would have cheered if he had spoken of Southern slavery. Instead, he spoke inclusively of *American slavery* and characterized slavery as an offence. Lincoln told his audience that a just God was judging America and was now the central actor who "wills to remove" slavery. What Lincoln had said in political language on February 1, he now said in both political and religious language in his Second Inaugural.

Lincoln, as a lawyer, had learned long before then to argue in court that if proposition A was true, then proposition B—its opposite—must be false. When Lincoln extolled freedom in his closely reasoned First Inaugural Address and his message to Congress of July 4, 1861, he was largely silent about slavery. With the passage of the Thirteenth Amendment as the backdrop, Lincoln, in his Second Inaugural Address, declared that if freedom was true, then slavery was false. He spoke with passionate eloquence, stating that the new birth of freedom and the abolition of slavery had become indivisible in a transformed American nation.

Notes

1. Response to a Serenade, February 1, 1865, in *The Collected Works of Abraham Lincoln,* ed. Roy P. Basler, 9 vols. (New Brunswick, N.J.: Rutgers University Press, 1953–55), 8:254.

2. Quoted in Robert W. Johannsen, *Stephen A. Douglas* (New York: Oxford University Press, 1973), 640–41.

3. John G. Nicolay and John Hay, *Abraham Lincoln: A History,* 10 vols. (New York: Century, 1890), 10:351.

4. William O. Stoddard, *Inside the White House in War Times: Memoirs and Reports of Lincoln's Secretary,* ed. Michael Burlingame (Lincoln: University of Nebraska Press, 1997), 130.

5. See Ronald C. White Jr., *The Eloquent President: A Portrait of Lincoln through His Words* (New York: Random House, 2005), 65, 68–69, 89–91.

6. Address before the Young Men's Lyceum of Springfield, Illinois, January 27, 1838, in *Collected Works,* 1:112.

7. Ibid., 1:108.

8. Ibid.

9. Ibid., 1:112.

10. Speech at Peoria, Illinois, October 16, 1854, in *Collected Works,* 2:276.

11. Ibid.

12. *Washington National Intelligencer,* December 2, 1862.

13. Annual Message to Congress, December 1, 1862, in *Collected Works,* 5:537.

14. Ibid.

15. David Wills to Abraham Lincoln, November 2, 1863, in Louis A. Warren, *Lincoln's Gettysburg Declaration: "A New Birth of Freedom"* (Fort Wayne, Ind.: Lincoln National Life Foundation, 1964), 45–46.

16. Gettysburg Address, November 19, 1863, in *Collected Works,* 7:23.

17. Psalm 90:10, King James Version.

18. Warren, *Lincoln's Gettysburg Declaration,* 106.

19. Address at Sanitary Fair, Baltimore, April 20, 1864, in *Collected Works,* 7:301–2.

20. Ibid., 7:302.

21. Second Inaugural Address, March 4, 1865, in *Collected Works,* 8:332–33.

10 Ballots over Bullets: Freedom and the 1864 Election

David E. Long

braham Lincoln ran for election many times in his life. Never would his victory at the ballot box be as important to the future of the nation as it was in 1864. Few moments and events in American history would so test the political will of the American people—and their resolve to be free—as the presidential canvass of 1864. It was a critical test of democracy, the final proof that a nation, not so overbearing as to jeopardize the personal liberties of its citizens, could nevertheless be strong enough to withstand a momentous attack on its legitimacy. This was one battle that was fought with ballots rather than bullets, and it could be argued that it was the greatest Union victory of the Civil War.

The 1864 presidential election was the most important electoral event in American history. It not only determined the outcome of the war but also, for millions, resolved whether they would spend their lives as enslaved workers or free citizens. It did more than any event since the adoption of the Declaration of Independence to define and expand the meaning of democracy in the United States. It answered the long-debated question of whether the Union was perpetual or merely a voluntary association of states existing for business advantage and subject to dissolution at the whim of its individual members. It affirmed that the Constitution created a bond that was indivisible. And the fact that it was held as scheduled in 1864 would make it improbable that future national elections would be postponed or suspended. There has never been—there will most likely never be—a crisis greater than the one presented by the American Civil War.

An election held during wartime is always a risky proposition. When war is fought internally, the risk increases exponentially. Prior to the existence of the

United States, there had been no historical precedent for holding a national referendum during wartime, certainly not during a civil war. The only wartime election in the brief history of the American republic had occurred in 1812, and that was during a war with a foreign nation. Congress had declared war less than six months prior to the vote. At the time of the election, few military actions had taken place, and the patriotism and jingoism that always attach to the national character early in wartime were still very much in place.

By contrast, the 1864 election took place following more than three and a half years of the bloodiest and most destructive war in American history. The government seemed adrift in a sea of uncertainty as battlefield defeats translated into failed policy, and revolutionary change that had been undertaken seemed more like acts of desperation than sound policy intended to secure victory. The human and material destruction of the war had mounted as the struggle dragged on. And a conflict that many had tried to wage in the traditional manner, with civility and forbearance toward the general population, had descended into a relentless and remorseless conflagration that increasingly failed to draw clear distinctions between military personnel and civilian noncombatants.

But the war had also made possible the Emancipation Proclamation and, by 1864, had raised the hopes and expectations of millions of enslaved people. For others, the potential loss of billions of dollars worth of human capital forced them to view the war differently than they had in 1861 and made the price of defeat far more costly. There was a sense that this long war, with its terrible toll and momentous issues—freedom or slavery, union or disunion, the future of America's democratic experiment in a hostile world—had transcended its time and that its effects would profoundly redound to the benefit or inure to the detriment of future generations still unborn. In the North, precious personal liberties, key to the ratification of the Constitution in 1787, had in 1861 been ignored or suspended due to the existence of a massive rebellion and the imminent threat to national security. People who had been arrested were often held in prison for weeks or months without charges being filed or the opportunity to be heard in court. Extraordinary legislative enactments had impacted people's lives in a way unprecedented in American history. Conscription had been enacted, and its first attempted implementation in 1863 had led to the most violent urban riot in American history. And the president, acting in a manner many claimed was dictatorial and without either legislative or judicial sanction, had set his name to a presidential proclamation ordering immediate freedom for millions of people who had been born into permanent bondage. Lincoln, claiming extraordinary powers based on the existence of a state of war, had done something nobody could have imagined at the beginning of the conflict. And now, in 1864, the man who had been the steward of the ship of state during those years was constitutionally compelled to come before the people to be measured for fitness in a national referendum in which he could only promise more of the same.

But beleaguered as the Lincoln administration was, and as incompetent as newspapers and politicians across the land declared this president to be, the government was actually sitting in a very strong position as 1864 began. Confederate armies had suffered terrible losses in 1863, and the drain on the available manpower had bled the South dry. Having expanded the draft age several times already, the Confederacy was in 1864 "robbing both the cradle and the grave" to fill out the ranks. There was much questioning as to just how long rebel soldiers could—or would—fight in support of an increasingly hopeless cause.

Republican Dissension

Difficult though it may be to believe today, while Lincoln was president he had much less than overwhelming support from within his own party. Radical Republicans had been unhappy with his policies for some time, as they wanted a more aggressive war policy against slavery. But who could challenge the incumbent? The man who seemed most promising was the secretary of the treasury, Salmon P. Chase. Chase was a Radical and had long been the Radicals' mole in the cabinet. When speculation about him as a candidate began circulating during the winter of 1863–64, Chase did nothing to discourage it. Senator Samuel Pomeroy of Kansas, who had been very unfriendly toward Lincoln, became chairman of a central committee formed early in 1864 to orchestrate efforts to make Chase a candidate. Pomeroy oversaw the drafting of a "confidential circular" intended to block the renomination of Lincoln. It praised the virtues of Chase and hailed him as the best and strongest nominee the party could put forward.[1]

When the confidential circular was printed in the *National Intelligencer* on February 22, it appeared much earlier than Chase had wanted and proved to be very bad timing. He immediately wrote to Lincoln, somewhat disingenuously, claiming that he had not known of the circular until it was in print. Lincoln replied that he had no intention of even reading the circular, and that if Chase performed his duties as secretary of the treasury as he had in the past, the president saw no reason to change his status. All across the country, Republican state committees, Republican legislatures, and Republican newspapers all rushed to endorse the president, not so much because of any affection felt toward him as in condemnation of the blatant disloyalty shown by Chase. The final blow came when the Ohio General Assembly, the legislature of Chase's home state, joined with others in making a pro-Lincoln declaration. The brief surge for Chase was dead in the water at that moment—at least temporarily.[2]

The Republican Party that met in Baltimore on June 7 no longer called itself the Republican Party. It was now the National Union Party. Republicans were hoping to win the support of "war" Democrats who were thoroughly disgusted with the peace wing of their own party. But the Republicans were far from enthralled with their elected leader, and there were many who came to Baltimore in the hope that somebody would emerge as a stronger candidate than Lincoln once they got there. The Chase balloon had already burst, and nobody else had emerged as a viable or attractive alternative. Lincoln won the nomination with all the votes on the first ballot, save for Missouri, where a heavily Radical delegation gave its first ballot vote to Ulysses S. Grant before coming around. The shallowness of Lincoln's support and the bad news that had been coming from the battlefield since early May meant that a military catastrophe might have been all it would take for the convention to reject a second term for Lincoln and to nominate another candidate, assuming the delegates could find someone they felt would be stronger.

In fact, a battlefield disaster did take place on June 3 at the Virginia crossroads known as Cold Harbor. On that morning, Grant ordered an all-out attack on Confederate lines by three corps of Union troops. The attack should not have been made, as Lee's troops were well entrenched and waiting for the early assault. In a matter of minutes, seven thousand soldiers were hit by Confederate fire. Given the length of time the attack lasted, it was perhaps the worst Union military defeat of the war. There had never been such concentrated minutes of killing in American history. And yet the public never found out about it. Grant was a politically savvy commander who believed in the importance of having Lincoln at the head of the government during this war. He also understood how vulnerable the president was to swings of public opinion. The only telegraphic communication Grant ever sent to the War Department about the attack on the morning of June 3 read, "We assaulted at 4:30 this A.M., driving the enemy into his entrenchments at all points, but without gaining a decided advantage. We now occupy a position close to the enemy and in some places within fifty yards. Our loss was not severe, nor do I suppose the enemy lost heavily. We captured over three hundred prisoners, mostly from Breckenridge's command."[3]

That report was not an accurate reflection of what had happened on the battlefield that morning. But Grant never sent anything more, and this was all that newspaper reporters had to rely on when they reported the battle. It received very little attention in the press, and yet it had been a disaster. And what followed during the four days after the battle was worse. Since neither side called for a truce, there was nothing to prevent continued firing at any movement that occurred on that open field where thousands of wounded Federal soldiers lay. It was a nightmarish scene that newspaper reporters would have described in all its gory detail, had they known. When terms for a truce were finally reached on June 7 and stretcher bearers went forward, they found just two men still alive. As I have written elsewhere:

> Occurring when it did, the Battle of Cold Harbor could have resulted in Republican disharmony in Baltimore, threatening the renomination of Lincoln, or at least diminished the appearance of almost universal Union support for the president's second term. It would certainly have triggered a tremendous outcry from the Democratic press. There would probably have been an increase in the activities of the [militant antiwar organization] Sons of Liberty, Confederate agents in Canada, and enhanced support for the already substantial peace movement in the North.[4]

Grant's cover-up of this operation probably saved Lincoln's renomination. But it certainly did not guarantee his reelection.

The other business of the convention was the nomination of a candidate for the vice presidency. Hannibal Hamlin of Maine was cast aside so the "Union" party could make a statement by nominating Andrew Johnson, the antebellum Tennessee senator who had refused to leave when his state had seceded and who became one of the leading Democrats to join with the Republicans during the war. When a delegation went to the White House on June 8 to inform the president he had been nominated again, Lincoln surprised the visitors by telling them, "I do not allow myself to suppose that either the convention or the League have concluded . . . that I am either the greatest or best man in America, but rather they have concluded it is not best to swap horses while crossing the river, and have further concluded that I am not so poor a horse that they might not make a botch of it trying to swap."[5] Only a few weeks after the convention adjourned, a disagreement about a patronage appointment in the Treasury Department caused Chase to submit his resignation for the fifth time. This time Lincoln accepted it.

Then on the Fourth of July, Congress hurriedly passed a reconstruction bill sponsored by Senator Benjamin Franklin Wade of Ohio and Representative Henry Winter Davis of Maryland. It set a much higher bar for a state's restoration than Lincoln had announced in his 1863 annual message and was intended by the Radicals as a rebuke to him for not having consulted them before proceeding into an area they considered a prerogative of Congress. When Lincoln pocket vetoed the bill, the Radicals exploded. Wade and Davis prepared a manifesto in which they concluded, "A more studied outrage on the legislative authority of the people has never been perpetrated."[6] The Wade-Davis Manifesto was so scathing that, coming as it did during a presidential election year, it is almost unimaginable that members of Lincoln's own political party had composed it.

The virtual avalanche of bad omens for Lincoln's reelection prospects continued to mount that summer—almost from the moment the Baltimore convention had adjourned. Some Radical Republicans began promoting the idea of a new convention that would dump Lincoln and nominate somebody else. Leading this movement was Representative James Ashley of Ohio, who divined the notion that a new meeting, to be held at the Cooper Union in New York, could nominate Major General Benjamin F. Butler, the former Democrat from Massachusetts, who would be acceptable to both the Radical Republicans and to the War Democrats. The movement gained strength in the days that followed and eventually numbered among its supporters both Wade and Davis, editor Horace Greeley, Mayor George Opdyke of New York, Senator Charles Sumner and Governor John Andrew, both of Massachusetts, and a number of other leading Republican figures.

Democrats Meet in Chicago

Following the Republican/Union convention in early June, nearly three months would elapse before the party had an opponent. The meeting of Democrats was one of the latest nominating conventions in American history, and it did not convene until August 29 in the Wigwam in Chicago, the hall that, ironically enough, had been constructed for the 1860 Republican convention that put Lincoln's name in nomination. The Democrats, who normally held their conventions in the late spring of a presidential election year, chose to delay the holding of a convention in 1864, because so long as Lincoln had no specific opponent, the Democrats could remain on the offensive. And given what was happening on the battlefield that spring, voters were turning against the president with each passing day, and the bloodletting showed no sign of letting up. The Democrats were in that very uncomfortable position that the opposition party often experiences in wartime, knowing that battlefield success furthers the prospect of their electoral defeat, and yet trying to avoid at all cost giving the appearance of disloyalty or lack of patriotism. It can be a delicate tightrope to walk.

Among the tens of thousands of Democrats who came to Chicago that last week of August were many members of the Sons of Liberty, a large grassroots organization of Midwestern antiwar Democrats ready to undertake much more than simple political action in their determination to stop the war and oust the Lincoln administration. Also present were a number of out-of-uniform Confederate soldiers, pursuant to the covert operation that had been planned in Jefferson Davis's office the previous March. Their official contact person was Jacob Thompson, a Confederate agent in Canada who had been bankrolled very generously to stir up whatever trouble he could in the North. He had met with Clement Vallandigham, a leading Copperhead and former congressman from Ohio, who had literally been banished from the North in 1863. When they met, Vallandigham had formally initiated Thompson into the Sons of Liberty, an act that cheered the Confederates and raised their hopes. Thompson had written a draft for $25,000 to the Sons of Liberty with the understanding that the money would be used to purchase weapons for an attack on Camp Douglas that was scheduled to occur during the convention. Jacob Thompson ordered all Confederate agents operating in the North to be in Chicago that week. The attack on Camp Douglas was to take place simultaneously with an uprising by the twelve thousand prisoners inside the facility. Union military and intelligence sources from multiple sources established that this plot was far more serious than the usual election-year scuttlebutt that circulates about great conspiracies being hatched to overthrow the government.

If the rumored events were to take place, the eight hundred Union home guard troops protecting the camp might easily be overwhelmed. Chicago became a very nervous city as that final week of August began. On the fashionable North Side, men armed themselves, and many women and children left town for Wisconsin until the convention was over. Then, on the eve of the convention, trains pulled into Chicago, and three thousand regular army soldiers marched off and filed into defensive trenches surrounding Camp Douglas. Any possibility that an attack would actually materialize ended with the arrival of those troops. Only the seventy or so plainclothes Confederates were inclined at that point to still consider an attack on the encampment—and without the anticipated assistance of the Sons of Liberty, even these battle-hardened rebels balked at the prospect of confronting three thousand well-armed Union veterans. The attack on Camp Douglas, and the so-called Northwest Uprising, never took place. Though many historians have claimed over the years that the threat of an actual uprising and the genuine danger to the government were greatly overplayed in 1864 and never constituted much more than a paper dragon, they dismiss a great deal of historical evidence, some of it primary and some of it circumstantial, that establishes the Copperhead threat was both real and substantial. In late August, for example, crates containing several thousand pistols shipped from New York to Indianapolis and addressed to a leading Indiana Copperhead, H. Harrison Dodd, arrived at his business, where they were immediately seized by state officials. Another leading Copperhead, John C. Walker, had purchased the guns in New York using Indiana state funds (Walker was the Indiana state purchasing agent in New York). He immediately dispatched a letter to Clement C. Clay, the other Confederate agent in Canada, seeking immediate reimbursement.

Some modern historians, led by the respected Frank Klement, have accused the Lincoln administration of orchestrating a campaign of hyperbole and grossly exaggerated claims as a way of ensuring its continued existence. Klement wrote of a supposed "great Civil War myth of conspiracies and subversive secret societies" that was nothing but a "fairy tale," a "figment of Republican imagination" compounded of "lies, conjecture, and political malignancy."[7]

The truth of the matter is there was a great deal of activity of a treasonable nature that went on, and it represented a serious threat to the war effort, the Lincoln presidency, and the future of freedom. In his definitive one-volume history of the war, *Battle Cry of Freedom,* James McPherson responded to Klement's claim of a "great Civil War myth":

> This carries revisionism a bit too far. There was some real fire under that smokescreen of Republican propaganda. The Sons of Liberty and similar organizations did exist. A few of their leaders—perhaps only a lunatic fringe—did conspire with rebel agents in Canada, receive arms for treasonable purposes, and plot insurrections against the government. Although Vallandigham and other prominent Democrats probably did not participate actively in these plots, some of them did confer with Jacob Thompson in Canada. Vallandigham was "Supreme Grand Commander" of the Sons of Liberty, and he lied under oath when he denied all knowledge of conspiracies at the treason trials of the Chicago conspirators in early 1865.[8]

Virginia's Dark and Bloody Ground

It can be difficult to comprehend all the disasters that befell the Lincoln administration that summer. Probably nothing damaged Lincoln's prospects as much as the appearance that Confederate armies were winning on the battlefield, or at least were not losing. Beginning in early May, when Grant's large army plunged into the Wilderness, Robert E. Lee delivered a devastating punch to the ribs of the Union force, compelling it to claw and scratch simply to hold its position against an army half its size. In the days and weeks to follow, as Grant refused to consider retreat, Lee, operating at one point with every one of his corps commanders out of action either sick or badly wounded, the Gray Fox was at his very best. Ill and fatigued by a war that had taken a tremendous toll on his body, Lee continued for the next month to successfully parry every thrust and movement by a Union commander who brought the same brilliance to his command responsibilities in the East that he had demonstrated for the previous two years in Mississippi and Tennessee.

Lee was so successful in blunting the advance of the Union army on Richmond that in June he dispatched one of his three army corps to the Shenandoah Valley under the command of Major General Jubal A. Early. Early enjoyed great success that month and even marched his army north, all the way to the Potomac River. Then he crossed the river, marched across Maryland, and by July 11 was actually inside the District of Columbia. Grant had to rush troops back from Petersburg, but in the meantime, Lincoln became the only president in history to come under enemy fire while in office. After becoming a target of Confederate sharpshooters while standing on the parapet at Fort Stevens, he and his family were forced to vacate the nearby summer cottage, return to the White House, and prepare to be evacuated from Washington by boat. It appeared the Confederates might actually take the city. Nothing could have injured Lincoln's public standing more than the approach of this army, literally inside the city limits, on the verge of capturing the nation's capital and the government in one fell swoop. At the moment the government was telling the people that the United States was winning the war and that the Rebels could not hold on much longer, a small Confederate army had marched to the city gates of the nation's capital.[9]

August Agonistes

August 1864 was certainly a low point of Abraham Lincoln's political career. He had to make difficult choices that required him to weigh the best interests of the country against what was in the best interest of his own political career. The issues that weighed him down were nothing less than the survival of the nation he had been elected to serve, the extirpation or continuation of slavery in the United States, and the sovereignty of the Constitution. The cumulative weight of the blows struck against his presidency, including a few by members of his own party, had brought Lincoln to that moment in his political life when he had to wonder whether he had any friends whatsoever. One of Lincoln's closest friends from Illinois, Leonard Swett, had been out stumping during August, and on August 22, he wrote his wife:

> The malicious foes of Lincoln are calling or getting up a Buffalo convention to supplant him. They are Sumner, Wade, Henry Winter Davis, Chase, Fremont, Wilson, etc. The Democrats are conspiring to resist the draft. We seized this morning three thousand pistols going to Indiana for distribution. The war Democrats are trying to make the Chicago nominee a loyal man. The peace Democrats are trying to get control of the Government, and through alliance with Jefferson Davis, to get control of both armies and make universal revolution necessary. The most fearful things are possible. I am acting with Thurlow Weed, Raymond, etc., to try to avert. There is not much hope. Unless material changes can be wrought, *Lincoln's election is beyond any possible hope. It is probably clean gone now.*[10] (emphasis added)

Even Lincoln himself seemed to accept the inevitability of his defeat. In reply to a comment from Wendell Phillips about the possibility of reelection, the president stated, "Oh, Mr. Phillips, I have ceased to have any personal feelings or expectation in that matter,—I do not say I never had any,—so abused and borne upon as I have been."[11]

It is at this lowest of all moments in the political life of Abraham Lincoln that most historians have lost their clear eye with regard to the character of this president. Historian James A. Rawley got it wrong when attempting to interpret the remarkably complex and seemingly inconsistent statements and actions of the president in August. "It was in August that the astounding probability arose," wrote Rawley, "that Lincoln was willing to accept slavery as the price of peace. To this time one might think of emancipation as the *sine qua non* for accepting Confederate surrender. The Emancipation Proclamation had appeared unequivocal in freeing all in regions in rebellion against the United States. Was it Lincoln's policy there would be no peace without the ending of slavery? Had the war become an abolitionist war? Had emancipation become an obstacle to the cessation of bloodshed?"[12]

Rawley recounted the concerns of a Wisconsin editor of a War Democratic newspaper, James Robinson, who wrote to Lincoln in August after reading the president's "To Whom It May Concern" memorandum in July, in which Lincoln had gone on record demanding two conditions for peace: affirmation of the Constitution and recognition of emancipation. Robinson chastised him for expanding the aims of the war by making emancipation a condition for peace and threatened that if such were the case it would be difficult for War Democrats to vote for his reelection.

In his response to Robinson, Lincoln wrote, "To me it seems plain that saying re-union and abandonment of slavery would be considered, if offered, is not saying nothing *else* or *less* would be considered, if offered. . . . If Jefferson Davis wishes to know what I would do if he were to offer peace and reunion, saying nothing about slavery, let him try me."[13] This was hardly a spread-eagle example of what Rawley claims was Lincoln's willingness to sacrifice emancipation in order to gain peace. By reading the entire text of the letter, rather than just the one sentence that seems to support such a notion, it is clear that Lincoln was saying precisely the opposite—that emancipation was a promise that could not be withdrawn. He also considered the occasion ripe for putting the onus for the continuation of the war back on Jefferson Davis's shoulders. And if nothing else, the simple fact that Lincoln never sent the letter should be the best indication that he did not wish to have it read as a statement of his intentions in August of 1864. If he wasn't willing to consider scuttling the promise of freedom then, it is inconceivable that there would have been any other time he would have been willing to do it.

On August 19, Lincoln met with two other Wisconsinites, a judge and a former governor. During that meeting, Lincoln said, "There have been those who have proposed to me to return to slavery the black warriors of Port Hudson

& Olustee to their masters to conciliate the South. I should be damned in time & in eternity for so doing. The world shall know that I will keep my promises to friends & enemies come what will."[14] Why Rawley chose to disregard this meeting and the words that Lincoln reportedly spoke then, but to focus on one line in a letter composed only two days earlier and never sent, is difficult to understand. A much stronger case for what Rawley argued can be made, based on what happened several days later.

During the fourth week of August, glum Republican state chairmen gathered in Philadelphia to discuss a strategy for the final two months leading up to the election. On the morning of August 23, Henry Raymond, the party's national chairman, sent Lincoln a telegram that had to be the absolute rock-bottom moment of his presidency:

> I am in active correspondence with your staunchest friends in every state and from them all I hear but one report[:] The Tide is setting strongly against us. Hon. E. B. Washburne writes that "were an election to be held now in Illinois, we should be beaten." Mr. Cameron writes that Pennsylvania is against us. Gov. Morton writes that nothing but the most strenuous can carry Indiana. This State (New York), according to the best information I can get, would go 50,000 against us tomorrow. And so of the rest. . . . Two special causes are assigned for this great reaction in public sentiment—the want of military successes, and the impression in some minds, the fear and suspicion in others, that we are not to have peace *in any event* under this administration until slavery is abandoned. In some way or other the suspicion is widely diffused that we *can* have peace with Union if we would.[15]

Then Raymond suggested that it might still be possible to revive the foundering prospects for reelection. Lincoln should appoint a special commission "to make [a] distinct proffer of peace to Jefferson Davis as the head of the rebel armies, on the sole condition of recognizing the supremacy of the Constitution, all other questions to be settled in a convention of the states." Raymond was suggesting that Lincoln withdraw emancipation as a condition for peace. To save his reelection, his campaign manager warned, Lincoln would have to sacrifice the one thing about his presidency that he felt would establish his name in history.[16]

After receiving that dire news, Lincoln sat down and composed a memorandum. What he wrote, and what he did with the memorandum, remains perhaps the most baffling act of his political life—from the perspective of most historians. After folding the memorandum in letter-style, he applied a wax seal and took it into in his noon cabinet meeting, where he passed it around the table, asking each of his ministers to sign the back of it, *sight unseen*. The baffled secretaries looked at one another in confusion and asked what it was.

The president told them they did not need to know, they simply needed to sign it, per his instruction. Each one did so. When it had been signed, he instructed his secretary to take it and place it in the White House safe. It was not opened until November 11, after he had been reelected. Just as it had been signed at a cabinet meeting, it was opened at a cabinet meeting as well. What he had written that morning in August was as follows: "This morning, as for some days past, it seems exceedingly probable that this administration will not be re-elected. Then it will be my duty to so cooperate with the President-elect as to save the Union between the election and the inauguration; as he will have secured his election on such ground that he cannot possibly save it afterwards."[17] The blind memorandum, as it has become famously known, certainly settled any doubt as to what he thought his prospects for reelection were in late August. "Exceedingly probable" may fall short of "absolutely certain," but it does not present a positive view. It was in this same state of mind that Lincoln composed an order consistent with what Raymond had proposed to him. Dated August 24, the day after receiving the Raymond telegram and meeting with his cabinet, it directed Raymond to obtain, if possible, an immediate conference with Jefferson Davis:

> At this conference you will propose, on behalf of this government, that upon the restoration of the Union and the national authority, the war shall cease at once, all remaining questions to be left for adjustment by peaceful modes. If this be accepted hostilities to cease at once. If it be not accepted, you will then request to be informed what terms, if any embracing the restoration of the Union, would be accepted. If any such be presented you in answer, you will forthwith report the same to this government, and await further instructions. If the presentation of any terms embracing the restoration of the Union be declined, you will then request to be informed what terms of peace would be accepted; and on receiving any answer, report the same to this government and await further instructions.[18]

The political dilemma required Lincoln either to stand by the principle that emancipation was an act of such staggering importance that it could not be offered as a bargaining chip under *any* circumstance or to take the path of political expediency and offer up the most important act ever performed by a president of the United States, knowing that it would never be accepted anyway. This was the most dangerous intersection ever encountered in the nation's journey to freedom. It was that defining moment in the history of the republic when everything that was good and decent about the government, about the act of extending freedom to millions of people yearning to breathe free, about a nation struggling to find a better kind of democracy while twisting in the uncertainty of how great a price it was willing to pay, hung in the balance. No other moment in American history would loom so ominously or weigh quite so heavily.

When Raymond arrived at the White House on August 25, Lincoln informed him that he could not authorize the commission after all. That same day, he had discussed it with the most trusted members of the cabinet, William H. Seward, Edwin M. Stanton and William Pitt Fessenden, and they had all concluded that to offer up emancipation by sending the peace commission to Richmond would be worse than losing the election. It would amount to an ignominious surrender. To claim that Lincoln was willing to renege on the promise of freedom to the slaves based on this writing is to make a wrong interpretation and to misunderstand this president. Like the letter to the Wisconsin editor, written but never sent, this demonstrates a commitment to *not* sacrifice emancipation, however dire the circumstances. This was a president who always made the most difficult of his decisions by applying Euclidean logic and considering every side of an issue, even to the point of reducing the merits of each position to writing so that it was revealed ever more clearly and could then be placed on the balance scale of logic and morality. Lincoln could only answer his own conscience. The nation had trusted that he would do just that, and on August 25 he did. There would be no peace, no election victory, that did not include emancipation.

The Tide Turns

It might seem unscholarly to hint that Divine Providence played a role in deciding the fate of great struggles in history. But Abraham Lincoln trusted in a Higher Being, especially so during the final year of the Civil War, when he seemed forever to be reading from the Bible, and when his greatest speeches and writings made clear that he believed the war was squarely in the hands of God. However, within days of the incomprehensibly bleak situation that bowed this president's shoulders during that last week in August, several things took place that changed the complexion of the war completely. During the last three days of August, the Democrats finally met in Chicago and nominated George B. McClellan as their candidate for president. Then, having nominated a famous Union general, the Democrats saddled him with a peace platform that condemned the war as a failure and called for a cessation of hostilities at the earliest practicable moment. As their final act of self-destruction, they then nominated one of the most outspoken Peace Democrats in the country, George Pendleton of Ohio, as McClellan's running mate.[19]

Most Democrats had not even arrived home from Chicago yet when a short telegraphic message from Georgia roused the public like nothing since the firing on Fort Sumter. It came from the headquarters of Major General William T. Sherman, whose army had been campaigning in northern Georgia for four months without striking a death blow against the Confederate Army of Tennessee. For the entire month of August, Sherman's army had been encamped in trenches stretching part way, but not completely around, this second-most important city still controlled by the Confederacy. Sherman broke the inert stalemate on the first of September when he managed to steal a giant flanking march and get a sizeable portion of his army astride the only remaining railroad line into Atlanta, before rebel commander John Bell Hood realized what had happened and could move his forces to protect the line. Hood evacuated the city immediately to save his army, and on September 3, Sherman's message to the War Department was short and direct: "Atlanta is ours, and fairly won."[20] Northerners celebrated as though the end of the war had been announced. Lawyer and diarist George Templeton Strong in New York wrote, "Glorious news this morning—Atlanta taken at last!!! . . . If it be true, it is . . . the greatest event of the war."[21] Southern diarist Mary Chesnut wrote, "Since Atlanta, I have felt as though all within me is dead, forever."[22]

Around the same time that Sherman sent word of his victory at Atlanta, word arrived in Washington of another stirring victory for the Union. At Mobile Bay, on August 5, Rear Admiral David Farragut led a flotilla of warships, including four monitors, between the barrier islands guarding the entrance to the bay, almost directly beneath the guns of Fort Morgan, and through a field of torpedoes. When the lead monitor, *Tecumseh,* struck a torpedo and sank in a matter of seconds (taking almost the entire crew down with her), the other ships began to slow in the water and even turn away from the frightening scene that had just occurred in front of them. They were absorbing a deadly fire from the guns of the Confederate fort. Farragut, his flagship being fourth in line, could not see what was happening ahead nor understand why the lead ships were slowing down. When he demanded an explanation, the reply was "Torpedoes ahead." Farragut shouted in response, "Damn the torpedoes. Full speed ahead." Almost instantly, it became one of the most famous orders in U.S. Navy lore. The rest of his flotilla passed Fort Morgan, subdued the small Confederate flotilla, and shut down Mobile Bay to the Confederacy. Three weeks later, combined army and navy operations resulted in the fall of the forts that protected the harbor. Farragut had closed down the South's last seaport on the Gulf of Mexico, and the account of his victory provided spectacular headlines across the North.[23]

The change in attitude about the war was nothing short of remarkable. The light at the end of the proverbial tunnel suddenly came into view and illuminated for many voters the choice they were about to make. The tide had already swung, but then in a series of battles in the Shenandoah Valley in September and October, a final exclamation point was appended to the resurgence of the Union war effort. At the end of August, Grant had appointed

Major General Philip H. Sheridan to take command of the Union Army in the Shenandoah. He had given him instructions that were twofold: go after Early "and follow him to the death" and then turn "the Shenandoah Valley [into] a barren wasteland . . . so that crows flying over it for the balance of the season will have to carry their provender with them."[24]

Sheridan performed his assignments well and efficiently. In mid-October, when it looked as though Early had ceased to be a threat, Sheridan personally returned to Washington for a meeting. While he was gone, Early, reinforced with another division of infantry and brigade of cavalry sent to the valley by Lee, performed a surprise attack in the early morning hours of October 19. Taken totally by surprise, two inexperienced divisions of Federals were routed. Within a short time, virtually the entire Army of the Shenandoah was fleeing north along the Winchester Pike. Sheridan was eating breakfast in Winchester when he heard the distant sound of artillery. He immediately saddled up and rode into legend.

As he approached the battlefield at a full gallop, he began to encounter hundreds of soldiers fleeing north. But when they saw Sheridan, they stopped running and began cheering. Their commander, known for his ferocity, was galloping straight toward the enemy, right through the middle of his fleeing army, cursing them with every breath he could muster. "God *damn* you, don't cheer me. If you love your country, come up to the front! . . . There's lots of fight in you men yet! Come up, God damn you! Come up!"[25] And come up they did. In the war's most outstanding example of battlefield leadership by an army commander, Sheridan rallied his army, re-formed it, and then ordered it to attack the Confederates who had only a few hours earlier completely routed a fair portion of the Union force. The Rebels, who were celebrating the harvest of goods they had gained by overrunning the Union camp, were driven from the field and pursued south by a relentless Sheridan determined to end Confederate resistance in the Shenandoah Valley.

News of the victory was celebrated by a joyous Northern press and public, and one newspaper even held a contest for the best poem written about the Battle of Cedar Creek. The end was near. In November, the final official and symbolic act of Northern victory took place in thousands of polling places. On battlefields in north Georgia and the Shenandoah Valley, and in the deep waters of Mobile Bay, soldiers and sailors in blue had written the final scene for this great American tragedy. On November 8, their loyal countrymen would ratify and ennoble their effort.

What It Meant

Because the 1864 election took place, democratic government in the United States passed its greatest test, which had posed one of the greatest quandaries that would ever face a free country: could a government that was not so strong as to threaten and undermine the basic liberties and freedom of its own people be strong enough to survive its own greatest crisis (especially when that crisis came from its own people)? The answer was a resounding yes. Nothing so stilled the life of a stubborn and combative Confederacy as the dagger that was plunged into the heart of the beast on November 8, 1864. A dozen Gettysburgs or Antietams could not in their sum total approach in importance the seminal event necessary for the existence of truly democratic government—a free and fair election and the universal freedom that soon resulted in the passage of the Thirteenth Amendment.

Notes

1. David E. Long, "The Election of 1864," in *American Presidential Campaigns and Elections*, ed. William G. Shade and Ballard C. Campbell, 3 vols. (Armonk, N.Y.: M. E. Sharpe, 2003), 2:407.

2. Ibid., 407–9.

3. *The War of the Rebellion: Official Records of the Union and Confederate Armies*, 128 vols. (Washington, D.C.: Government Printing Office, 1880–1901), 1st ser., 1 (pt. 3): 254.

4. David E. Long, *The Jewel of Liberty: Abraham Lincoln's Re-election and the End of Slavery* (Mechanicsburg, Pa: Stackpole, 1994), 204.

5. *Presidential Campaigns and Elections*, 409.

6. *New York Tribune*, August 5, 1864. See Long, *Jewel of Liberty*, 183–85.

7. Frank L. Klement, *Copperheads in the Middle West* (Chicago: University of Chicago Press, 1960), 202–3. See also *Dark Lanterns: Secret Political Societies, Conspiracies, and Treason Trials in the Civil War* (Baton Rouge: Louisiana State University Press, 1984).

8. James M. McPherson, *Battle Cry of Freedom: The Civil War Era* (New York: Oxford University Press, 1988), 783.

9. See Long, *Jewel of Liberty*, 207–8.

10. Leonard Swett to "My Dear Wife," August 22, 1864, in Ida M. Tarbell, *The Life of Abraham Lincoln*, 3 vols. (New York: S. S. McClure Co., 1895), 3: 200–201.

11. David Herbert Donald, *Lincoln* (New York: Simon and Schuster, 1995), 426.

12. James A. Rawley, *Turning Points of the Civil War* (Lincoln: University of Nebraska Press, 1966), 185–86.

13. Lincoln to James Robinson, August 17, 1864, in *The Collected Works of Abraham Lincoln*, ed. Roy P. Basler, 9 vols. (New Brunswick, N.J.: Rutgers University Press, 1953–55), 7:499–501.

14. Quoted in Rawley, *Turning Points of the Civil War*, 507.

15. Ibid., 517.

16. Long, *Jewel of Liberty*, 187–88.

17. John Nicolay and John Hay, *Abraham Lincoln: A History*, 10 vols. (New York: Century, 1886), 9:251.

18. *Collected Works*, 7:517.

19. Long, *Jewel of Liberty*, 283.

20. William Tecumseh Sherman, *Memoirs of General W. T. Sherman* (New York: Library of America, 1990), 583.

21. George Templeton Strong, *Diary of the Civil War, 1860–1865: George Templeton Strong* (New York: Macmillan, 1962), 480–81 (entry for September 3, 1864).

22. C. Van Woodward, ed., *Mary Chesnut's War* (New Haven, Conn.: Yale University Press, 1981), 648.

23. Long, *Jewel of Liberty*, 209.

24. *War of the Rebellion*, 1st ser., 37 (pt. 2): 558, 43 (pt. 2): 202, 40 (pt. 3): 223.

25. Bruce Catton, *A Stillness at Appomattox* (Garden City: Doubleday, 1956), 314.

11 The Constitution, the Amendment Process, and the Abolition of Slavery

Herman Belz

peculiar ambiguity appears in scholarship concerning the abolition of slavery in the United States. The principal agency of slave emancipation and the means by which it was accomplished are unclear. The Emancipation Proclamation, once the most famous freedom document in American history, is routinely questioned with respect to its liberating force and effect.[1] Responsibility for slave emancipation is further problematized in the proposition that the slaves themselves, not President Abraham Lincoln and the Union high command, were the "prime movers" in the abolition of slavery.[2] Whether the Emancipation Proclamation be viewed as futile or effective, the Thirteenth Amendment is perceived as neither decisive in securing slaves' freedom nor conclusive in extinguishing slavery from American public law.[3]

The meaning and significance of the Thirteenth Amendment are called into question in still another sense that is constitutional in nature. The abolition amendment was ratified by former Confederate states that were excluded from the deliberative process that framed it. From this fact, a question arose at the time concerning its constitutionality. Like other constitutional questions of the Civil War era, the propriety of the abolition amendment was settled in practice without a definitive theoretical resolution of its legitimacy as a construction of the Article V amending power. The power conferred in that article is a formal embodiment of the constituent authority on which the Constitution was founded. Exercise of the amending power in the framing and ratification of the Thirteenth Amendment implicated the exercise of constituent national sovereignty not only in the reconstruction of the Union but also in the construction of Article V as a foundation principle of American constitutionalism.

With respect to the Constitution and the amendment process, three questions epitomize interpretive controversy over the Thirteenth Amendment: Why was Article V chosen as the means of abolishing slavery? What was the substantive policy of the amendment? And was the exercise of the Article V amending power, in the form of the Thirteenth Amendment, constitutionally legitimate? This essay attempts to answer these three questions.

At the time of the Missouri Compromise of 1820, John Quincy Adams reflected on the disposition of the slavery question in the United States. Adams wrote in his diary: "Slavery is the great and foul stain upon the North American Union, and it is a contemplation worthy of the most exalted soul whether its total abolition is or is not practicable: if practicable, by what it may be effected, and if a choice of means be within the scope of the object, what means would accomplish it at the smallest cost of human suffering." Adams speculated that "A dissolution, at least temporary, of the Union, as now constituted, would be certainly necessary. . . . The Union might then be reorganized on the fundamental principle of emancipation."[4]

The framing and ratification of the Thirteenth Amendment addressed the series of questions that provoked Adams's concern. At one level, the issue in dispute was the existence of slavery as a system of labor and domestic personal relations in the United States. At another level—as it presented itself to statesmen such as Adams—slavery raised questions that, in the deepest sense, were constitutional in nature.

The status of slavery as a domestic institution under the Constitution and in relation to the federal union was indeterminate. Properly understood, the United States Constitution, in many explicit and implicit references, recognizes and hence includes the state constitutions. In eleven of the twenty-two states in the Union, slavery was legally recognized and established; in the other states, public law and policy prohibited slavery. Division of opinion over slavery at the state level was mirrored at the national level. The Constitution stipulated rules, forms, and procedures concerning the powers of the federal and state governments in relation to slavery. Administration of the federal government presented practical questions concerning slavery for which the text of the Constitution provided no clear answer.

The Constitution, in vague, nominally inexplicit language, recognized the existence of slavery.[5] Without specifically defining their respective powers, the document authorized both the national and state governments to act upon the subject of slavery. As a gloss on the constitutional text, a convention of understanding arose in the early national period according to which, on the one hand, states had exclusive power to recognize, abolish, prohibit, or otherwise regulate slavery within their jurisdictions, and on the other hand, the federal government would adopt an attitude of neutrality toward slavery as a municipal institution.[6] This so-called federal consensus was hortatory and prudential, not constitutionally binding nor legally obligatory.[7] The convention did not require that, in the conduct of national government, expressions of opinion concerning slavery or considerations of federal policy indirectly affecting the institution be prohibited unless authorized by an amendment of the Constitution. Under the text of the Constitution, in other words, the status of slavery in relation to the national government was indeterminate. Questions concerning slavery might arise in the forum of national legislative politics that would be subject to deliberation and decision by ordinary majority rule. As an intrinsic matter, policy debate and decision on slavery did not formally require an exercise of supermajoritarian politics, as the Article V amendment process directed.[8]

Why, then, was the abolition of slavery in the United States accomplished by means of an exercise of the Article V amending power, rather than by alternative means of revising constitutional meaning, including legislative and executive branch constitutional construction?[9] To answer this question, it is necessary to distinguish between the amendment process and constitutional construction as means of determining and revising the meaning of the Constitution.[10]

Provision of a systematic procedure for amending the fundamental political law of the nation was perhaps the most distinctive element in the improved science of politics that the framing and ratification of the Constitution signified.[11] The adoption of a written constitution demonstrated the ability of the people to "establish good government from reflection and choice," rather than depend "for their political constitutions on accident and force."[12] In the Pennsylvania ratification convention, James Wilson argued that the power of the people to control their constitutions, changing them whenever they pleased, was a substitute for what elsewhere was associated with calamity and war. Americans, said Wilson, presented to the world "a gentle, a peaceful, a voluntary, and a deliberate transition from one constitution of government to another."[13]

The Article V amendment process prescribed the means by which the people of the United States, in a manner analogous to that employed in the making of the Constitution, could alter or revise the fundamental law through the exercise of their constituent sovereign authority. President George Washington summarized the doctrine of peaceful constitutional revision from within the system in his Farewell Address. Washington stated, "The basis of our political systems is the right of the people to make and to alter their Constitutions of Government." If, in the opinion of the people, the distribution of constitutional powers was "in any particular wrong, let it be corrected by an amendment in the way the Constitution designates." The procedure was required by respect for the authority on which true liberty depended. Declared Washington, "The very idea of power and the right of the People to establish Government presupposes the duty of every Individual to obey the established Government." Accordingly, "the Constitution which at any time exists till changed by an explicit and authentic act of the whole People, is sacredly obligatory upon all."[14]

Article V presents itself as the exclusive and authoritative method of revising or altering the meaning of the Constitution. When one considers, however, that in practice the Constitution is not self-enforcing but requires interpretation and construction in its application, the possibility of revision of constitutional meaning outside the amending process arises. On the one hand, the primacy of the text might reasonably be seen as placing the burden of proof on alternative methods of determining constitutional meaning to demonstrate their legitimacy.[15] On the other hand, interpretation and construction by the judicial and political branches, respectively, have been accepted as alternative means of determining constitutional meaning. These forms of revision introduce elements of flexibility and responsiveness into the activity of constitutional maintenance that are otherwise precluded by exclusive reliance on Article V.[16]

In the light of these considerations, we are justified in asking whether a constitutionally correct means existed to resolve the controversy over the status of slavery under the Constitution and in relation to the federal government. As between revision by the amendment process and constitutional construction by the political branches, did the Constitution, properly understood, indicate one or the other as the preferred means of settling the slavery controversy consistent with the integrity of republican government?

From a practical standpoint, the answer to this question might well be considered constitutional construction. The objectives of neither proslavery Southerners nor antislavery Northerners were so implausible in relation to the existing Constitution as to necessitate settlement of the sectional conflict by means of the Article V amending process.[17] Believing the Constitution supported their objectives, and in view of the difficulty, if not impossibility, of organizing the supermajoritarian political coalition required to pass a constitutional amendment, both sides sought to gain decisive advantage through adoption of national policy based on constitutional construction of the text, history, and principles of the fundamental law. Of course, the import of these sources of constitutional meaning was precisely the matter in dispute. They were no less controversial whether considered from the standpoint of construction by the legislative and executive branches, interpretation of constitutional law by the judiciary, or the exercise of the amending power under Article V.[18]

As the slavery conflict entered its penultimate phase from 1846 to 1860, both North and South appealed more directly to the Constitution for justification of their policy proposals.[19] Practical reason and republican responsibility disposed lawmakers, executive officers, and opinion leaders to settle disputed questions of constitutional meaning through constitutional construction. The political barriers implicit in the supermajority requirements of Article V precluded its use as a means of settling the slavery controversy.[20]

As a matter of constitutional theory and republican political philosophy, the power to amend the Constitution was of a piece with the power to make the Constitution. Authority to ordain and establish fundamental political law was a manifestation of national sovereignty. The constitution-making power derived from the right of the people to alter or abolish their form of government when it became destructive of the ends for which it was created. In the words of the Declaration of Independence, it was the power "to institute new Government, laying its Foundation on such Principles, and organizing its Powers in such Form, as to them shall seem most likely to effect their Safety and Happiness."[21]

The amendment process, as we have noted, was conceived as a peaceful and orderly alternative to constitution-making based directly on the exercise of the right to revolt. Unlike the original constituent sovereignty as it was exercised in acts of rebellion and revolution, however, the amendment power in the design of the Constitution was given a specific institutional form. The procedure stipulated in Article V for revising the text of the Constitution was intended to recognize the constituent sovereignty of the people, while limiting the exercise of this power in a manner consistent with the ends and objects of the nation's fundamental political law. More precisely, Article V was conceived as a formally defined or special exercise of constituent sovereignty in a union that was partly federal and partly national in nature.

As a political association, the people of the United States formed neither a unitary nation nor a confederation of independent sovereign states. The sovereignty of the nation as a whole inhered in the people and states united—that is, in their integrated and mutually responsible character. The people were at once citizens of the states in which they resided and of the United States. Under Article V, the people, as constituent authority in their particular states, limited the exercise of the constituent sovereignty they possessed as citizens of the United States as a whole. In the view of Donald S. Lutz, "the amendment process invented by the Americans was a public, formal, highly deliberative decision-making process that distinguished constitutional matters and normal legislation, and that returned to roughly the same level of popular sovereignty as that used in the adoption of the constitution."[22] The distinctly federal character of the amendment process caused it to be a rarely used instrument of deliberative democracy and means of resolving constitutional controversies.

From a post–Civil War perspective, it seems obvious that the political and economic development of the country in the first half of the nineteenth century, much of it centered on slavery, necessitated some kind of constitutional revision. The question is whether Americans' decision to resolve the slavery controversy through armed conflict signified constitutional failure, as many scholars contend. With respect to the amendment process and the abolition of slavery, David Kyvig states that because the process was based on shared assumptions and goals, the fundamental conflict over slavery was not something that Article V was designed to resolve. Indeed, Kyvig concludes that the "truly monumental constitutional problem of the age could be settled only by revolution."[23]

The amendment process was intended to avert violent revolution and effect constitutional change by peaceful means. The power embodied in Article V, however, notwithstanding its formal institutional definition, was in essence the constituent authority of the people to alter or abolish their government and make a new constitution to protect their safety and happiness. That the election of 1860 forced these fundamental issues into public consciousness, and that Article V, notwithstanding its previous disutility, appeared to implicate them, can be seen in the sudden appeal to the amending process as a means of dealing with the constitutional crisis that the secession movement created.

During the secession winter 1860–61, fifty-seven resolutions, proposing upward of two hundred constitutional amendments, were introduced into Congress. Their subject matter included prohibition of secession, protection of slavery, fugitive slaves, the status of slavery in the territories, acquisition of new territories, admission of states, colonization of free Negroes, and the guarantee of republican government.[24] One proposal, the proslavery Corwin, or "original," Thirteenth Amendment, was approved by Congress as a compromise measure.[25] It was ratified by three Northern states in the early months of the Civil War. In December 1863, the first abolition amendment was introduced into Congress, and in January 1865, Congress approved the Thirteenth Amendment prohibiting slavery in the United States.

The ambiguity in scholarship concerning the end of slavery in the United States, referred to at the outset of this essay, focuses on whether slavery was abolished by constitutional or revolutionary means. It appears in Kyvig's account that the slavery question was beyond the scope of the amending power and required a revolutionary solution.[26] Kyvig points a different interpretive direction, however, in summarizing the constitutional significance of the war. He writes, "The force of arms crushed not only slavery but also the argument that individual states possessed the power to alter the Constitution." The nature of the Union was shown not to be a compact of states, and "the northern victory was, among other things, a victory for Article V. When the guns fell silent, it stood as the sole means of formally altering the Constitution."[27]

To arrive at a clear understanding of how the amendment process affected or was employed in the abolition of slavery, it is necessary to consider the meaning and import of formal alteration of the Constitution among means of constitutional revision. The Article V amendment process is one way in which political facts and ideas "g[e]t into our constitutionalism"[28] and "enter the fabric of the Constitution."[29] Constitutional construction and interpretation are other ways. Without putting too fine a point on it, for purposes of the present analysis it suffices to say that, whatever the method of determining constitutional meaning, the central issue is the relationship between constitutional forms and political reality.

A written constitution is designed for the purpose of securing the ends, principles, values, and goods of the political community. Constitutional forms need to be distinguished from political reality, without being divorced from it. When an unbridgeable gap exists between the constitution and political life, the result is weak government leading to the subversion of the ends of the community. When constitutional forms are reduced to empty formalities, incentives exist to exercise power informally outside the constitution and the laws.[30]

Although the election of 1860 was constitutionally orthodox in a procedural sense, it signaled a radical disjunction between constitutional form and political reality. Secession long threatened began in practical and passionate earnest. In retrospect, it is apparent that constitutional adjustment or reconfiguration of some sort was required; the flood of constitutional amendment proposals in Congress suggested as much.

The country was divided into hostile sectional blocs not recognized in the form and structure of the Constitution. Each section accused the other of violating the bond of constitutional trust on which the Union rested: the North, in Southern eyes, guilty of forming an antislavery party that threatened the security of their domestic institutions; the South, in Northern eyes, guilty of insurrection and treason in the form of the secession movement. What can be viewed as a crisis of constitutional fidelity was transformed into an operational constitutional crisis by the Confederate government's attack on Fort Sumter and the Union government's decision to resist armed secession.[31]

Through no fault of its own—other than the inescapable problem of the self-enforcing nature of the written Constitution—the constitutional system failed to function as intended. Political reason of state, in combination with partisan and ideological passions, supervened over constitutional forms and procedures. Article V, the key to peaceful constitutional change in the framers' vision of deliberative democracy, proved to be irrelevant.

In the first two years of the war, Article V did not recommend itself to Republican lawmakers and constitutional lawyers as a means of settling the slavery controversy.[32] A critique by Republican constitutional writer Sidney

George Fisher explained why the amendment process appeared a useless formality. Article V was intended to give the people the power to revise the Constitution. The manner of exercising the power was so difficult, uncertain, and slow, however, that it was doubtful the Constitution could be altered when alteration was necessary. Fisher warned, "the exigencies of the future may require great and organic changes; the best opinion of the country may demand them, and the necessity for them may be obvious to all men able to think upon the subject, which nevertheless may not be three-fourths of the people of the States." The amendment article "has not preserved us from civil war, though the war turned on construction as to the power of Congress over the Territories." According to Fisher, "The rebellion has tested and illustrated its merits as a means of peacefully altering the Constitution." The amendment process did not, as the framers hoped, "prevent the explosion of the passions of the people in revolutionary violence."[33]

Indeed, the amendment process was a relatively untested constitutional procedure, notwithstanding the practice throughout the antebellum era of introducing amendment proposals into Congress as expressions of public opinion. The adoption of the first ten amendments was intended to clarify and confirm principles of federal-state relations implicit in the Constitution as ratified. Fisher was correct in observing that "This part of the Constitution was new, and had, therefore, never been tried by experience." The audacity of the proposed method of constitutional revision inspired doubt in legalists like Fisher: "Reserved powers of the people, dormant till roused by a great crisis, on profound and difficult questions of constitutional law and political science, surely this was a new thing under the sun."[34]

To consider the first of the three questions that frame this inquiry: What explains the turn to Article V as the means for effecting the constitutional elimination of slavery, rather than reliance on construction of the Constitution through policy and practice? In the view of historian Michael Vorenberg, "The Thirteenth Amendment was, above all, a product of historical contingency." Neither part of a political strategy, nor "a natural product of prevailing legal principles," nor an expression of popular thought, the amendment was "an expedient solution to the problem of making emancipation constitutional."[35] While at the level of historical narrative this view is accurate, as far as it goes, in a deeper sense, reliance on the Article V amending power fulfilled theoretical and practical requirements of American constitutionalism. Article V was used as the means of determining constitutional meaning concerning the status of slavery because, in the wartime crisis, maintenance and preservation of the Constitution required the direct exercise of the constituent power of the people.

The disruption of the Union caused by secession was analogous to the crisis of the Union in the Revolutionary era, when the Constitution of 1787 was established on the basis of the people's constituent sovereignty. The difference was that, in the Civil War crisis of national existence, the founding of a new constitution was not necessary. Preservation of the Union and the Constitution required reform and reconstruction through the exercise of constituent sovereignty from within the system. In their attempt to overthrow the government of the Union, the seceding states became practically disorganized as republican political societies. What was needed, as Lincoln, with customary precision, said in describing reconstruction, was "the re-inauguration of the national authority."[36]

The secession of eleven slave states dramatically altered the structure and agenda of constitutional politics. Article V now became a practicable means of constitutional revision. Revolutionary secession, in Unionist eyes a perverse exercise of states' rights that was tantamount to state suicide, was the practical reason why the amendment process was used to settle the slavery question as a matter of public law and policy.

In the first two years of the war, constitutional construction by Congress and the president resulted in the adoption of emancipation policies in national territories and in areas under Union control. Construction as a means of determining constitutional meaning might have continued as the preferred instrument for reforming the fundamental political law with respect to slavery. Under a written constitution, however, appeal to the documentary text commands ultimate authority as the standard of legitimacy for procedural and substantive purposes.

Lincoln recognized this basic fact in his conduct of constitutional politics. In December 1862, he proposed to use the amending process to inaugurate a federally sponsored program of gradual and compensated emancipation, by which the states would remodel their constitutions and laws to abolish slavery.[37] Aimed at loyal border state opinion in particular, the plan received little support.[38] The signing of the Emancipation Proclamation on January 1, 1863, signaled an escalation in executive construction of the war power toward antislavery ends. Throughout 1863, the Lincoln administration made abolition of slavery through state constitutional revision an essential element in its evolving reconstruction policy. In a national union that depended on the interrelation of federal and state constitutions, the practical reason of written constitutionalism dictated use of the Article V amending power to confirm and establish emancipationist constitutional constructions.

The second issue this study of the Thirteenth Amendment addresses concerns the construction of Article V as a substantive exercise of the constituent power of the people. From the standpoint of constitutional theory, the question is whether there are implicit limits on what can be done through use of the amending process. The Constitution, as ratified, limited the amending power in two respects: amendment of the importation and migration clause was prohibited for twenty years; and no state, without its consent, could be deprived of its equal suffrage in the Senate.[39] Did Article V, by analogy to the exercise of constituent national sovereignty in the federal convention, authorize additional limitations on the exercise of the amending power?

Debate on the framing of the Thirteenth Amendment posed this issue for the first time in national politics outside the context of the original constitutional settlement. An inherent tension in American constitutionalism presented itself. If the Constitution rested on and signified an exercise of the right of revolution based on the constituent sovereignty of the people, could future use of that sovereignty be limited by the forms and procedures of the Article V amending process? Previous to ratification of the Constitution in 1787, exercise of constituent national sovereignty was not institutionalized and regularized in fixed constitutional forms. Ratification of the Constitution under the nine-state rule of Article VII was intended by the federal convention as a unique event.[40] For the first time since 1810, when an amendment concerning titles of nobility was sent to the states for ratification, the ratification process was set in motion by congressional approval of the Corwin amendment in March 1861, and the question arose whether Article V authorized enactment of an unamendable amendment. That is to say, could Congress, under Article V, preclude "an appeal to the ultimate source of political and legal authority"?[41]

As a charter of fundamental political law, the Constitution would be incoherent if, in establishing a system of republican government, it authorized exercise of the right of revolution to alter or abolish that government.[42] A solution to this theoretical problem was to regard the amending process as prudentially limited by recognition of essential constitutional principles beyond the constructive reach of Article V power. The rationale for limiting the amending process was to prevent the overthrow of the Constitution, by adopting a rule of construction holding that an amendment "must be in harmony with the thing amended."[43]

The question of implicit limits on the Article V amending process was raised in debate in Congress over the substantive policy of the Thirteenth Amendment. Would the amending power be used in a revolutionary way to subvert essential constitutional principles? Or was the purpose of the amendment to reinaugurate the national authority on a more truly republican basis? In the latter view, the Thirteenth Amendment would place additional limits on the power of the states over the rights of individuals, bringing them under national authority in a manner consistent with the design and intent of the original Constitution.

Democrats argued for implicit limits on the amending process. In effect regarding slavery as the bond of union, they contended that state sovereignty over municipal institutions and domestic relations was the core constitutional value. By depriving states of the power to determine the status and rights of persons dwelling within their jurisdictions, the proposed Thirteenth Amendment, they insisted, would destroy the principle on which the nation was founded.[44]

Republicans denied the argument for intrinsic limits on Article V as an embodiment of the constituent power of the people. The proposed abolition amendment declared, "Neither slavery nor involuntary servitude, except as a punishment for crime whereof the party shall have been duly convicted, shall exist within the United States, or any place subject to their jurisdiction." Republicans viewed this prohibition as a limitation on the power of both states and private individuals to recognize and establish property in human beings. The amendment withdrew from the states "one single subject more in addition to those which were withdrawn by the original Constitution," a Republican lawmaker contended.[45]

As a construction of Article V, the Thirteenth Amendment signified a limited exercise of the inherently unlimited constitution-making authority of the people. Congress employed the constituent power of Article V as a means of affirming the core principle of liberty in the founding of the nation. If the liberty and natural rights of individuals, recognized in the Declaration of Independence, formed the essential principle of the Union and American nationality, as Republicans believed, then the Thirteenth Amendment, as a determination of constitutional meaning, was affirmative and declaratory in nature.

In the context of nineteenth-century natural law thinking, the antislavery amendment presented itself as a clarification and confirmation of the natural liberty and rights of persons on which republican government was founded.[46] In support of this reading, the key constructive feature of the Thirteenth Amendment was the narrow conception of slavery as the possession of human chattel. That is to say, slavery was not viewed broadly as the denial or deprivation of all the rights and liberties that a free person might conceivably claim. This meaning can be inferred from the language of the Thirteenth Amendment, which was drawn almost verbatim from the Northwest Ordinance of 1787.[47] The ordinance had been construed narrowly to prohibit the master-slave relationship, not to confer civil or political rights on emancipated slaves.[48]

Contemporary understanding of the Thirteenth Amendment as a limited exercise of the unlimited amending power is found in Sidney George Fisher's discussion of Article V in *The Trial of the Constitution*. An admirer of the unwritten English constitution and the principle of legislative sovereignty, Fisher, as noted, questioned the practicability of Article V as an effective means of constitutional revision. Nevertheless, he recommended its application for the purpose of reinaugurating national authority in a reformed and reconstructed Union. Fisher reasoned that exercise of the ultimate sovereignty vested in the government was intended for extraordinary occasions only. It should be employed "when demanded by a great emergency" and "solicited by public opinion." He advised, "Even then, if the proposed measure involve the fundamental principles of the Government, resort should be had, if possible, to the process of amendment authorized by the Fifth Article." Fisher believed that "Such a course would silence factious opposition, and satisfy honest scruples. It would maintain and cherish a wholesome reverence for the Constitution, and tend to establish it more and more firmly, as time advances, on custom, the only sure basis for law."[49]

Fisher said slavery, mistakenly, was permitted and protected by the Constitution in states where it existed. The principle of state power over local interests was also established in the Constitution as a principle essential to union. Article V provided a way by which the country could eliminate slavery without affecting the local power of the states. Although not the only way to abolish slavery, the amendment process was, in Fisher's view, "the best way, simply because it is the one expressly pointed out by the Constitution, whilst others are impliedly authorized. Therefore we should follow it if we can."[50]

Fisher's argument reflected the assumption implicit in written constitutionalism that the Article V amendment process trumps other means of constitutional revision.[51] In practice, this assumption often breaks down because of the inability of the Constitution, especially in situations of acute political controversy, to enforce itself. The debate in Congress over implicit limits on the amending power, in relation to the substantive policy of the Thirteenth Amendment, illustrates the inescapability of construction with respect to the intrinsic meaning of Article V. Furthermore, during and after the ratification process, another and more serious question was presented concerning the constitutional legitimacy of the Thirteenth Amendment. Arising from the irregular and uncertain status of the former seceded states and their relationship to the federal government, the lawfulness of the Thirteenth Amendment is the third question this study considers.

In its affirmation of the right of individual liberty, the Thirteenth Amendment was conceived as the basis of a settlement of the issues over which the war was fought. Those issues—the nature of the Union and the relative powers of the federal and state governments with respect to the status of persons—could not, however, be bracketed while the work of Reconstruction proceeded. Indeed, they defined Reconstruction as a political and constitutional problem and were implicated in the exercise of the Article V amending power.

The formality and seeming clarity of Article V permitted it to appear, abstractly, as a self-enforcing provision in the conduct of constitutional politics. The extraordinary circumstances of the postwar period could be viewed, however, as constituting a condition of duress that rendered legally vulnerable the construction of Article V on which the Thirteenth Amendment rested. The question that confounded constitutional lawyers during the war persisted afterwards: were the seceded states members of the Union, and were their legislatures legally qualified to act for them in ratifying the amendment as Article V presumed? Second, was the role of the federal government in the exercise of the amending power excessive and constitutionally improper?

Although excluded from the deliberative process that framed the measure in Congress, the legislatures of nine seceded states ratified the Thirteenth Amendment in 1865. These ratifications could be viewed as directed, if not coerced, by federal policy in order to qualify for readmission to the national legislature. The result might be seen to violate the principle of state autonomy and voluntary consent that formed the premise of the amending process.[52] The claim of constitutional impropriety in the application of Article V was the procedural parallel to the substantive objection that the Thirteenth Amendment violated the exclusive right of states to legislate the status of persons.[53]

The legitimacy of the Thirteenth Amendment as an exercise of the Article V amending power was premised on the sovereign authority of the Union to resist secession as an unjustified rebellion and an unconstitutional exercise of the reserved powers of the states. Lincoln developed this argument throughout the war. He declared in the First Inaugural that "in view of the Constitution and the laws, the Union is unbroken."[54] In a practical sense, secession caused the disorganization and delegitimation of governments in the rebellious states, depriving them of their republican character in the sense of the Constitution. This delinquency resulted in suspension of the right of autonomous consent implicit in the constitutional guarantee of a republican form of government to every state in the Union.[55]

In accepting the nomination for president from the National Union Convention in 1864, Lincoln discussed the force and effect of these propositions in relation to the proposed Thirteenth Amendment. He explained that in the Preliminary Emancipation Proclamation, "the people in revolt" were given "a hundred days of explicit notice" that they could resume their allegiance without the overthrow of slavery, "and that they could not so resume it afterwards." Nevertheless, they "elected to stand out." At that point, "such [an] amendment of the Constitution as [is] now proposed, became a fitting, and necessary conclusion to the final success of the Union cause." Lincoln stated, "Such alone can meet and cover all cavils. Now, the unconditional Union men, North and

South, perceive its importance, and embrace it. In the joint names of Liberty and Union, let us labor to give it legal form, and practical effect."[56]

Controversy over the legitimacy of the Thirteenth Amendment as an exercise of the amending power illustrates the tension between form and substance in American constitutionalism. Fidelity to the Constitution requires political judgment concerning the right relationship between the forms of the Constitution and the ends of the political community. In the controversy leading to the Civil War, specific provisions of the Constitution gave formal, if inexplicit, recognition to slavery in states where it existed. Opinion differed over whether this degree of formal recognition signified affirmation of slavery as a principle of union, republican government, and national existence. This was a political and constitutional question in the deepest sense. The practical reason of constitutionalism required that, in dealing with it, concern for the substantive ends of the fundamental law be given primacy over regard for procedural forms.[57]

Lincoln spelled out his understanding of constitutional practical reason in relation to the ultimate extinction of slavery in the Hodges letter, dated April 4, 1864. Defending his construction of the executive power in the policy of military emancipation, he wrote, "I aver that, to this day, I have done no official act in mere deference to my abstract judgment and feeling over slavery. I did understand, however, that my oath to preserve the constitution to the best of my ability, imposed on me the duty of preserving, by every indispensable means, that government—that nation—of which that constitution was the organic law."[58]

That is to say, the oath of office as a constitutional form and the Constitution of which it is a part exist to the end of preserving the life of the nation, of which the government of the Union is the institutional embodiment. Government is a means of maintaining the Constitution; the Constitution is a means of preserving the nation. The Constitution as form and means, however, consists in principles and goods that define American nationality, giving it not merely instrumental but also intrinsic value. In a practical sense, preservation of the Constitution becomes an end in itself identical to the end of preserving the life of the nation.

Lincoln asked, "Was it possible to lose the nation, and yet preserve the constitution?" In characteristic fashion, his answer expressed the force of practical reason:

> By general law life *and* limb must be protected; yet often a limb must be amputated to save a life; but a life is never wisely given to save a limb. I felt that measures, otherwise unconstitutional, might become lawful, by

becoming indispensable to the preservation of the constitution, through the preservation of the nation. Right or wrong, I assumed this ground and now avow it. I could not feel that, to the best of my ability, I had even tried to preserve the constitution, if, to save slavery, or any minor matter, I should permit the wreck of government, country, and Constitution altogether.[59]

In the Hodges letter, Lincoln presented a determination of constitutional meaning on the slavery question based on a prudential judgment concerning the right relationship between form and substance in constitutional maintenance. The same kind of practical reasoning justified the framing and ratification of the Thirteenth Amendment as an exercise of the Article V amending power. At the time of its adoption by Congress in January 1865, Lincoln addressed the relationship between constitutional form and political reality in the Thirteenth Amendment. He said the amendment was "a King's cure for all the evils" posed by the slavery question. Lincoln "wished the reunion of all the States perfected and so effected as to remove all causes of disturbance in the future; and to attain this end it was necessary that the original disturbing cause should, if possible, be rooted out." The Thirteenth Amendment was "the fitting if not indispensable adjunct to the consummation of the great game we have been playing."[60]

In the drastically altered political situation following his assassination, the confidence Lincoln expressed in the Thirteenth Amendment as a Reconstruction settlement proved unrealistic. As a vindication of the equality principle in the Declaration of Independence, the force and effect of the amendment were inadequate for the protection of the freed people's civil rights and liberties. The Fourteenth Amendment, a more explicit revision of the relative powers of the federal and state governments, was required as a constitutional foundation for the protection of civil rights of citizens of the United States.

Although at times criticized for failing to fulfill its civil rights potential, the Thirteenth Amendment has made an essential and enduring contribution to the libertarian tradition in American constitutionalism. Legislative construction and judicial interpretation have adhered to the original understanding of the amendment as a prohibition of slavery and involuntary servitude, defined in personal libertarian terms with respect to conditions of enforced compulsory service.[61] The amendment has resisted transformation into an instrument of egalitarian redistribution based on the theory that its enforcement requires affirmative protection against the "badges and incidents" of slavery.[62] The history of the Thirteenth Amendment is testimony to the wisdom and practicability of a limited exercise of the constituent sovereignty conferred by Article V on the people of the United States.

Notes

1. Michael Vorenberg reiterates the now standard claim that, although it defined the Civil War as a war for black freedom, "the Emancipation Proclamation did not free a single slave." Michael Vorenberg, *Final Freedom: The Civil War, the Abolition of Slavery, and the Thirteenth Amendment* (New York: Cambridge University Press, 2001), 1.

2. Ira Berlin, Joseph P. Reidy, and Leslie S. Rowland, eds., *Freedom: A Documentary History of Emancipation, 1861–1867* (Cambridge: Cambridge University Press, 1985), 2–3. Berlin et al. assert: "Once the evolution of emancipation replaces the absolutism of the Emancipation Proclamation and the Thirteenth Amendment as the focus of study, the story of slavery's demise shifts from the presidential mansion and the halls of Congress to the farms and plantations that became wartime battlefields. And slaves—whose persistence forced federal soldiers, Union and Confederate policy makers, and even their own masters onto terrain they never intended to occupy—become the prime movers in securing their own liberty."

3. Legal historian Gerald T. Dunne, noting the "primacy" and "hegemony" of the Fourteenth Amendment, states, "True, the Thirteenth did formally cleanse the legitimation of human slavery from the euphemisms of the original document. Nonetheless, a case can be made that it was largely unnecessary inasmuch as the twin forces of the Emancipation Proclamation and state action at the grass roots had effectively wiped slavery from the American scene, both de jure and de facto, well before Georgia ratified the Thirteenth Amendment on December 5, 1865." Gerald T. Dunne, "The Reconstruction Amendments: A Bicentennial Remembrance," in *Our Peculiar Security: The Written Constitution and Limited Government*, ed. Eugene W. Hickok Jr., Gary L. McDowell, and Philip J. Costopoulos (Lanham, Md.: Rowman and Littlefield, 1993), 179.

4. Quoted in William Lee Miller, *Arguing about Slavery: John Quincy Adams and the Great Battle in the United States Congress* (New York: Vintage Books, 1998), 187–88.

5. See, for example, Article I, Section 9, referring to "the Migration or Importation of such Persons as any of the States now existing shall think proper to admit"; Article I, Section 2, referring to apportionment based on "the whole Number of free Persons . . . [and] three fifths of all other Persons"; Article IV, Section 2, referring to "Persons[s] held to Service or Labour in one State, under the Laws thereof."

6. Don E. Fehrenbacher, *The Slaveholding Republic: An Account of the United States Government's Relations to Slavery*, ed. Ward M. McAfee (New York: Oxford University Press, 2001), 10–11.

7. William M. Wiecek, *The Sources of Antislavery Constitutionalism in America, 1760–1848* (Ithaca, N.Y.: Cornell University Press, 1977), 15–16.

8. Article V states: "The Congress, whenever two thirds of both houses shall deem it necessary, shall propose Amendments to this Constitution, or, on the Application of the Legislatures of two thirds of the several States, shall call a Convention for proposing Amendments, which . . . shall be valid . . . when ratified by the Legislatures of three fourths of the several States, or by Conventions in three fourths thereof, as the one or the other Mode of Ratification may be proposed by the Congress."

9. In his 1820 analysis of slavery, John Quincy Adams seemed to envision, as one method of disposing of the question, a constitutional convention. Adams expressed the opinion that the Missouri Compromise Act, in which Congress prohibited slavery from the Louisiana Purchase north of latitude 36°30′, was "all that could be effected under the present Constitution." He supported the act for that reason and "from extreme

unwillingness to put the Union at hazard." Adams nevertheless speculated whether it might not have been "a wiser as well as a bolder course to have persisted in the restriction upon Missouri [i.e., deny it admission as a slave state] till it should have terminated in a convention of the States to revise and amend the Constitution." Adams supposed that such a course of action would have "produced a new Union of thirteen or fourteen states unpolluted with slavery," with the object of "rallying to their standard the other States by the universal emancipation of their slaves." It seems unlikely that Adams envisioned an Article V convention. The division of the Union into an equal number of free and slave states would seem to have made reliance on the orthodox amendment process a political impossibility. Considering his reference to a dissolution of the Union, as noted, Adams may have been thinking in the terms of "right-of-resistance" politics, analogous to the politics of the American Revolution. "If the Union must be dissolved," he wrote, "slavery is precisely the question upon which it ought to break." Adams's meaning seems to be that should dissolution of the Union occur, peacefully or otherwise, the free states, in an original convention analogous to that of 1787, might make a new constitution in which slavery was prohibited. Miller, *Arguing about Slavery*, 190.

10. Keith E. Whittington, *Constitutional Construction: Divided Powers and Constitutional Meaning* (Cambridge, Mass.: Harvard University Press, 1999), 1–19.

11. *The Federalist Papers*, no. 9, ed. Clinton Rossiter (New York: Mentor, 1961), 72.

12. Ibid., no. 1, 33.

13. David E. Kyvig, *Explicit and Authentic Acts: Amending the U.S. Constitution, 1776–1995* (Lawrence: University Press of Kansas, 1996), 68.

14. Henry Steele Commager, ed., *Documents of American History*, 7th ed. (New York: Appleton-Century-Crofts, 1963), 1: 172.

15. The preeminence of Article V in determining constitutional meaning is affirmed in Kyvig's study of the amendment process. Arguing that the concept of written constitutionalism lay at the heart of American republicanism, Kyvig says, "at its core [was] the dynamic device whose presence enhanced the chances of republican agreements on government achieving lasting success: a mechanism for formal amendment" (Kyvig, *Explicit and Authentic Acts*, 65).

16. The adoption of ten constitutional amendments between 1789 and 1791 might appear to support the belief that "routine constitutional change by specific, prearranged, extralegislative means was a particularly remarkable new concept" (Kyvig, *Explicit and Authentic Acts*, 2). Nevertheless, the supermajoritarian requirements of the amending process rendered impractical the idea of "routine constitutional change" under Article V.

17. Whittington, *Constitutional Construction*, 14.

18. The distinction between interpretation and construction as methods of determining constitutional meaning arises from the nature of the Constitution as fundamental political law, considered in relation to the structural principle of the separation of powers. In the view of political scientist Keith E. Whittington, both interpretation and construction "seek to elaborate a meaning somehow already present in the text, making constitutional meaning more explicit without altering the terms of the text itself." The difference between them is that construction, unlike interpretation, "provides for an element of creativity in construing constitutional meaning." According to Whittington, "It is a necessary and essentially political task, regardless of the particular institution exercising that function, to construct a determinate constitutional meaning to guide government practice" (ibid., 5–6).

19. Although slavery was a contentious issue in the federal convention, for the sake of intersectional harmony it was placed in a subordinate position in national politics. The

Missouri Compromise was the exception that proved the rule, until territorial expansion and the Mexican War elevated the slavery question to national prominence. In the view of Don E. Fehrenbacher, "it became the fashion and almost a necessity to justify any sectionally controversial proposal in constitutional terms. The crucial change in the slavery controversy . . . was therefore not the introduction of new principles or formulas, but rather the constitutionalizing of the argument." Don E. Fehrenbacher, *The Dred Scott Case: Its Significance in American Law and Politics* (New York: Oxford University Press, 1978), 140.

20. Of four hundred constitutional amendment proposals introduced into Congress from 1803 to 1859, only eight were addressed to the subject of slavery. Herman V. Ames, "The Proposed Amendments to the Constitution of the United States during the First Century of Its History," in *Annual Report of the American Historical Association for the Year 1896* (Washington, D.C.: Government Printing Office, 1897), 193.

21. A. Christopher Bryant, "Stopping Time: The Pro-Slavery and 'Irrevocable' Thirteenth Amendment," *Harvard Journal of Law and Public Policy* 26 (2003): 505–8.

22. Donald S. Lutz, "Toward a Theory of Constitutional Amendment," in *Responding to Imperfection: The Theory and Practice of Constitutional Amendment*, ed. Sanford Levinson (Princeton: Princeton University Press, 1995), 240. Article VII provided for establishment of the Constitution upon ratification by the conventions of nine states.

23. Kyvig, *Explicit and Authentic Acts*, 134.

24. Ames, "Proposed Amendments to the Constitution," 194–208.

25. It stated: "No amendment shall be made to the Constitution which will authorize or give to Congress the power to abolish or interfere, within any States, with the domestic institutions thereof, including that of persons held to labor or service by the laws of said State" (ibid., 196).

26. Kyvig, *Explicit and Authentic Acts*, 134.

27. Ibid., 153.

28. Kermit L. Hall, Harold M. Hyman, and Leon V. Sigal, eds., *The Constitutional Convention as an Amending Device* (Washington, D.C.: American Historical Association and American Political Science Association, 1981), 64 (quoting Jack Peltason).

29. Kyvig, *Explicit and Authentic Acts*, 187.

30. Robert Eden, "Executive Power and the Presidency," in *Leo Strauss, the Straussians, and the American Regime*, ed. Kenneth L. Deutsch and John A. Murley (Lanham, Md.: Rowman and Littlefield, 1999), 59.

31. Keith E. Whittington, "Yet Another Constitutional Crisis?" unpublished ms. (Princeton University, 2001), 7–13.

32. Vorenberg, *Final Freedom*, 29–30, 40.

33. Sidney George Fisher, *The Trial of the Constitution* (1862; repr., New York: Negro Universities Press, 1969), 26.

34. Ibid., 28.

35. Vorenberg, *Final Freedom*, 3

36. *The Collected Works of Abraham Lincoln*, ed. Roy P. Basler, 9 vols. (New Brunswick, N.J.: Rutgers University Press, 1953–55), 8:400.

37. Ibid., 5:530–31.

38. Vorenberg, *Final Freedom*, 30–31.

39. U.S. Constitution, Article V.

40. U.S. Constitution, Article VII: "The Ratification of the Conventions of nine States, shall be sufficient for the Establishment of this Constitution between the States so ratifying the Same."

41. Bryant, "Stopping Time," 508.

42. Jeffrey K. Tulis, "Constitution and Revolution," in *Constitutional Politics: Essays on Constitution Making, Maintenance, and Change*, ed. Sotirios A. Barber and Robert P. George (Princeton: Princeton University Press, 2001), 116–27.

43. John R. Vile, "The Case against Implicit Limits on the Constitutional Amending Process," in Levinson, *Responding to Imperfection*, 193–94. Kyvig lends support to this rule of construction in stating that the decision to enumerate amendments separately from the original constitutional text conveyed the idea that "the core of the system articulated by the Founders was not to be touched." He adds, "The conservatism of American constitutional arrangements rests, in some part, upon this perception" (Kyvig, *Explicit and Authentic Acts,* 102).

44. Herman Belz, *A New Birth of Freedom: The Republican Party and Freedmen's Rights, 1861–1866* (New York: Fordham University Press, 2000), 122.

45. Ibid., 123.

46. Howard Jay Graham, *Everyman's Constitution: Historical Essays on the Fourteenth Amendment, the "Conspiracy Theory," and American Constitutionalism* (Madison: State Historical Society of Wisconsin, 1968), 298–300.

47. The ordinance of 1787 stated: "There shall be neither slavery nor involuntary servitude in the said territory, otherwise than in the punishment of crimes, whereof the party shall have been duly convicted" (Commager, *Documents of American History*, 1:132).

48. Belz, *New Birth of Freedom*, 126.

49. Fisher, *Trial of the Constitution*, 314–15.

50. Ibid., 315.

51. Keith E. Whittington's observation is apt: "In many ways, it is the striking presence of a written constitutional text that has blinded us to the complexity of our constitutional discourse" (Whittington, *Constitutional Construction*, 9). Although Article V presents itself as the exclusive means of constitutional amendment, the practical reason of written constitutionalism discloses the existence of a choice of means of revising constitutional meaning. In modern constitutionalism, legislative construction and judicial interpretation are recognized as alternative modes of constitutional revision. Nevertheless, depending on circumstances, they are subject to challenge as lacking the legitimacy of formal Article V amendment. Lutz, "Toward a Theory of Constitutional Amendment," 237.

52. John Harrison, "The Lawfulness of the Reconstruction Amendments," *University of Chicago Law Review* 1, no. 68 (2001): 375–80.

53. This view was widely held in the South during Reconstruction and to varying degrees appears in modern accounts. Kyvig states that in the post–Civil War era the Reconstruction amendments "appeared to depart, at least in spirit, from the procedures laid out in 1787 for constitutional revision. Thus they came to be thought of as amendments that could not have been achieved in normal circumstances. This perception had lasting effects in regard to the Thirteenth, Fourteenth, and Fifteenth Amendments as well as on general attitudes toward the amending process and constitutionalism itself" (Kyvig, *Explicit and Authentic Acts*, 156). Bruce Ackerman, a constitutional theorist, argues that "The Reconstruction Amendments—especially the Fourteenth—would never have been ratified if the Republicans had followed the rules laid down by Article Five of the original Constitution." According to Ackerman, Republicans challenged the basic premise for constitutional revision, namely, the principle of federalism itself, which holds "that a constitutional amendment must obtain the support of both the national government and the states, acting independently of one another, before it could be recognized as a legitimate

addition to our higher law." Ackerman says, "the first breach of federalist premises occurred during the ratification of the Thirteenth Amendment" and was expanded in the adoption of the Fourteenth Amendment. "To prevent the South from using the Federalist rules of Article Five to defeat the proposal and ratification of the amendment, the Reconstruction Republicans elaborated a new, and more nationalistic, system of constitutional decision making—one in which the states played only a secondary role. It was this revised process, and not the one designed by the Founding Federalists, that determined the legitimacy of the constitutional solution we now identify as the Fourteenth Amendment." Bruce Ackerman, *We the People: Foundations* (Cambridge, Mass.: Harvard University Press, 1991), 45.

54. *Collected Works*, 4:265.

55. U.S. Constitution, Article IV, Section 4: "The United States shall guarantee to every State in this Union a Republican Form of Government."

56. *Collected Works*, 7:380.

57. Defending the Constitution against the charge of illegality in the ratification debate, on the ground that the federal convention violated provisions of the Articles of Confederation, James Madison wrote in *The Federalist*, no. 40, "They must have reflected that in all great changes of established governments forms ought to give way to substance; that a rigid adherence in such cases to the former would render nominal and nugatory the transcendent and precious right of the people to 'abolish or alter their governments [. . .] as to them shall seem most likely to affect their safety and happiness.'" (Rossiter, *Federalist Papers*, no. 40, 252–53).

58. *Collected Works*, 7:281.

59. Ibid.

60. Ibid., 8:254.

61. Herman Belz, "The Thirteenth Amendment," in *The Heritage Guide to the Constitution* (Washington, D.C.: Regnery, 2005), 380–84.

62. Criticism of judicial interpretation is presented in Alexander Tsesis, *The Thirteenth Amendment and American Freedom: A Legal History* (New York: New York University Press, 2004).

12 The Thirteenth Amendment Enacted

Michael Vorenberg

ith his overwhelming victory in the election of 1864, Abraham Lincoln found his pockets full of political capital, and he chose to spend much of it making sure that the constitutional amendment abolishing slavery was enacted as quickly as possible. He declared the vote a sign that the people now were united behind the emancipation program he had helped to launch more than two years earlier. "It is the voice of the people now, for the first time, heard upon the question," he wrote in his message to Congress one month after the election.[1] In the five months following his election, Lincoln did more than any president before him, and more than any after, to secure freedom for African Americans in the form of a constitutional amendment abolishing slavery.

Before examining what Lincoln actually did on behalf of the amendment, it is worth pondering why he believed it so important that *this* House of Representatives, which already had failed to carry the amendment in a vote during the summer, adopt the amendment. Why not wait for the convening of the next House, which he could call into session as early as March 1865, and which would have the two-thirds majority needed to make adoption certain? Obviously, Lincoln wanted slavery abolished legally and quickly for the sake of those living as slaves. But, also, he wanted the *issue* of slavery taken out of his hands as quickly as possible, which is exactly what the amendment would do. Ever since July 1864, when he had written the "To Whom It May Concern" letter, which said that he would enter into peace talks with Confederates only on the terms of union *and* emancipation, Lincoln had been hounded by the false charge that his insistence on emancipation was the only obstacle to an immediate peace. In fact, as Lincoln well knew, it was the Confederate insistence on separation from the Union that kept the war going. The sooner that Congress adopted the amendment and sent it to the states for ratification, the sooner that Lincoln could say that his position on emancipation was irrelevant, for the people were deciding the matter on their own in the state legislatures. It was precisely this position that Lincoln would take at the Hampton Roads peace conference in February 1865, just after Congress adopted the amendment.[2]

Also, Lincoln preferred that the amendment be a product of a bipartisan effort rather than a purely Republican one. Democrats and border state Unionists, who had usually voted against emancipation, held about 40 percent of the seats in the House of Representatives; about a quarter of that group would have to vote in favor of the amendment for it to be adopted by the requisite two-thirds majority. Adoption of the amendment would thus symbolize an end to old party divisions over slavery and would allow for the solidification of a larger, lasting Union party, the sort of broad coalition that Lincoln had been striving to create for years. "The next Congress will pass the measure if this does not," Lincoln wrote in his annual message. "Hence there is only a question of *time* as to when the proposed amendment will go to the States for their action. And as it is to so go, at all events, may we not agree that the sooner the better?"[3]

After pleading with Congress to pass the amendment now rather than later, Lincoln took careful steps that would leave no political tracks. Even before Congress convened, he had begun to contemplate means to secure the amendment's adoption. In October, he had improved the measure's chances by securing Nevada's admission to the Union. The solidly Republican state would send one pro-amendment representative to the second session of Congress and would later vote in favor of ratification. If we can believe Charles A. Dana, the assistant secretary of war, Lincoln engineered the congressional act for Nevada statehood early in 1864 precisely because he wanted another state in the Union that would ratify the amendment. But Dana's account, written more than thirty years after the war, overstated the president's interest in the amendment prior to his renomination, and it confuses Lincoln's involvement in the Nevada statehood act with his sponsorship of the Thirteenth Amendment later that winter. Certainly, politicians recognized early on that Nevada's admission, as well as the readmission of Southern states such as Louisiana and Arkansas, would aid the passage of the amendment.[4] But the president's main interest in Nevada during 1864 had been in the electoral votes the new state could give him in the presidential contest. The coming election, rather than the impending decision on the amendment, led the Lincoln administration to hasten the admission of Nevada. Yet Lincoln's efforts in behalf of the Western state, even if driven by a somewhat unrelated motive, did help ensure the amendment's eventual adoption.[5]

With the new Congress in session again, the president attended to the amendment more deliberately. On December 7, he talked strategy with Abel Rathbone Corbin. A former congressional clerk, Corbin was a wealthy New York City financier with powerful friends in city politics. After the war, he made a name for himself by marrying the sister of President Ulysses S. Grant and then, with his friend Jay Gould, using his connection to the president to try to corner the gold market—a clumsy effort culminating in the financial panic known as "Black Friday." In late 1864, Corbin played for smaller stakes, promising to secure a few votes for the amendment in exchange for Lincoln's gratitude (and the later favors that gratitude might bring). The president told Corbin of his wish to see the amendment adopted prior to his second inauguration, in March; he did not want to call a special session of Congress. The New Yorker thought he could change the votes of some Democratic congressmen from his state, or at least guarantee their absence for the final vote. Lincoln, uncertain about the rules for adopting an amendment, had to be assured by Corbin that absences would indeed be helpful, that passage required approval of only two-thirds of the members in attendance, rather than two-thirds of the whole House.

The president also listened to the businessman's thoughts on how to win the support of Austin A. King and James S. Rollins, two Missouri congressmen who had voted against the amendment in June. Lincoln was scheduled to appoint a new federal judge in Missouri. Corbin asked him to leave the place vacant so that King and Rollins might earn some say in the appointment by voting correctly on the amendment. In this way, the president would not commit himself to anyone, but he would use the vacant judgeship—"a serpent hanging up on a pole," Corbin called it—to manipulate votes.[6] No evidence exists suggesting that Lincoln took Corbin's plan seriously, though it seems the president did fail to appoint someone to the Missouri post before his death. Rather than use subterfuge to sway the border state representatives, Lincoln preferred more direct methods. According to James Rollins, the president called him into the White House some weeks before the final vote and told him to inform all border state men of Lincoln's "anxiety to have the measure pass." Would Rollins, "an old Whig friend," lend his support? The Missouri slave owner delighted Lincoln by telling him that he already planned to back the amendment. When the president asked if Rollins could obtain King's support as well, the congressman seemed optimistic.[7] Corbin's ploy, apparently, was unnecessary. When the amendment was debated the next month, King and Rollins delivered two of the most eloquent speeches in its defense.

Less willing to reverse their positions on slavery were Sunset Cox of Ohio and John Todd Stuart of Illinois, two other lame-duck congressmen who consulted with Lincoln about the amendment. Both of these men thought that peace should take priority over abolition. During the holiday recess of Congress, Cox persuaded Stuart, Lincoln's former law partner and Mrs. Lincoln's cousin, to join him in asking the president to recommend peace negotiations with the Confederates. When the two congressmen arrived at the White House, Lincoln listened to their suggestion, but then shifted the subject to the antislavery amendment. Cox, and perhaps Stuart as well, promised to support the amendment if the president made a "sincere effort" toward peace and was rebuffed by the Confederates. Perhaps the offer made Lincoln think more approvingly of the plan of Francis P. Blair Sr., who had been asking to go to Richmond to negotiate with Jefferson Davis. If the president let the old man go and Davis rejected all terms short of Confederate independence, as Lincoln knew he would, then the conditions of Cox and Stuart would be met and more Democratic votes would be assured for the amendment. The president, if he conceived of such a strategy, kept it to himself. He knew that Union military victories, not peace delegations, must convince the Confederates to renounce their ideal of independence. Only after the fall of Savannah in late December did Lincoln allow the elder Blair to visit Richmond. When Blair returned from his meeting with Jefferson Davis, he carried an ambivalent message that the Confederate president had agreed to negotiate, but only "with a view to secure peace to the two countries."[8] Those final words signaled Davis's firmness on the demand for independence and made the prospect of reunion unlikely. Lincoln wrote out a careful reply explaining that he also was ready to negotiate, but "with the view of securing peace to the people of our one common country."[9] He sent the note, and Blair, back to Richmond.

The president probably thought that his message would squelch any further willingness by the Confederacy to negotiate a peace; if Jefferson Davis agreed to peace talks concerning "one common country," he would surely invite the fury of those Southerners insistent on independence. But perhaps the Confederate leader would be swayed by Blair's suggestion to send envoys to Washington on the pretext of designing a joint military venture to Mexico. Lincoln had rejected Blair's Mexico project, though he had not prohibited the veteran politico from discussing the plan with Davis. Whatever Blair decided to tell Confederate authorities, Lincoln was sure of one thing: he did not want to make an ultimatum on slavery, and the best way to remove slavery from the bargaining table was to secure the amendment's adoption.

Therefore, the president now worked harder than ever to win a few more votes for the amendment. To one representative whose brother had died in the war, Lincoln said, "your brother died to save the Republic from death by the slaveholders' rebellion. I wish you could see it to be your duty to vote for the Constitutional amendment ending slavery."[10] According to John B. Alley, a Republican congressman from Massachusetts, the president called two members of the House to the White House and told them to find two votes for the measure (it is not clear in Alley's story whether they already supported the amendment). When the congressmen asked for more specific instructions, Lincoln supposedly responded, "I leave it to you to determine how it shall be done; but remember that I am President of the United States clothed with great power, and I expect you to procure those votes."[11]

Alley's recollection, published twenty-three years after the event, was one of many reminiscences that implicated the president in the unseemly political bargaining that occurred during the last days before the final vote on the emancipation amendment. Such tales have helped fix Lincoln in the minds of revisionist historians as a president willing to forsake ethical means to achieve noble ends. But the evidence in this case does not bear out the image. There is not one reliable source, nor even an unreliable one, that reports that the president made any specific promise in exchange for a vote in favor of the amendment.

Still, Alley's account, while difficult to believe in its specifics—Lincoln was not the sort of chief executive to say, "I am President . . . clothed with great power"—does suggest the role the president played in the final drive to secure votes for the amendment. By endorsing the amendment in his annual message, and by directly confronting certain congressmen, Lincoln sent a clear signal that he would look kindly on opposition members who lent their support to the legislation. The message was certainly received in the House. "The wish or order of the President is very potent," said an opponent of the amendment during the debate. "He can punish and reward."[12] Yet Lincoln probably did not give specific promises to potential converts. Instead, he most likely let his lieutenants make the bargains and allowed them to use his name to seal the agreement. This arrangement kept the president uninvolved in shady negotiations, while giving tremendous bargaining power to Representative James Ashley of Ohio, Secretary of State William H. Seward, and others working for the amendment's adoption.

Probably a few deals were designed in this fashion, and at least one is well documented. Congressman Anson Herrick, a New York Democrat, already approved of the amendment in principle (his paper, the *New York Atlas*, had published editorials in its favor), but he was reluctant to break with the majority of his party by voting for it. Patronage from the Lincoln administration, however, might compensate for the castigation that Herrick could expect to receive if he broke from party ranks. From James Ashley and many others working for the amendment—but not from the president—Herrick received a promise of an appointment for his brother as a federal revenue assessor in exchange for his vote. Only after Congress adopted the amendment did Lincoln assure Herrick that "whatever Ashley had promised should be performed," and the president sent the recommendation for Herrick's brother to the Senate. (Unfortunately for the congressman, Lincoln died after recommending his brother, and when the Senate refused to confirm the appointment, neither President Andrew Johnson nor Seward was willing to assist Herrick further.)[13]

While Ashley and his allies generally did not inform the president of the details of their negotiations until after the amendment was adopted, on at least one occasion they sought Lincoln's help before the final vote. One day in mid-January, Ashley called at the White House bearing an offer of assistance for the amendment from agents of the Camden and Amboy Railroad. Under a state incorporation law, the New Jersey company enjoyed a monopoly, controlling the only line running the length of the state. For years, New Jersey residents had protested against the monopoly, and eventually, the fight was taken up by reform-minded politicians who had come to look upon any monopoly with the same disdain that they regarded another state-controlled institution, slavery. At the moment, the leading crusader against the Camden and Amboy was Senator Charles Sumner. The Massachusetts senator had sponsored a bill establishing a competitive railroad in New Jersey, and the measure was now in the hands of the Senate Commerce Committee, of which Sumner was not a member. The Camden and Amboy agents were determined to keep the measure in committee until the Thirty-eighth Congress expired. To Ashley, the railroad lobbyists suggested a swap: they would procure votes for the amendment if he would persuade Sumner to drop his bill. Ashley, no doubt skeptical of his or anyone's influence with Sumner, took the proposal to Lincoln. According to John G. Nicolay, the president rejected the offer, saying he could "do nothing with Mr. Sumner in these matters."[14]

The matter probably did not end there, however. After the House voted to adopt the antislavery amendment, rumors circulated that the influence of the Camden and Amboy had helped secure some votes. The failure of the Senate Commerce Committee to report the antimonopoly bill before the end of the session fueled accusations. Many years later, veteran politicians still gossiped about a possible deal. In 1898, James Scovel, a longtime opponent of the rail-road monopoly, reported that Congressman Thaddeus Stevens had told him that Lincoln secured votes against Sumner's bill and "these same votes helped Mr. Lincoln's amendment for permanent emancipation." The amendment, said Stevens, "was passed by corruption, aided and abetted by the purest man in America."[15]

When considered next to Nicolay's record of the president's reaction to the Camden and Amboy proposition, Stevens's account of Lincoln's involvement, reported secondhand more than forty years after the fact, seems dubious. A bargain between Republican congressmen and Camden and Amboy represen-tatives certainly did not require the president's approval. Perhaps Ashley gave the railroad lobbyists a false impression that Lincoln would comply with their wishes. Or maybe Republican senators on the Commerce Committee were convinced by Camden and Amboy agents, and not by Lincoln, that postponing Sumner's bill would lead to some positive result, such as the passage of the amendment in the House, New Jersey's election of a Republican senator, or the ratification of the amendment by the New Jersey legislature. One lobbyist for the railroad wrote to Joseph P. Bradley, a lawyer for the Camden and Amboy and a future Supreme Court justice, that he had spoken to members of the Commerce Committee and other senators, and "with all, the *political* view of the question was the one in which they seemed most interested." The monopoly's agent was "well satisfied" that any antimonopoly bill could be defeated, and that the present proposal by Sumner would not be hastily reported out by the committee because of the "wheels within wheels which must first be reached and tested."[16] Either James Ashley, Senate Republicans, or simply their own judgment persuaded the lobbyists for the Camden and Amboy that helping the antislavery amendment would keep Republicans favorable toward the monopoly. Almost certainly, the railroad's influence was behind the decision of Representative Andrew J. Rogers to stay away from the House on the day of the final vote. Congressman James S. Rollins told the House that the New Jersey member "had been confined to his room several days by indisposition." That the report of Rogers's alleged illness should come from Rollins, who, with Lincoln's encouragement, had become one of the amendment's overseers, suggests that the absence was part of a prearranged strategy.[17]

On January 31, 1865, after weeks of debate, arm-twisting, and soul-searching, the work of Lincoln and his political operatives finally bore fruit: the House of Representatives adopted the resolution for the Thirteenth Amendment. The only glitch came when rumors circulated that Confederate peace envoys were on their way to meet with Lincoln in Washington. Indeed, Francis P. Blair Sr. had persuaded Jefferson Davis that Lincoln might postpone the issue of reunion to discuss a joint expedition to Mexico, a project that the president had in fact rejected, and Davis had sent three messengers to Washington. But Union military officials had held them up in City Point, Virginia. Opposition congressmen had warned that the amendment would inhibit negotiations; if they knew that commissioners were on the way, they would demand a postponement of the final vote. Quickly, Ashley sent a messenger to the president for a note denying the rumor. Lincoln, who knew that any negotiations would occur outside of Washington, wrote out a clever reply: "So far as I know, there are no peace commissioners in the city, or likely to be in it."[18] Ashley showed the deceptive message to opposition members and silenced the peace murmurs. The vote went forward, and the resolution for the amendment received the two-thirds majority it needed for enactment. As they cast their votes, Republican congressmen were aware that they were making history. Representative George Julian of Indiana later recalled that, after the vote, he felt "born into a new life, and that the world was overflowing with beauty and joy."[19] Representative Cornelius Cole of California wrote to his wife, "the one question of the age is *settled*. Glory enough for one session, yes, even for a life."[20]

The president agreed. To a crowd of celebrants outside the White House the day after the vote in Congress, Lincoln admitted that the "[Emancipation] proclamation falls far short of what the amendment will be when fully consummated." He was so genuinely pleased with the measure that he had signed it that morning. Constitutional law did not require the president's signature on a proposed amendment, and congressmen who were already worried about the swelling of presidential power would later scold him for his action. But Lincoln was determined to leave his mark on the amendment for posterity. He may also have wanted to redress the wrong done by his predecessor, James Buchanan, who signed the "first" Thirteenth Amendment of 1861, the one that would have given slavery eternal life. The present amendment, the president told the serenaders before him, ended all questions about the status of enslaved Americans who still resided in rebellious states; it was "a King's cure for all the evils." Beyond the issue of slavery, however, the president would say nothing of the future of African Americans. What rights would they have after the war? What evils, if any, would be left uncured? These questions were not foremost in Lincoln's mind. Union—or as he put it now, "the reunion of all the states perfected"—was still the immediate goal.[21]

One evil cured by the amendment that Lincoln did not mention, but which he must have had in mind, was that slavery complicated peace negotiations. The action of Congress made it possible for the president to tell Confederates that the future of slavery was solely in their hands, not his, because the only way to halt the amendment was for the seceded states to pledge loyalty to the Union and then vote against ratification. Soon Lincoln would have an opportunity to press the advantage the amendment gave him. As the joyful crowd serenaded the president, Secretary of State Seward was already on his way to Hampton Roads, Virginia, to meet with three Southern envoys. The president joined him the next day.

The negotiations at Hampton Roads were unusual, for both Jefferson Davis and Abraham Lincoln were almost certain beforehand that an arranged peace was impossible. Davis welcomed negotiations not because he countenanced reunion but rather because he sought a temporary cease-fire to allow Southern forces to regroup before renewing their fight for Confederate independence. Even if the three commissioners dispatched by Davis—Alexander H. Stephens, the Confederate vice president, Robert M. T. Hunter, ex-secretary of state of the Confederacy, and John A. Campbell, a former U.S. Supreme Court justice—hoped to secure a permanent peace on the basis of reunion, Davis's instructions explicitly ordered them to negotiate for an armistice between "two countries."[22] Lincoln surely doubted that the Confederates had renounced their aim of independence, but he feared that rejecting the peace overture would make him appear overly intractable, a position that could damage the fate of the Thirteenth Amendment, which was now before the states for ratification.

On February 3, Lincoln and Seward met the three Confederate commissioners on the *River Queen*, a Union ship moored in the James River just off the shore of Hampton Roads. After some preliminary discussions, in which Lincoln expressed skepticism at the idea of a joint expedition to Mexico and explained that the Union's wartime acts of emancipation would have to be respected by the Southern states as a condition of reunion, Seward told the commissioners that Congress had adopted the constitutional amendment abolishing slavery. If the war should go on, said the secretary of state, the measure would certainly be ratified by the requisite states and slavery abolished; but if the rebel states surrendered, they could vote against it and postpone emancipation.[23]

The commissioners were surprised, not only because this was the first that they had heard of Congress approving the amendment, but also because Seward's statement suggested that federal authorities still counted the Confederate states as members of the Union. Stephens asked Lincoln for reassurance about the status of the rebel states. Would they indeed be allowed to send representatives to Congress? The president gave his standard reply to this question. In his opinion, the rebel states would resume their "practical relations to the Union" as soon as they surrendered to the national authority. Stephens, who was well aware that Congress might take a different view of the Confederate states, asked the president why he could not bring the Southern states back into the Union by a presidential proclamation, such as he had used against slavery. In response, the president told Stephens that if he were in the Georgian's place, he would persuade the governor of his state to assemble the legislature and instruct the newly elected body to recall the state's troops, elect members to Congress, and ratify the antislavery amendment "*prospectively*, so as to take effect—say in five years."[24]

Abolitionists would have been shocked to learn that Lincoln made this statement—assuming that he did indeed make it. They also would have been taken aback by his suggestion to R. M. T. Hunter that the federal government might appropriate up to four hundred million dollars to those states freeing their slaves voluntarily.[25] Although Congress early in the war had passed legislation compensating loyal owners for the loss of their emancipated slaves, it had rejected all proposals for compensation during the debates on the antislavery amendment. The idea of paying for slaves now offended most Northerners,

THE THIRTEENTH AMENDMENT ENACTED 189

who viewed Southern slaveholders' loss of property in slaves as a necessary price of their treason. Northern lawmakers might have been willing to provide compensation, but the conventions of property law had been ground down by the friction of four years of destructive war.

After four hours of increasingly unproductive conversation, the meeting disbanded. Lincoln told Stephens that he would consider the proposal for a joint military expedition, but he confessed that his mind was unlikely to change. The conference was a failure, as the president knew it would be. Yet, the meeting served Lincoln's ends perfectly. By introducing the issue of the antislavery amendment, Seward and his chief had convinced the Confederate commissioners that the president was powerless to revoke his emancipation policy. Just days after the conference, in a message picked up by Northern newspapers, Jefferson Davis reported to the Confederate Congress that his counterpart had told the peace commissioners of the amendment to demonstrate that "the question of slavery was wholly removed from his control and placed beyond negotiation."[26] As a result of the Hampton Roads conference, all now understood that the constitutional amendment made it pointless to protest against the administration's emancipation policy.

While it is easy to see why Lincoln and Seward mentioned the amendment at Hampton Roads, it may seem odd that they took such an outmoded approach to the question of emancipation. Did the two Union leaders really think the slaves could be freed gradually, despite what the amendment itself said? Did they truly hope that Congress would appropriate millions of dollars to compensate not only the loyal but also the rebellious owners of slaves? Apparently, the president was sincere in at least one of the statements he made at the meeting. When he returned to Washington from Hampton Roads, he read to the cabinet a draft proposal to Congress that four hundred million dollars should be distributed to the rebellious states, with each state receiving money in proportion to its slave population of 1860. Half of the funds would be distributed by April 1 if the rebellion ceased; and the other half would be given by July 1 if the antislavery amendment had been ratified by three-quarters of the states. The war would cost the Union about three hundred million dollars during the next one hundred days, explained Lincoln, so why not pay roughly the same sum to end the war immediately? Seward was not present to comment on the plan, but all the other cabinet members rejected the proposal because they thought, quite rightly, that Congress would not adopt it, and because they knew that only military victory, and not financial incentives, could end the war. The president, who seemed saddened by the rejection, declared, "you are all against me."[27]

Lincoln's dejection was probably genuine, not simply because he preferred that loyal Unionists be compensated for the loss of their slaves, but because he regretted that his government would miss an opportunity to drive deeply into

Southern morale a wedge he had helped set at Hampton Roads. The strategy of the president and Seward at the Virginia conference had been to offer the most generous terms possible for reunion, while knowing full well that they would be rejected. By demonstrating magnanimity, even on the issue of slavery, Lincoln hoped to turn war-weary Southerners against the Confederate leaders who demanded independence at any cost. Appeasement, thought the president, would weaken even further the popularity of Southern fire-eaters. In a sense, the plan was no different from those he had proposed during the secession crisis and the first years of the war. But in that earlier period, he made conciliatory proposals with the belief that they might be accepted and with the regret that they would allow slavery to linger. Now, however, he knew that any proposal short of Confederate independence would be rejected, and, because of the constitutional amendment, he was sure that slavery would not last long beyond the war. Since emancipation was soon to be a fact, Lincoln felt free to offer concessions on slavery.

The cabinet's rejection of the compensated emancipation plan confirmed for the president what he must already have suspected: that any suggestion of compromise on slavery, no matter how hollow, would be rebuffed by the majority of Northerners. Lincoln decided not to deliver his proposal to Congress. Also, when he issued his public account of the Hampton Roads conference to the House of Representatives, he repeated nothing he had said to the peace commissioners about slavery. Instead, the president highlighted the intransigence of the Southerners, claiming that they sought "an indefinite postponement" of reunion.[28] Seward, in a separate statement to the Senate, reported that Lincoln did not negotiate on emancipation, and that the two Union leaders told the Southerners that Congress had approved the constitutional amendment, which he predicted was to be "soon accepted" by three-fourths of the states. Neither Seward nor the president mentioned advocating a policy of gradual, compensated emancipation.[29]

Whatever was in fact said at Hampton Roads, Lincoln almost certainly did not propose "prospective" ratification of the amendment, as Alexander Stephens later claimed that he did. As a Georgian writing during the period of military reconstruction, Stephens had obvious political motives for claiming that the late president meant to give the Southern states complete control over emancipation and the freed people. If Lincoln did in fact counsel "prospective" ratification, he did so disingenuously. He knew that neither Congress nor the Supreme Court, now commanded by the devoted antislavery activist Salmon P. Chase, would accept anything but immediate emancipation under the abolition amendment.

Although ratification was a hotly contested issue in a number of Union state legislatures, the partisan nature of the debates made it possible to make some predictions about the results. Even if all the states that went for Lincoln in the election of 1864 voted for ratification, the amendment would receive approval from only twenty-two states, five short of the twenty-seven needed for ratification. The number twenty-seven, however, was based on the assumption that there were thirty-six states in the Union. If one assumed instead that the eleven seceded states were out of the Union, then the approval of only seventeen states was needed. As federal lawmakers faced the reality of the ratification process, they were forced to confront an issue they had barely considered, and certainly not resolved, during their debates on the amendment: Were the Southern states to be counted in the Union, and if so, were votes for ratification by provisional state governments in the South to be accepted as legitimate?

The attitude of the Lincoln administration toward ratification by the Southern states was clear. At Hampton Roads, the president and the secretary of state had told the Southern commissioners that a state's previous decision on secession was irrelevant; so long as a newly formed legislature pledged itself to the Union and the Constitution, it could vote on ratification. Unionist legislatures in Southern states undergoing Reconstruction certainly had no doubts about their qualifications to vote on the amendment. In Louisiana, Tennessee, and Arkansas, new legislatures all demonstrated their commitment to the Union by giving unanimous, or near-unanimous, votes in favor of ratification. Also deciding in favor of the amendment was the Unionist "legislature" of Virginia. Early in the war, this tiny body (eleven members in the house, five in the senate) had been formed by the Unionist governor, Francis H. Pierpont, and recognized by the Lincoln administration so that a "state" ordinance might be passed creating the separate, Unionist state of West Virginia. The legislature of West Virginia and the "loyal" legislature of Virginia, now residing in Alexandria, both ratified the amendment days after Congress approved it. The State Department duly counted all of the ratifications by the Southern states, even that of the Pierpont government in Virginia. A small number of congressmen, led by Senator Sumner, took the position that the seceded states were out of the Union and thus could not vote on ratification and should not be counted in the calculation of how many state ratifications were needed. But Sumner's group met with strong opposition, and the congressional session adjourned on March 3, 1865, without issuing an official policy on the role of the Southern states in ratification.[30]

That left the oversight of ratification in the hands of the Lincoln administration, at least until the new Congress convened in December. Two days after Robert E. Lee's surrender to Ulysses S. Grant at Appomattox Court House, the president pushed for ratification in a speech that many anticipated would be the first of a series on Reconstruction. In it, Lincoln challenged the claim of those such as Sumner who had argued that ratification required "no more than three fourths of those States which have not attempted secession." "Such a ratification would be questionable," said Lincoln, "while a ratification by three fourths of all the States would be unquestioned and unquestionable." Lincoln also challenged the Radicals' position on states like Louisiana that were undergoing Reconstruction. While Sumner and others wanted to treat these states as outside of the Union and not accept ratifications of the Thirteenth Amendment made by Unionist legislatures there, the president wanted Louisiana quickly readmitted. "If we reject Louisiana," said Lincoln, who mentioned that the state already had decided for ratification, "we also reject one vote in favor of the proposed amendment." The president understood the amendment's power not only as a guarantee of African American freedom but also as a potential catalyst for speedy Reconstruction.[31] Three days after the speech, the president was assassinated. There would be no more words by Lincoln on the Thirteenth Amendment.

The pistol shot of John Wilkes Booth gave the nation its greatest martyr to the causes, now twinned, of restoring the Union and enacting emancipation. As a side effect, the death of Lincoln made the ratification of the Thirteenth Amendment almost certain, for the state legislatures would be loath to dishonor the memory of the slain president by allowing slavery to live. Many of those who had once opposed the amendment, or who had simply treated the measure with indifference, knew that they must now change their course. Reflecting on Lincoln's death, Calvert Comstock, a Democratic editor in upstate New York, advised a fellow publicist, "from this point let us refuse to allow the Dem. party to ever *seem* in a disloyal position or as the defenders of Slavery. If we avoid such issues we shall soon have the political ascendancy."[32] Members of the loyal opposition in the New York state assembly shared Comstock's opinion. Although the state senate had voted for ratification, Democrats in the assembly prior to Lincoln's death were united against the antislavery amendment. Now, a number of Democratic legislators, anticipating the arrival of Lincoln's funeral train in Albany in late April, decided that they could not honorably oppose ratification while memorializing the president. On April 22, four days before Lincoln's casket arrived in the state capital, a Democratic faction led by Smith Weed agreed to back the amendment, and the New York assembly finally voted for ratification.[33] Other states, North and South, would follow, and on December 18, 1865, Seward issued a proclamation declaring the amendment ratified. In death, as in life, Lincoln coaxed reluctant emancipators to embrace constitutional freedom.

Notes

1. *The Collected Works of Abraham Lincoln*, ed. Roy P. Basler, 9 vols. (New Brunswick, N.J.: Rutgers University Press, 1953–55), 8:149. Much of the account in this essay is drawn

directly from Michael Vorenberg, *Final Freedom: The Civil War, the Abolition of Slavery, and the Thirteenth Amendment* (Cambridge: Cambridge University Press, 2001), 176–210.

2. Michael Vorenberg, "The Deformed Child: Slavery and the Election of 1864," *Civil War History* 47 (September 2001): 240–57.

3. *Collected Works*, 8:149.

4. See, for example, D. L. Gregg to Elihu B. Washburne, Washington, March 25, 1864, Elihu B. Washburne Papers, Library of Congress.

5. Charles A. Dana, *Recollections of the Civil War* (New York: D. Appleton, 1898), 174–77. See Earl S. Pomeroy, "Lincoln, the Thirteenth Amendment, and the Admission of Nevada," *Pacific Historical Review* 12 (December 1943): 362–68.

6. Abel R. Corbin to Abraham Lincoln, December 8, 1864, Abraham Lincoln Papers, Library of Congress.

7. Isaac N. Arnold, *The Life of Abraham Lincoln* (Chicago: Jansen, McClurg, 1885), 358–59.

8. Edward C. Kirkland, *The Peacemakers of 1864* (New York: Macmillan, 1927), 223.

9. *Collected Works*, 8:221.

10. Isaac N. Arnold, *The History of Abraham Lincoln and the Overthrow of Slavery* (Chicago: Clarke, 1866), 469.

11. Allen Thorndike Rice, ed., *Reminiscences of Abraham Lincoln by Distinguished Men of His Time* (New York: North American Review, 1888), 585–86.

12. Speech of Rep. Aaron Harding of Kentucky, *Congressional Globe*, 38th Cong., 2nd sess. (January 9, 1865), pt. 1, 180, 53–54.

13. Anson Herrick to William H. Seward, July 3, August 8, 29, 1865, February 5, 1867, and Homer Nelson to William H. Seward, July 29, 1865, November 20, 1866, William H. Seward Papers, Special Collections, University of Rochester.

14. John G. Nicolay and John Hay, *Abraham Lincoln: A History*, 10 vols. (New York: Century, 1890), 10: 84–85; Helen Nicolay, *Lincoln's Secretary: A Biography of John Nicolay* (New York: Longmans, Green, 1949), 220–21.

15. James M. Scovel, "Thaddeus Stevens," *Lippincott's Monthly Magazine*, April 1898, 550.

16. J. R. Freese to Joseph P. Bradley, January 16, 1865, Joseph P. Bradley Papers, New Jersey Historical Society, Newark, N.J..

17. *Congressional Globe*, 38th Cong., 2nd sess. (January 31, 1865), pt. 1, 530. On Rollins's role in passing the amendment and his friendship with Lincoln, see *New York Evening Post*, January 14, 1865; Elizabeth Blair Lee to Samuel Phillips Lee, February 2, 1865, in *Wartime Washington: The Civil War Letters of Elizabeth Blair Lee*, ed. Virginia Jeans Laas (Urbana: University of Illinois Press, 1991), 472.

18. *Collected Works*, 8:248; S. S. Cox to Manton M. Marble, February 1, 1865, Manton M. Marble Papers, Library of Congress; Kirkland, *Peacemakers of 1864*, 226–37.

19. George W. Julian, *Political Recollections, 1840–1872* (Chicago: Jansen, McClurg, 1884), 251.

20. Cornelius Cole, *Memoirs of Cornelius Cole* (New York: McLoughlin Brothers, 1908), 220.

21. *Collected Works*, 8:254.

22. Kirkland, *Peacemakers of 1864*, 226.

23. Alexander H. Stephens, *A Constitutional View of the Late War between the States*, 2 vols., (Philadelphia: National Publishing, 1870), 2:610–11.

24. Ibid., 611–14.

25. Ibid., 617; John A. Campbell, *Reminiscences and Documents Relating to the Civil War during the Year 1865* (Baltimore: John Murphy, 1887), 25.

26. *New York Tribune*, February 9, 1865.

27. John G. Nicolay, Memorandum of conversation with J. P. Usher, October 11, 1877, John G. Nicolay Papers, Library of Congress; Francis Fessenden, ed., *Life and Public Services of William Pitt Fessenden*, 2 vols. (Boston: Houghton, Mifflin, 1907), 2:8; Howard Beale, ed., *The Diary of Gideon Welles: Secretary of the Navy under Lincoln and Johnson*, 3 vols. (New York: W. W. Norton, 1960), 2:237; *Collected Works*, 8:261.

28. *Collected Works*, 8:285.

29. Ibid., 8:286–87n1.

30. Vorenberg, *Final Freedom*, 224–26.

31. *Collected Works*, 8:399–405.

32. Calvert Comstock to Manton Marble, April 21, 1865, Marble Papers, Library of Congress.

33. *Journal of the Assembly of the State of New York*, 88th sess., 1865, 1387–89; *New York Evening Express*, April 24, 1865; *New York Herald*, April 24, 1865.

13 "That Which Congress So Nobly Began": The Men Who Passed the Thirteenth Amendment Resolution

Ron J. Keller

n otherwise ordinary session of the House of Representatives was disrupted on June 27, 1922. The House adjourned for five minutes to receive an honored guest. Cornelius Cole, visiting the U.S. Capitol for the first time in more than fifty years, stood to address the chamber. The members sat respectively attentive to the frail man, who was one of their own. Just shy of his one hundredth birthday, this former representative and senator from California recalled proudly his experiences in Congress. This occasion was a particular honor, considering that Cole was the last surviving member of the Thirty-eighth Congress, which met from 1863 to 1865. That Congress left a legacy by passing one of the most significant pieces of legislation in American history.[1]

President Lincoln and Congress began administering a death sentence to the institution of slavery by 1863, but something more substantive was needed. In his annual message to Congress on December 8, 1863, Lincoln called for emancipation to be extended to include the border states. A ready and deliberate move, it stopped short of embracing the suggestion of Representative Isaac N. Arnold of Illinois—asking Congress to pass a constitutional amendment abolishing slavery. That would come soon enough.[2]

The Thirty-eighth Congress largely did not need prodding to advance the antislavery movement. Republicans dominated in both chambers—thirty Republicans, twelve Democrats, and seven border state Unionists comprised the Senate; eighty-six Republicans, seventy-two Democrats, and twenty-four border state Unionists in the House. While their views represented the spectrum from conservative to radical, vocal antislavery advocates dominated the

Senate. And the powerful and famous Charles Sumner from Massachusetts eclipsed them all. One of the most ardent antislavery advocates ever to inhabit Congress, Sumner was well regarded for his powerful oratory, if not a bit of vanity.[3] Though beaten unconscious in the Senate chamber in 1856 following an antislavery speech, he continued fervently to pursue not only the abolition of slavery but the cause of black equality as well. He often criticized Lincoln's reluctance on emancipation, but the two maintained a friendship. Another champion of the antislavery cause was Michigan's Zachariah Chandler, who also frequently communicated with Lincoln on emancipation issues.[4]

Forceful antislavery proponents inhabited the House of Representatives as well. The "apostle of freedom," Pennsylvania's Thaddeus Stevens, was one.[5] Stevens personally abetted the freedom of many slaves through the Underground Railroad before his election to Congress. Like Sumner, he radically pushed for legal rights and not just freedom. Another slavery opponent was Ohio's James A. Garfield, a skilled debater who had risen to the rank of brigadier general before accepting a congressional seat in 1863 upon a resignation. As expected, the men in the Thirty-eighth Congress represented their various parties, philosophies, and populations but would be called upon to nobly expel slavery from the country.

Only a week after the president's annual message, Republican James Ashley from Ohio took the initiative and on December 14, 1863, introduced in the House, as one of the session's first actions, a bill to make the abolition of slavery part of "the organic law of the land." Ashley set in motion what eventually became the Thirteenth Amendment to the U.S. Constitution. A month later, Missouri Democrat John B. Henderson introduced a similar joint resolution in the Senate.[6]

While war matters consumed the attention of the Senate, Sumner stepped forward there and on February 8, 1864, introduced his own joint resolution, which included the clause "all persons are born equal under the law."[7] Concerned that such wording on equality might derail the chances for passage, Lyman Trumbull of Illinois—also a firm protagonist of black rights—offered his own phraseology, omitting Sumner's controversial language but adding Congress's power to enforce the abolition of slavery. Trumbull's wording was accepted. Sumner at first held out for his own version, although he finally acquiesced.[8]

Despite overwhelming Democratic Party opposition to the proposal, it was a foregone conclusion that the Senate would achieve the necessary two-thirds vote to pass it. Unlike the more contentious debate to follow in the House, the Senate witnessed little persuasive opposition. Sumner indicated the lack of divisiveness and "impatience of the Senate" at the end of debate when he wrote, "Senators wished to vote and get to their dinner."[9]

While some Democrats argued that private property could not be taken away under a constitutional amendment, other Democrats relented. One such Democrat was Reverdy Johnson from Maryland, who had been instrumental in preventing his state from seceding from the Union.[10] Here was a former Whig turned War Democrat, who opposed emancipation, now speaking for a constitutional amendment. Johnson declared, "I never doubted the day must come when human slavery must be terminated. I am called upon to decide what is best to be done to rid an institution so full of peril."[11]

In some respects, even more extraordinary was the position of John Henderson of Missouri. A former Democrat born in Virginia, he had personally experienced involuntary servitude after he was orphaned as a child. He had been a strong supporter of President James Buchanan, but as a moderate, he opposed secession. Elected to the Senate as a Unionist in 1862, Henderson advised President Lincoln on border state and emancipation policy.[12] In proposing the Thirteenth Amendment to the Senate, Henderson hoped for a revitalization of the Democratic Party if it embraced the antislavery measure. Earnestly declaring the "inalienable right of liberty belongs to all men," Henderson signaled a sea change in the long-standing Democratic Party position on slavery.[13]

On April 8, 1864, by a margin of 38 to 6, the Senate passed the joint resolution abolishing slavery. All Republicans cast votes in favor, as did six Unionists and four Democrats: Reverdy Johnson, Lyman Trumbull, and Oregon's James Nesmith and Benjamin Harding. Only Thomas Hendricks of Indiana, James McDougall of California, George Riddle and Willard Saulsbury of Delaware, and Lazarus Powell and Unionist Garrett Davis of Kentucky voted against it.[14]

Approval of the proposed amendment would be easily obtained in the Senate as compared to the House of Representatives, where opposition was strong. The work fell back again to Congressman Ashley, who was up to the task.

Striking in appearance, James M. Ashley was an ambitious political organizer. In his youth, he had witnessed the detestable treatment of slaves as a cabin boy on a riverboat and later aided briefly in bringing slaves to freedom across the Ohio River. Ashley allied himself strategically with Salmon P. Chase, attracted to Chase's firm stances on temperance and antislavery. In the House, Ashley introduced an emancipation resolution as early as 1861, but it was defeated at that time. Now, in 1864, he returned to his fight.[15]

The necessary support for passage, however, was not yet present in the House, and the joint resolution was soundly rejected on June 15, 1864. It fell nearly along party lines, with 65 Republicans voting yes, and 93 Democrats voting no.[16] Democrats Joseph Baily of Pennsylvania, Ezra Wheeler of Wisconsin, and John Griswold and Moses Odell of New York voted in favor, as did most Republicans. Ashley was amazed at the solid Democratic vote, but, not ready to concede, he voted no to save the amendment, under an obscure

House rule that it might be reintroduced in the second session of the Thirty-eighth Congress.[17] Ashley recognized his charge now would be to convince Democrats to abandon cherished party traditions for a greater moral cause.

President Lincoln had previously given minimal attention to the amendment but now promptly and vigorously embraced it. He began publicly and privately challenging the Republican Party faithful, encouraging Democrats also to support the "expected" constitutional amendment.[18] At Lincoln's suggestion, the June 1864 Union (Republican) National Convention included in its platform a firm and sweeping commitment to a constitutional amendment abolishing slavery.[19] Accordingly, when Lincoln was reelected that November, he viewed his victory as a mandate for action.

In his annual message to Congress on December 6, 1864, Lincoln again stressed the imperative for the House to pass the resolution as the Senate had done. The recent election had emboldened the Republican Party, which would enjoy a larger majority in the new, Thirty-ninth Congress meeting in 1865. It was thus only a matter of time before the amendment would be sent to the states. Yet the president appealed to the outgoing Thirty-eighth Congress to tackle the immense task in its final days: "May we not agree the sooner the better? Unanimity of action among those seeking a common end is desirable."[20]

In response to the president's call, Representative Ashley again led the fight for passage, even threatening to hold a special session of Congress if enough votes could not be mustered. He opened the final session of the Thirty-eighth Congress on January 6, 1865, with a forcible speech that made "thoughtful men pause and consider." Addressing his comments to the "enlightened judgment and Christian philanthropy" of every member, he declared that only a constitutional amendment could make the Republic finally free.[21] Echoing the words of Abraham Lincoln, Ashley noted that the founders did not intend the nation to be half slave and half free. Immediately after his declaration, a firestorm of demands to speak on the issue erupted from both sides of the aisle. Debate in the House brought a crowd of observers and reporters, who filled the galleries and hung onto every word, although earlier speeches suggested that the division along party lines was only growing firmer.[22] There appeared little indication that anything different from the previous year's result would transpire. Likelihood of change seemed in the first few days of 1865 "a matter of grave doubt."[23]

Democrats held fast to the slogan "the Union as it was, the Constitution as it is." Representatives William Finck of Ohio, Daniel Voorhees and Charles Eldridge of Indiana, Fernando Wood of New York, and Robert Mallory of Kentucky all led protracted debate, each denying that the abolition of slavery should be achieved through amending of the Constitution.[24] Republicans responded by arguing the moral incumbency of immediate action. Representative Elihu Washburne of Illinois, from General Ulysses S. Grant's hometown of Galena, reminded his foes that in his own state "staunch Democrats are prepared to amend and wipe out the wicked and infernal slavery which has brought untold horrors onto the nation."[25] Cornelius Cole from California offered that the United States had always been an example to the world and could resume that role again by adopting the proposal. James Patterson of New Hampshire followed eloquently: "The voices of our murdered heroes sleeping on a thousand victorious battlefields and still other voices from the dim but glorious hereafter of our history call for our immediate and decisive action. This is a solemn[,] earnest[,] terrible revolution."[26] Concluding that he lacked at least six, and perhaps as many as fourteen votes necessary to secure passage, Ashley decided to postpone the vote until the last day of January.[27] This would buy him only a little time. But that time would prove to be one of the most significant months in the history of Congress.[28]

Ashley immediately sent letters and circulars to Republican members, urging their lobbying support and imploring their presence and their vote on January 31 as "absolutely essential."[29] Concurrently, an amazing and vast myriad of behind-the-scenes lobbying efforts was engineered to ensure victory, involving members of Congress, political bargains, and President Lincoln himself. Lincoln, in fact, had begun diligently lobbying soon after the November 1864 election. From this time, historian Michael Vorenberg asserts, "No piece of legislation during Lincoln's presidency received more of his attention than the Thirteenth Amendment."[30]

Lincoln and Ashley teamed up to target border state and liberal Democrats who appeared to vacillate on their slavery sympathies. Their goal was to find members who would "follow their conviction, even to political death, provided they know that their votes would pass the measure."[31] For example, Lincoln met with New York financier Abel Corbin, who promised to help obtain votes from New York Democrats in exchange for Lincoln's "gratitude."[32] Ashley approached Frank Blair of Missouri, Henry Winter Davis of Maryland, and Reuben Fenton and Augustus Frank of New York, seeking out those who might now risk their political popularity. They, in turn, provided names of more possibilities. Well over half of them would ultimately vote for the resolution.[33]

Lincoln's success proved greater with border state conservatives than with Democrats. The border states of Maryland and Missouri, while Unionist, harbored some strong Southern sympathies. With that in mind, Lincoln promised at least one congressman that, in return for support of the amendment, he would endorse a Reconstruction plan that included lenient amnesty to the South.[34] Hoping to induce the border state support, Lincoln invited Missourian James Rollins, a personal friend, to his White House office. There, the president expressed his deep anxiety about the possible failure of the measure. After Rollins informed Lincoln that he was in full support, the president recruited him to entice the rest of the Missouri delegation.[35]

Representative John Alley from Massachusetts later testified that Lincoln called two House members to the Executive Mansion and directed them, too, to find the necessary votes. When they inquired as to how they were to achieve that, Lincoln responded, "I leave it to you to determine how it shall be done; but remember that I am the President of the United States, clothed with immense power, and I expect you to procure these votes."[36]

Secretary of State William H. Seward also engineered lobbying efforts of his own behind the scenes. He recruited prominent and well-connected Tennessee lawyer W. N. Bilbo, who solicited the support of every Democrat he knew who had any influence with members of Congress. He relied on New York representatives Homer Nelson and Augustus Frank to pressure others to pledge their allegiance.[37]

Allegations persist that patronage and even bribery were utilized at the highest levels of government to induce votes. Indeed, George Yeaman from the border state of Kentucky and Anson Herrick and Moses Odell from New York, Seward's home state, all received posh appointments following the congressional session. However, appointments such as these were not unusual, and no certain evidence exists of a trade-off.[38] It has also been alleged that Lincoln utilized patronage to promise statehood for Nevada if it delivered amendment support.[39] Undoubtedly, successful persuasions of Congress depended on negotiating, and according to Representative George Julian from Indiana, "the particulars . . . never reached the public."[40] As Representative Alley noted, while Lincoln practiced politics and may have used patronage and other means of persuasion "where he thought it might do the most good," he felt justified if it might help the "down-trodden race."[41] He largely left negotiation to subordinates, and no evidence exists that Lincoln himself struck any unethical promise or bargain in exchange for securing votes.

Lincoln also sought out the support of Ohio Democrat Samuel "Sunset" Cox, whom he distrusted. The former newspaper owner and editor was widely regarded as a clever, intelligent statesman who also exercised significant influence among his colleagues.[42] Recognizing Cox's political weight, Lincoln personally pleaded with him that his vote was vital to passing the amendment. A moderate, Cox had been asked by longtime Democrat and prominent historian George Bancroft to throw his support behind the amendment proposal. Bancroft reasoned that the Southern economy could rebound only with the removal of slave labor.[43] "Slavery to me," Cox asserted, "is the most repugnant of all human institutions."[44] Rumors circulated of an envoy of Confederate peace commissioners being sent to meet with the Lincoln administration, and Cox assured the president he would not oppose the resolution unless peace negotiations commenced. He worried that talk of an amendment might jeopardize successful peace talks.[45] Cox came through for Lincoln by publicly admitting that the power to abolish slavery could be granted by constitutional amendment.[46] Cox then summoned party colleagues to his quarters one by one to persuade them to expel the slavery question "from the political arena."[47]

The intense congressional saga came to its climax on January 31, 1865. The House of Representatives was scheduled to vote on the resolution later that afternoon. Fully recognizing the importance of the action, Cox noted, "The last day of January is here."[48] Representative Julian from Indiana would later describe what was about to occur as "one of the grandest events of the century."[49]

On the House floor, the winds were changing. First, Democrat Archibald McAllister from Pennsylvania, defeated in his reelection bid the previous November, spoke to his members: "When this measure was before the House on a former occasion, I voted against it. In voting now for the measure, I cast my votes against the cornerstone of the Confederacy."[50]

Then Alexander Hamilton Coffroth stood to address the body. The former publisher of a well-read Democratic Party newspaper, like McAllister he was an ardent Pennsylvania Democrat who had voted against the amendment proposal the year before.[51] But unlike the other man, Coffroth was not a lame-duck congressman.

First impressions would not have led anyone to assume that Coffroth would help instigate a turning point in the history of the Thirteenth Amendment. Though he was potentially sacrificing his political career on this one upcoming vote, there he now stood—soft-spoken, seemingly nervous and timid, with his hands stuck in his pockets.[52] But if his composure was lacking, his clarity was not: "I have been a Democrat all my life, and I assure my politically associated colleagues my political life has been spent defending and supporting measures which I thought were for the good of the party and the country." Contemplating the gravity of the moment and of the future—especially his future—he resolved, "If by my action I dig my political grave, I will descend into it without a murmur knowing I am justified and that I am doing what will ultimately prove to be a service to my country!"[53] When Coffroth finished, cheers erupted.[54]

Moved by Coffroth's selfless display, the mood of the House seemed energized and emboldened. Representative Herrick, Democrat from New York, then stood to record his sentiments: "Last session, I voted against this resolution from a solemn conviction of duty. I shall now vote for it from a similar conviction. . . . I feel it to be my very duty to vote for it and I shall, whatever may be the consequences to me politically or otherwise."[55] The mood was electric.

Down to the last few hours before the crucial vote, Ashley was still counting the likely ayes. He had exhausted almost every possible lobbying effort at his disposal but was confident now he had barely enough. Then a last-minute incident arose to complicate the picture. Cox, who was ready to cast his vote in a few hours in favor, was informed that Confederate peace commissioners were waiting to meet with General Grant. Cox asked Ashley if he could send word to the president asking whether he could confirm the rumor and reminding him that his crucial vote hinged on its substantiation or denial. Ashley promptly inquired of Lincoln, who sent a note back insisting that there were no such peace commissioners in Washington.[56] Ashley seized the moment and circulated Lincoln's note to skeptical members to shore up further support.[57] Cox viewed it incredulously, however, believing that "other sources" in Congress were more knowledgeable about these matters than either Ashley or even the president. Cox was certain that Lincoln was either "mistaken or ignorant" of possible proceedings at Grant's headquarters.[58] Yet Ashley remained certain that Cox was with them on the vote.

Finally, Speaker of the House Schuyler Colfax called for a vote to be taken on the joint resolution. Representatives Mallory and Eldridge attempted to delay the vote so as to regain strength for the opposition, but Thaddeus Stevens angrily protested to Ashley, and the latter called for the debate to close.[59] The hour was at hand, and the fate of this long, noble crusade was about to be decided. Ashley had once believed he would not "live long enough to see" it happen.[60] But now he would.

Before a packed gallery of spectators that afternoon desiring to witness this historic and suspenseful occasion, the roll call was requested, and one-by-one the votes were announced. A crescendo of repeated applause met the numerous "ayes." The joint resolution passed, 119 to 56, with 8 not voting. An enthusiastic and sustained applause erupted following the announcement, more boisterous than any that Congress had ever heard and loud enough that it carried outside.[61] The final passage was complete. The Thirty-eighth Congress had done its duty. Representative Julian most certainly captured the sentiment of many of his colleagues when he later recalled, "I was inexpressibly thankful for the privilege of recording my name on so glorious a page of the nation's history."[62]

The following day, February 1, an elated Abraham Lincoln signed the resolution with pride, even though a presidential signature was not necessary on a proposed constitutional amendment.[63] However, it seemed only natural that Lincoln should sign a document he had worked so hard, alongside Congress, to secure. After a procession outside the White House, Lincoln spoke from his balcony and stated that it was up to the states to now consummate "that which Congress so nobly began."[64] In response, that very day, Lincoln's home state of Illinois became the first to ratify the amendment.

Every Republican member of the House had voted affirmatively on the proposed amendment, and thirteen more Democrats had joined the four who had voted yes in the June 1864 vote. The success of this measure is rightly owed to the vision, pressure, and fortitude of Lincoln, Ashley, and other Republican leaders. But it was also due to the number of Democrats who disregarded partisanship in order to extend freedom to all. As Michael Vorenberg has asserted, "The most powerful provision against slavery owes its existence in part to slavery's onetime defenders."[65] Also, the border state congressmen, who could have easily ridden the fence, provided crucial support, and they deserve credit alongside the Republicans. Historians James G. Randall and Richard Nelson Current concluded that "the slaveholder [James] Rollins rather than the self-proclaimed egalitarian Stevens, was the real spokesman for Lincoln in the House."[66] Had the border state members and the Democrats who voted in favor not done so, the measure would have failed by sixty-five votes. Had even five Democrats not voted in favor, it would have failed as well.[67]

A few other incidentals might be noted in the congressional vote. Michigan, Minnesota, Oregon, Kansas, and West Virginia were unified in the amendment's support. Not surprisingly, the New England states gave almost unanimous support—save for New Hampshire's Daniel Marcy, who did not vote. New Jersey, New York, Ohio, and Pennsylvania, from which much of the heated January debate emanated, were almost evenly split.[68] Less than half the delegations from Illinois, Indiana, and Ohio voted for it. The delegation from the slave state of Missouri demonstrated it was more united than those states, with ten of its twelve members of the Senate and House submitting affirmative votes.

Sunset Cox, whom Seward later said deserved credit "more than any other member . . . [for] the passage of the Constitutional Amendment in Congress abolishing slavery," had brought forth crucial Democratic votes and persuaded other Democrats not to be absent. Yet, in the end, he cast an opposing vote.[69] Cox believed in the rumors of peace negotiations, which actually proved true. Moreover, Lincoln had known about them. Since the Confederate emissaries had not yet reached Washington, he was technically truthful in his note stating he was not aware of any peace commissioners *in the city*. Had Lincoln not sent this assurance to Ashley in the manner he did, several more members would likely have voted in opposition. That almost certainly would have doomed any prospect for the amendment's passage.[70]

This historic final session of the Thirty-eighth Congress was remarkable for both its actions and its members: Those such as Ashley, who carried the mantle of leadership to a freedom-affirming conclusion. Those such as Coffroth, who escaped the ideological shadow of their party. Those such as Cox, who considered it their patriotic duty to bring colleagues aboard. These men are prototypes for many others in Congress in 1864 and 1865; yet, each was exceptional. Political decisions carry political repercussions. These three leaders considered other factors more important than awaiting the political judgment of their constituents and being rewarded or punished accordingly at the ballot box. Consider that, of the nineteen border state representatives that Ashley met with, thirteen voted for the amendment, and all paid the ultimate political price by being defeated in the next election.[71] James Rollins and Samuel Knox of Missouri, Delaware's Nathaniel Smithers, Maryland's John Creswell, and others were unseated for unpopular but courageous stances. Because the slavery resolution had been a campaign issue in the 1864 election on the eve of the House vote, Ashley, Coffroth, and Cox were also coarsely rebuked in their home districts for their sentiments.

Cox had been caught in the crossfire in the 1864 election. The Ohio Democratic Party was badly split, and the party's gubernatorial candidate, Clement Vallandigham—the Peace Democrat previously banished by Lincoln from the Union—refused to endorse the moderate Cox. General party support eroded, and Cox's support suffered as well. Democrats had held fourteen of the state's nineteen seats in the House of Representative before the 1864 elections. Afterward, they lost all but two, Cox's included. The demoralized statesman had worked with passionate zeal, and his political future was then uncertain. Still, when it came time to vote on the amendment, the lame-duck congressman voted his conscience, justifying his "nay" upon proper patriotic principle.[72]

It was rare even for a Republican to make black freedom the primary issue in his campaign, but James Ashley did so in his 1864 reelection bid. Coming off the failure of the antislavery amendment resolution the previous June, he relentlessly pushed the amendment to the voters in his district as hard as he had in the House of Representatives. And while many Republicans preached the evils of slave labor, few proposed black equality as did Ashley. His astonishingly progressive foresight won him few friends and many political enemies. Though Ashley was likable, many of his constituents resented his adamant antislavery position, castigating him for his "love for niggers."[73] The Unionist newspaper *Toledo Blade* refused to endorse him for reelection in 1864, berating him as a traitor to the Unionist platform.[74] Ashley refused, however, to abandon these convictions. As well regarded as he was, his actions nearly cost him his congressional seat in the 1864 election, as he narrowly squeaked by his opponent.[75]

Alexander Coffroth had known the political repercussions might be detrimental to his career when he broke with many of his party members and constituents to side with the Republicans. Though he did claim victory in his close 1864 reelection, his opponent, William Koontz, successfully contested the ballot returns, and Coffroth was not allowed to be seated. His bold support of the resolution was not greatly welcomed as the *Franklin (Pa.) Repository* reflected:

Among these [who disregarded party interests] the name of Gen. A. H. Coffroth is found, and his vote is severely critisised by his former friends. We could not refrain from exposing the folly of Gen. Coffroth's speech against the success of this amendment delivered during the last session. . . . General Coffroth is *not* elected to the next Congress, and he knows it. . . . It is enough of us to know that Gen. Coffroth has cast a most righteous vote, and he is entitled to full credit for it. He will soon retire from official position, in obedience to the voice of the people of his district, and when the charges of the unscrupulous men who but recently sustained him have been forgotten, he will live in history, as one of the men who aided in consummating the greatest moral victory achieved in the history of Nations.[76]

One hundred and nineteen members of the House of Representatives of the Thirty-eighth Congress, elected to serve their vastly different constituents, political expectations, and ideologies, accomplished the improbable, submitting themselves to a greater good for the country. Agreeing to abolish forever the catalyst for the Civil War was not an easy task, but this Congress prescribed freedom for all by writing it into the "organic law of the land." Historical consternation may linger over the deal- making and behind-the-scenes bargaining to secure congressional votes. The fact that "the great moral victory" was attained through some arguably illicit deals strikes many as unpalatable and ignoble. But such judgment misses a crucial point. In the case of the congressional passage of the Thirteenth Amendment resolution, the art of compromise—for the elevation of a long-excluded race of people, with few personal rewards attached, and nothing illegal committed—was more accurately a great moral achievement. To be sure, its passage required political posturing and pandering, but the visible and unshakable moral convictions of those aforementioned, among others, cannot be discounted.

John G. Nicolay and John M. Hay, Lincoln's White House secretaries and biographers, put the issue in perspective when they later wrote, "Here was a great revolution of ideas, a mighty sweep of sentiment, which could not be explained away by the stale charge of sectional fanaticism, or by alleging irregularities of political procedure."[77] The war for preservation of the Union ended with a victory for the greatest of moral causes—liberty for all. The further road to equality would be difficult; but the first step was taken. The names and achievements of the Thirty-eighth Congress are testament to a great moment when a new course was charted for the nation. That which Abraham Lincoln and Congress so nobly began, gave to the republic a new birth of freedom.

MEMBERS OF CONGRESS WHO VOTED IN
FAVOR OF THE THIRTEENTH AMENDMENT

Members of the Senate

Henry S. Lane (Indiana)
James W. Grimes (Iowa)
James Dixon (Connecticut)
Waitman T. Willey (West Virginia)
La Fayette S. Foster (Connecticut)
Lot M. Morrill (Maine)
Henry B. Anthony (Rhode Island)
Peter G. Van Winkle (West Virginia)
Daniel Clark (New Hampshire)
John Conness (California)
Jacob Collamer (Vermont)
John P. Hale (New Hampshire)
Edwin D. Morgan (New York)
John C. Ten Eyck (New Jersey)
John Sherman (Ohio)
William Sprague (Rhode Island)
Ira Harris (New York)
Henry Wilson (Massachusetts)
Charles Sumner (Massachusetts)
James H. Lane (Kansas)
Reverdy Johnson (Maryland)
Solomon Foot (Vermont)
Samuel C. Pomperoy (Kansas)
Timothy O. Howe (Wisconsin)
James Harlan (Iowa)
Morton S. Wilkinson (Minnesota)
B. Gratz Brown (Missouri)
Zachariah Chandler (Michigan)
Alexander Ramsey (Minnesota)
Edgar Cowan (Pennsylvania)
John B. Henderson (Missouri)
Benjamin F. Wade (Ohio)
James W. Nesmith (Oregon)
Jacob M. Howard (Michigan)
Lyman Trumbull (Illinois)
James R. Doolittle (Wisconsin)
William P. Fessenden (Maine)
Benjamin F. Harding (Oregon)

Members of the House of Representatives

Leonard Myers (Pennsylvania)
James M. Ashley (Ohio)
Ignatius Donnelly (Minnesota)
James G. Blaine (Maine)
M. Russell Thayer (Pennsylvania)
John F. Farnsworth (Illinois)
Thaddeus Stevens (Pennsylvania)
De Witt C. Littlejohn (New York)
Henry C. Deming (Connecticut)
Ithamar C. Sloan (Wisconsin)
Augustus Frank (New York)
Henry Winter Davis (Maryland)
John H. Hubbard (Connecticut)
William B. Allison (Iowa)
John F. Driggs (Maryland)
Glenni W. Schofield (Pennsylvania)
Sidney Perham (Maine)
Ebon C. Ingersoll (Illinois)
James W. Patterson (New Hampshire)
John D. Baldwin (Massachusetts)
John M. Broomall (Pennsylvania)
Daniel Morris (New York)
Thomas T. Davis (New York)
Nathan F. Dixon (Rhode Island)
Henry L. Dawes (Massachusetts)
Ephraim R. Eckley (Ohio)
Joseph Baily (Pennsylvania)
Francis Thomas (Maryland)
James S. Rollins (Missouri)
Sempronius H. Boyd (Missouri)
Cornelius Cole (California)
Fernando C. Beaman (Michigan)
Frederick A. Pike (Maine)
Nathaniel B. Smithers (Delaware)
Samuel F. Miller (New York)
James T. Hale (Pennsylvania)
John Ganson (New York)
Samuel Knox (Missouri)
William G. Steele (New Jersey)
William Radford (New York)

Godlove S. Orth (Indiana)
Edward H. Rollins (New Hampshire)
Josiah B. Ginnell (Iowa)
Asahel W. Hubbard (Iowa)
Orlando Kellogg (New York)
William Higby (California)
Hiram Price (Iowa)
William B. Washburn (Massachusetts)
George S. Boutwell (Massachusetts)
Theodore Pomperoy (New York)
John F. Starr (New Jersey)
A. Carter Wilder (Kansas)
John F. Longyear (Michigan)
Joseph W. McClurg (Missouri)
James K. Moorhead (Pennsylvania)
William D. Kelley (Pennsylvania)
Amasa Cobb (Wisconsin)
Alexander H. Coffroth (Pennsylvania)
Henry T. Blow (Missouri)
John R. McBride (Oregon)
James M. Marvin (New York)
Anson Herrick (New York)
James E. English (Connecticut)
Austin A. King (Missouri)
Thomas D. Eliot (Massachusetts)
Alexander H. Rice (Massachusetts)
Charles Upson (Michigan)
William Windom (Massachusetts)
Justin S. Morrill (Vermont)
Thomas A. Jenckes (Rhode Island)
Schuyler Colfax (Indiana)
Leonard Myers (Pennsylvania)
Daniel Gooch (Massachusetts)
John A. Griswold (New York)
Wells A. Hutchins (New York)
John A. Kasson (Iowa)
Freeman Clarke (New York)
Samuel Hooper (New York)
Walter D. McIndoe (Wisconsin)
Portus Baxter (Vermont)
Oakes Ames (Massachusetts)
Elihu Washburne (Illinois)

James F. Wilson (Iowa)
Ambrose W. Clark (New York)
Jesse O. Norton (Illinois)
Calvin T. Hulburd (New York)
Frederick E. Woodbridge (Vermont)
Robert B. Van Valkenburg (New York)
Robert C. Schenck (Ohio)
Henry W. Tracy (Pennsylvania)
Henry G. Worthington (Nebraska)
Benjamin F. Loan (Missouri)
James A. Garfield (Ohio)
Thomas B. Shannon (California)
Charles O'Neill (Pennsylvania)
Isaac N. Arnold (Illinois)
Edwin H. Webster (Maryland)
Augustus C. Baldwin (Michigan)
Ezra Wheeler (Wisconsin)
George H. Yeaman (Kentucky)
Giles W. Hotchkiss (New York)
William H. Randall (Kentucky)
Francis W. Kellogg (Michigan)
John H. Rice (Maine)
Rufus P. Spalding (Ohio)
Homer A. Nelson (New York)
Kellian V. Whaley (West Virginia)
Jacob B. Blair (West Virginia)
Augustus Brandegee (Connecticut)
John B. Alley (Massachusetts)
Lucien Anderson (Kentucky)
Green C. Smith (Kentucky)
John A.J. Creswell (Maryland)
Archibald McAllister (Pennsylvania)
Thomas Williams (Pennsylvania)
George W. Julian (Indiana)
William G. Brown (West Virginia)
Moses F. Odell (New York)
Ebenezer Dumont (Indiana)

Notes

1. *Biographical Directory of the American Congress, 1774–1961* (Washington, D.C.: Government Printing Office, 1961), 719; additional information courtesy of the Cornelius Cole Family Papers, UCLA Serials Department of Special Collections.

2. Annual Message to Congress, December 8, 1863, in *The Collected Works of Abraham Lincoln*, ed. Roy P. Basler, 9 vols. (New Brunswick, N. J.: Rutgers University Press, 1953–55), 7:52. See also Hans L. Trefousse, *The Radical Republicans* (New York: Alfred A. Knopf, 1969), 298.

3. John G. Nicolay and John Hay, *Abraham Lincoln: A History*, 10 vols. (New York: Century, 1890), 10:75.

4. *Biographical Directory of the American Congress*, 680.

5. A. K. McClure, *Lincoln and Men of War-Times* (Philadelphia: Times Publishing, 1892), 99.

6. Henry Wilson, *History of the Rise and Fall of Slave Power*, 3 vols. (Boston: Osgood, 1877), 3:434–35. See also Nicolay and Hay, *Abraham Lincoln*, 10:75.

7. Nicolay and Hay, *Abraham Lincoln*, 10:75–76.

8. Wilson, *History of the Rise and Fall*, 436–37. See also Trefousse, *Radical Republicans*, 298; and James G. Randall and Richard Nelson Current, *Lincoln the President* (New York: Dodd, Mead, 1955), 304.

9. Charles Sumner to George William Curtis, in *Selected Letters of Charles Sumner*, ed. Beverly Wilson Palmer, 2 vols. (Boston: Northeastern University Press, 1990), 2:233–34.

10. J. Frederick Essary, *Maryland in National Politics*, 2nd ed. (Baltimore: John Murphy, 1932), 180.

11. *Congressional Globe*, 38th Cong., 1st sess. (April 5, 1864), 1149.

12. For more information on Senator Henderson, visit www.mrlincolnswhitehouse.org.

13. Michael Vorenberg, *Final Freedom: The Civil War, the Abolition of Slavery, and the Thirteenth Amendment* (Cambridge and New York: Cambridge University Press, 2001), 98.

14. *Congressional Globe*, 38th Cong., 1st sess. (April 8, 1864), 1424.

15. Sherman Jackson, "Representative James Ashley and the Midwestern Origins of the Thirteenth Amendment," *Lincoln Herald* 80 (Summer 1978): 83–85; additional information courtesy of Ohio Historical Society.

16. *Congressional Globe*, 38th Cong., 1st sess. (June 15, 1864), 2995.

17. Nicolay and Hay, *Abraham Lincoln*, 10:78. The rule was that if the sponsor of a bill voted no on it, it could be reintroduced in the next session.

18. Reply to Committee Notifying Lincoln of His Renomination, June 8, 1864, in *Collected Works*, 7:380; Proclamation Concerning Reconstruction, July 8, 1864, in ibid., 7:433; Letter to Henry Hoffman, October 10, 1864, in ibid., 8:41.

19. Randall and Current, *Lincoln the President*, 307.

20. Annual Message to Congress, December 6, 1864, in *Collected Works*, 8:149.

21. James G. Blaine, *Twenty Years in Congress* (Norwich, Conn.: Henry Bill Publishing, 1884), 536.

22. *Congressional Globe*, 38th Cong., 2nd sess. (January 6, 1865), 138. For more on Ashley, see William C. Harris, *Lincoln's Last Months* (Cambridge, Mass.: Belknap Press, 2001), 178; and Vorenberg, *Final Freedom*, 185.

23. Samuel Cox, *Three Decades of Federal Legislation* (Providence: J. A. & R. A. Reid, 1885), 321.

24. George W. Julian, *Political Recollections* (Chicago: Jansen & McClury, 1884), 250.

25. *Congressional Globe*, 38th Cong., 2nd sess. (January 15–28, 1865), 477–523.

26. Ibid.

27. Vorenberg, *Final Freedom*, 180. See also www.mrlincolnswhitehouse.org.

28. Julian, *Political Recollections*, 250.

29. Vorenberg, *Final Freedom*, 180.

30. Ibid., 180–81.

31. Jackson, "James Ashley," 88.

32. Vorenberg, *Final Freedom*, 181.

33. Jackson, "James Ashley," 88–89.

34. Harris, *Lincoln's Last Months*, 130; Vorenberg, *Final Freedom*, 181.

35. James S. Rollins, "The King's Cure for All Evils," in *Conversations with Lincoln*, ed. Charles M. Segal (New York: G. P. Putnam's Sons, 1961), 362–64.

36. Quoted by John B. Alley, in *Reminiscences of Abraham Lincoln by Distinguished Men of His Time*, ed. Allen Thorndike Rice (New York: North American Review, 1886), 585–86.

37. LaWanda Cox and John Cox, "The Seward Lobby and the Thirteenth Amendment," in *Politics, Principle, and Prejudice* (New York: Atheneum, 1969), 1–21. See also Harris, *Lincoln's Last Months*, 130.

38. Cox and Cox, "Seward Lobby," 28–29; Jackson, "James Ashley," 93.

39. Trefousse, *Radical Republicans*, 298.

40. Julian, *Political Recollections*, 250.

41. Quoted by John Alley, in Rice, *Reminiscences of Abraham Lincoln*, 586.

42. *Biographical Directory of the American Congress*, 745–46; additional information courtesy of Ohio Historical Society.

43. Harris, *Lincoln's Last Months*, 127.

44. Cox, *Three Decades of Federal Legislation*, 325.

45. Ibid., 327–28.

46. Ibid., 321.

47. Cox and Cox, "Seward Lobby," 18; David Lindsey, *Sunset Cox: The Irrepressible Democrat* (Detroit: Wayne State University Press, 1959), 93.

48. Cox, *Three Decades of Federal Legislation*, 326.

49. Julian, *Political Recollections*, 250.

50. *Congressional Globe*, 38th Cong., 2nd sess. (January 31, 1865), 523.

51. *Biographical Directory of the American Congress*, 717.

52. Vorenberg, *Final Freedom*, 206.

53. *Congressional Globe*, 38th Cong., 2nd sess. (January 31, 1865), 523.

54. Vorenberg, *Final Freedom*, 206.

55. *Congressional Globe*, 38th Cong., 2nd sess. (January 31, 1865), 525–26.

56. Cox, *Three Decades of Federal Legislation*, 327–28.

57. Vorenberg, *Final Freedom*, 206.

58. Cox, *Three Decades of Federal Legislation*, 327–28.

59. Randall and Current, *Lincoln the President*, 312.

60. Jackson, "James Ashley," 91.

61. *Congressional Globe*, 38th Cong., 2nd sess. (January 31, 1865), 531. See also Doris Kearns Goodwin, *Team of Rivals: The Political Genius of Abraham Lincoln* (New York: Simon & Schuster, 2005), 689.

62. Julian, *Political Recollections*, 251.

63. Randall and Current, *Lincoln the President*, 313–14.

64. *Collected Works*, 8:255.

65. Vorenberg, *Final Freedom*, 204.

66. Randall and Current, *Lincoln the President*, 312–13.

67. Jackson, "James Ashley," 92. See also Harris, *Lincoln's Last Months*, 132.

68. *Congressional Globe*, 38th Cong., 2nd sess. (January 31, 1865), 531.

69. Lindsey, *Sunset Cox*, 95.

70. Much discussion of this can be found in Cox, *Three Decades of Federal Legislation*, 327; Vorenberg, *Final Freedom*, 207; Harris, *Lincoln's Last Months*, 132; and Goodwin, *Team of Rivals*, 688.

71. Jackson, "James Ashley," 88–89.

72. See Sunset Cox, *Eight Years in Congress: 1857–1865* (New York: Appleton, 1865), 6.

73. Comments such as this one are recorded in Maxine Baker Kahn, "Congressman Ashley in the Post–Civil War Years," *Northwest Ohio Quarterly* 36:125 (Summer 1964).

74. Jackson, "James Ashley," 87.

75. Vorenberg, *Final Freedom*, 171.

76. "A Nation Disenthralled," *Franklin Repository*, February 8, 1865.

77. Nicolay and Hay, *Abraham Lincoln*, 10:822.

14 The End of the Beginning: Abraham Lincoln and the Fourteenth and Fifteenth Amendments

Frank J. Williams

> We hold these truths to be self-evident, that all men are created equal, that they are endowed by their Creator with certain unalienable Rights, that among these are Life, Liberty and the pursuit of Happiness. —Declaration of Independence

When Thomas Jefferson penned the Declaration of Independence, he eloquently defined the promise of America—freedom and equality for all. But putting this simple and cherished concept into practice required the blood and sweat of countless individuals in succeeding generations, black and white alike. Perhaps no other leader in American history fully appreciated the import of this human struggle more than our sixteenth president.

Even as a young lawyer in this country's heartland, Abraham Lincoln knew that the promise of the Declaration rang hollow for the millions of blacks held in slavery. Even after losing his 1855 and 1858 bids for the United States Senate, Lincoln maintained a quiet but keen interest in public affairs. He read proslavery publications, thereby maintaining a finger on the pulse of proslavery opinions, and he noted a shift in attitude toward slavery—a shift away from the thought that it was a necessary evil and toward the idea that it was a positive aspect of society. Privately, Lincoln decried this philosophy, writing in a personal memorandum, "although volume upon volume is written to prove slavery a very good thing, we never hear of the man who wishes to take the good of it, *by being a slave himself.*" Lincoln maintained an ongoing, albeit private, dialogue in which he dissected and contested the validity of common proslavery arguments. For example, he wrote, "If A. can prove, however conclusively, that he may, of right, enslave B.—why may not B. snatch the same argument, and prove equally, that he may enslave A?"[1]

The justification for slavery was contingent upon the unspoken rule that the masters were always white and the slaves were always black. On this, Lincoln wrote, "By this rule, you are to be slave to the first man you meet, with a fairer skin than your own." It was also commonly held that white men were more intelligent than their black counterparts. Lincoln warned, "By this rule, you are to be slave to the first man you meet, with an intellect superior to your own."[2]

By the summer of 1855, Lincoln's ruminations on the extent to which slavery was ingrained in American society led him to conclude, "The Autocrat of all the Russias will resign his crown, and proclaim his subjects free republicans sooner than will our American masters voluntarily give up their slaves." As he became further agitated by the state of the Union, Lincoln documented his concerns in writing. Among all that plagued Lincoln, one question rose above all others: "Can we, as a nation, continue together *permanently—forever*—half slave, and half free?" To that question, he had but one answer: "The problem is too mighty for me. May God, in his mercy, superintend the solution."[3]

When, as president-elect, Lincoln boarded the inaugural train headed for Washington, this country stood on the precipice of self-destruction—mired in a national crisis of unparalleled proportions. Lincoln set out to heal a country split by a racial chasm so deep that the Founding Fathers' dream of one new nation was unraveling, thread by thread.

Four years later, with eloquent confidence, Lincoln explained his commitment to uniting the people of the nation—both black and white. His message of equality still reverberates through the ages: "With malice toward none; with charity for all; with firmness in the right, as God gives us to see the right, let us strive on to finish the work we are in; to bind up the nation's wounds; to care for him who shall have borne the battle, and for his widow, and his orphan—to do all which may achieve and cherish a just, and a lasting peace, among ourselves, and with all nations."[4]

Lincoln's legacy for this nation is one of true emancipation. The Emancipation Proclamation and the Thirteenth Amendment are the cornerstones of America's freedom foundation. With its ratification in December 1865, the Thirteenth Amendment freed approximately four million slaves who remained in bondage despite the Emancipation Proclamation. At the same time, the legal landscape of every slave state was instantly and irrevocably altered.

By plowing his way through the politics and fears of prejudice, Lincoln left us an invaluable inheritance—the renewed promise of one nation, indivisible, with liberty and justice for all. We, in the twenty-first century, bask in the achievements of the heroes of our nation's history—Lincoln not the least among them. He might not have foreseen the need for additional alterations to the Constitution, in the form of the Fourteenth and Fifteenth Amendments, nor anticipated that these amendments would be passed by Congress and ratified by the states. But, undoubtedly, had Lincoln been alive, he would have used all legal, political, and military means to ensure passage of the last two Civil War amendments.

The Beginning: Lincoln Builds a Foundation for the Future

Almost from the beginning of his administration, Abraham Lincoln was pressured by abolitionists and Radical Republicans to issue an emancipation proclamation. In principle as well as in strategic military terms, Lincoln approved of such a policy. His opposition to slavery came partly from a deep and personal repugnance. But always the consummate lawyer, he shaped his political policy with an eye toward his constitutional responsibility to preserve the Union. Early on in Lincoln's administration, the political and philosophical line he drew in the vast American republic allowed for the continuation of slavery in the South. Thus, the extemporaneous remarks that he made in Philadelphia on his way to being inaugurated come as a surprise to some but serve to illustrate the depth of Lincoln's feelings about slavery—that he thought a Union with slavery might not be worth saving:

> [There was] something in that Declaration giving liberty, not alone to the people of this country, but hope to the world for all future time. It was that which gave promise that in due time the weights should be lifted from the shoulders of all men, and that *all* should have an equal chance. This is the sentiment embodied in that Declaration of Independence. Now, my friends, can this country be saved upon that basis? If it can, I will consider myself one of the happiest men in the world if I can help to save it. If it can't be saved upon that principle, it will be truly awful. But, if this country cannot be saved without giving up that principle—I was about to say I would rather be assassinated on this spot than to surrender it.[5]

By allowing border slave states to maintain the status quo until he secured their loyalty to the Union and by prohibiting the expansion of the institution into the territories, Lincoln believed that the ultimate result would be the extinction of slavery. He was shrewd in his strategic planning and postponed taking any overt action against slavery until he believed he had wider support from the American public.

During his 1858 campaign debates with Senator Stephen A. Douglas, Lincoln did not denounce those who held slaves. He recognized that his only proposals to end the practice at that time, colonizing slaves outside the United States or freeing them but keeping them strictly segregated, would be unacceptable to slave owners. But he made clear his position with a forceful attack against the spread of slavery in America.

Four years earlier, Lincoln and Douglas had begun disputing the issue of slavery. In Peoria, Illinois, the two men argued the pitfalls and benefits of Douglas's Kansas-Nebraska Act. In a two-hour-long response to the senator's defense of the new law he had sponsored, Lincoln said, "This *declared* indifference . . . for the spread of slavery, I can not but hate. I hate it because of the monstrous injustice of slavery itself. I hate it because it deprives our republican example of its just influence in the world—enables the enemies of free institutions, to taunt us as hypocrites—causes the real friends of freedom to doubt our sincerity, and especially because it forces so many really good men amongst ourselves into an open war with the very fundamental principles of civil liberty—criticising the Declaration of Independence, and insisting that there is no right principle of action but *self-interest*."[6] Lincoln repeated the position he had taken in an earlier speech: "[T]here is no reason at all furnished why the negro after all is not entitled to all that the declaration of independence holds out, which is, 'life, liberty, and the pursuit of happiness' and I hold that he is as much entitled to that as the white man. I agree that the negro may not be my equal and Judge Douglas' equal in many respects—certainly not in color, and in intellectual development, perhaps—but in the right to [eat] the bread which his own hand earns, he is my own equal and Judge Douglas' equal, and the equal of every living man."[7] Lincoln concluded his statement with a direct attack on Douglas's advocacy of "popular sovereignty":

> When [Judge Douglas] is saying that the negro has no share in the Declaration of Independence, he is going back to the year of our revolution, and, to the extent of his ability, he is muzzling the cannon that thunders its annual joyous return. When he is saying, as he often does, that if any people want slavery they have a right to have it, he is blowing out the moral lights around us. When he says that he don't [*sic*] care whether slavery is voted up or down, then, to my thinking, he is, so far as he is able to do so, perverting the human soul and eradicating the light of reason and the love of liberty on the American continent.[8]

Because Lincoln was so strongly committed to the democratic process and the Constitution as it then existed, he limited his early public criticisms to the expansion of slavery into the territories. Nevertheless, he became increasingly powerful in articulating his opinion. In the last debate with Senator Douglas, Lincoln likened the slavery debate to the timeless struggle between right and wrong: "They are the two principles that have stood face to face from the beginning of time; and will ever continue to struggle. It is the same spirit that says, 'You work and toil and earn bread, and I'll eat it.' No matter in what shape it comes, whether from the mouth of a king who seeks to bestride the people of his own nation and live by the fruit of their labor, or from one race of men as an apology for enslaving another race, it is the same tyrannical principle."[9]

Even after attaining the presidency, Lincoln initially limited his antislavery fight to the battle against extending it into the new federal territories. Because as a frontier lawyer he had limited experience and contact with blacks, his policy, like most politicians', was to do the least he had to do. He wanted the problem of slavery to go away, but from the beginning of his presidency, his primary goal was to preserve the Union. Whether or not that mission would include dismantling the institution of slavery depended upon whether taking such action was necessary to save the Union. As he wrote, even after drafting an emancipation proclamation, "I would save the Union. I would save it the shortest way under the Constitution. The sooner the national authority can be restored; the nearer the Union will be 'the Union as it was.' If there be those who would not save the Union, unless they could at the same time *save* slavery, I do not agree with them. If there be those who would not save the Union unless they could at the same time *destroy* slavery, I do not agree with them. My paramount object in this struggle *is* to save the Union, and is *not* either to save or to destroy slavery."[10]

As the war unfolded, Lincoln came to recognize the importance of publicly denouncing the entire institution of slavery—not just its expansion. Lincoln knew that the struggle of slaves was very much the same struggle of all people—the struggle for peace and freedom. By midsummer 1862, he was openly discussing with several of his cabinet members his growing conviction that military law and political necessity now required the emancipation of slaves by executive order. On July 22, the president read a rough draft of an emancipation proclamation to his cabinet. Artist Francis B. Carpenter called this cabinet meeting "a scene second only in historical importance and interest to that of the Declaration of Independence."[11] Ultimately, Lincoln agreed with Secretary of State William H. Seward that he must wait for a military victory before making his proclamation public. "I do not want to issue a document that the whole world will see must necessarily be inoperative, like the Pope's bull against the comet!" Lincoln said.[12]

And so it was months later, as a glowing sun set over the blood-soaked fields of Antietam on September 22, 1862, that President Lincoln publicly issued his preliminary proclamation: "[All] persons held as slaves within any state, or designated part of a state, the people whereof shall then be in rebellion against the United States shall be then, thenceforward, and forever free; and the executive government of the United States, including the military and naval authority thereof, will recognize and maintain the freedom of such persons."[13]

Until this point in his presidency, Lincoln viewed the Civil War as a rebellion and the federal response as a fight to preserve the Union without addressing the institution of slavery. But by issuing the Emancipation Proclamation, Lincoln threatened to crush the Confederacy by destroying slavery, the basis of its economy and society. This marked one of the few times in history in which the war aims were changed in the middle of war.

Black Americans, knowing that freedom was at last on the horizon, hailed Lincoln as a hero. Word quickly spread that there was an administration in Washington that finally supported and welcomed emancipation. Something as hopeful and dramatic as freedom cannot be contained. Thousands of slaves, even in territory still controlled by the Confederacy, fled to the protection of the Union lines.

A former Alabama slave, Wallace Turnage, who in the nineteenth century wrote an account of his years in bondage, recalled that in 1864 he escaped in a rowboat on Mobile Bay in Alabama, where he was rescued in rough weather by a Union gunboat: "I now dread the gun and handcuffs and pistols no more. Nor the blewing [sic] of horns and running of hounds; nor the threats of death from the rebel's authority. I can now speak my opinion to men of all grades and colors, and no one to question my right to speak."[14]

With the support of the administration, at least two hundred thousand slaves walked, ran, or rowed to freedom by February 1865. This perceived "mass exodus" caused some people great trepidation, as evidenced by Attorney General Edward Bates's reply to a letter from A.W. Bradford, governor of Maryland: "I am honored with your letter of yesterday informing me that large numbers of slaves owned in Maryland, are daily making their way into the District of Columbia from the neighboring counties of your State, which you assure me is producing great anxiety and complaint in your community. . . . In these distempered times, I am not at all surprised to hear that Slaves in the border States are using all available means to escape into free territory."[15]

No matter how many slaves were actually freed under the auspices of the Emancipation Proclamation, what proved essential to the war was that by issuing it, Lincoln made slave liberation a goal of the Union government. Not only did emancipation begin removing the useful labor of blacks from the home front of the Confederacy, it also added their labor power to the Union cause. Even though Lincoln described emancipation as a "necessary war measure," he also showed political shrewdness by making it a goal of his administration.

Official liberty for all slaves came in December 1865 with the ratification of the Thirteenth Amendment to the Constitution. Lincoln vigorously supported the Thirteenth Amendment, insisting that it be a part of the National Union

Party platform for the 1864 election. The effect of the Thirteenth Amendment validated Lincoln's dedication to freedom and his belief that our democracy was the "last best, hope of earth."[16]

As a onetime member of the Whig Party, Lincoln had begun his presidency, like his compatriots, opposed to reckless "tampering" with the Constitution. However, he evolved over the course of his tenure in the White House—personally and politically. His proposed constitutional amendments present perhaps the clearest examples of this metamorphosis. In his annual message to Congress in December 1862, Lincoln recommended the adoption of three constitutional amendments directed at the abolition of slavery. The first would offer federal funds to any existing slave state that abolished slavery any time before January 1, 1900. The second would guarantee "all slaves who shall have enjoyed actual freedom by the chances of the war, at any time before the end of the rebellion, shall be forever free; but all owners of such, who shall not have been disloyal, shall be compensated for them." And the third would authorize federal funds for colonization.[17] Colonization was, in many ways, nothing more than a humane form of ethnic cleansing—an out-of-sight, out-of-mind solution. It was an idea Lincoln had earlier articulated. In his address to a committee of black leaders on August 14, 1862, Lincoln had urged them to take advantage of $600,000 in congressional appropriations to fund colonization in Africa and the Caribbean.[18] He exhorted them to consider colonization, stating that "[t]he aspiration of men is to enjoy equality with the best when free, but on this broad continent, not a single man of your race is made the equal of a single man of ours. Go where you are treated the best."[19]

Even earlier, while eulogizing his political hero Henry Clay, Lincoln had referenced colonization, arguing that "There is a moral fitness in the idea of returning to Africa her children, whose ancestors have been torn from her by the ruthless hand of fraud and violence."[20] Lincoln took a long time before losing interest in this scheme. The 1862 annual message that included his proposed colonization amendment was given only one month before he issued the final Emancipation Proclamation.

In closing his address to Congress that December, Lincoln made these prophetic remarks:

> Fellow-citizens, *we* cannot escape history. We of this Congress and this administration, will be remembered in spite of ourselves. No personal significance, or insignificance, can spare one or another of us. The fiery trial through which we pass, will light us down, in honor or dishonor, to the latest generation. We *say* we are for the Union. The world will not forget that we say this. We know how to save the Union. The world knows we do know how to save it. We—even *we here*—hold the power, and bear

the responsibility. In *giving* freedom to the *slave*, we *assure* freedom to the *free*—honorable alike in what we give, and what we preserve. We shall nobly save, or meanly lose, the last best, hope of earth.[21]

And indeed, whatever one's position in a modern debate on Lincoln's methods, there can be no dispute that he accomplished what he set out to do: Lincoln saved the Union. By issuing the Emancipation Proclamation, he ran the first leg in a long relay toward full equality. And he set the stage for later emendations to our national Constitution, namely the Fourteenth and Fifteenth Amendments.

Lincoln, "Citizenship," and the Fourteenth Amendment

During the Civil War, every American's civil liberties were, at best, put on hold, and at worst, put one step backward. Without a doubt, Lincoln's unilateral suspension of the writ of habeas corpus is the most extreme example of freedom curtailed.[22] It was with sobriety that Lincoln took what some alleged were extraconstitutional actions, but these measures, whether strictly legal or not, were ventured upon under what Lincoln perceived to be a popular necessity.[23] Lincoln believed that once the Civil War ended, all abbreviated or suspended civil rights should and would be restored.

Perhaps no group has more acutely felt itself to be in an ambiguous position with regard to American citizenship than Civil War–era blacks. During that time, the nation's legal leadership concurred that the United States Constitution did not confer the rights and privileges of citizenship to blacks. Congressional legislation prohibited them from handling the mail for fear that, among several reasons put forward by Postmaster General Gideon Granger in 1802, they would be able to mix with other people and learn that a person's rights are not determined by his color.[24] The State Department, with few exceptions, denied the passport applications of black Americans.

The *Dred Scott* decision conferred full legality to such restrictions. In its decision, the United States Supreme Court ruled that Congress could not prohibit the introduction of slavery into any territory of the United States and that blacks could never be considered citizens of the United States, regardless of the laws set forth by any individual state. Writing for the majority, Chief Justice Roger B. Taney pronounced that blacks were considered "so far inferior, that they had no rights which the white man was bound to respect." So inferior was their race, Taney said, the Founding Fathers had not included them in either the Declaration of Independence or the Constitution.[25]

The *Dred Scott* decision drew swift, intense, and heated opposition. Such opposition was also vital to the platform of the Republican Party that nominated Abraham Lincoln for the presidency in 1860.[26] But even before his nomination, Lincoln forcefully attacked the Court's ruling. His first public statements denouncing the decision were made during a speech in Springfield, Illinois, on June 26, 1857. Lincoln was clear about his displeasure with the Court's conclusions and resolute in his conviction that they contradicted the basic tenets of the Declaration of Independence: "[W]e think the Dred Scott decision is erroneous. We know the court that made it, has often over-ruled its own decisions, and we shall do what we can to have it over-rule this . . . Judicial decisions are of greater or less authority as precedents, according to circumstances."[27]

Lincoln proceeded to speak eloquently about the negative effects of the *Dred Scott* decision and the way in which it conspired to form a hopeless situation for African Americans. "All the powers of earth seem rapidly combining against [the oppressed Negro]," Lincoln said. "One after another they have closed the heavy iron doors upon him, and now they have him, as it were, bolted in with a lock of a hundred keys, which can never be unlocked without the concurrence of every key; the keys in the hands of a hundred different men, and they scattered to a hundred different and distant places; and they stand musing as to what invention, in all the dominions of mind and matter, can be produced to make the impossibility of his escape more complete than it is."[28]

Lincoln then addressed the *Dred Scott* decision by name, arguing that the position taken by Chief Justice Taney, who authored the decision, and Stephen A. Douglas, who supported it, rested on false assumptions about the Declaration of Independence:

> Chief Justice Taney, in his opinion in the Dred Scott case, admits that the language of the Declaration is broad enough to include the whole human family, but he and Judge Douglas argue that the authors of that instrument did not intend to include negroes, by the fact that they did not at once, actually place them on an equality with the whites. Now this grave argument comes to just nothing at all, by the other fact, that they did not at once, *or ever afterwards*, actually place all white people on an equality with one or another. And this is the staple argument of both the Chief Justice and the Senator, for doing this obvious violence to the plain unmistakable language of the Declaration.[29]

Other groups also spoke out against the decision. In 1861, the State Department granted a passport to Henry Highland Garnet, a black man. The passport explicitly stated that Garnet was a "citizen of the United States—language in direct contravention of *Dred Scott*."[30] The following year, when an American revenue cutter detained a vessel in the coastwise trade because the captain was a man of color,[31] Lincoln's secretary of the treasury, Salmon P. Chase, addressed a formal inquiry regarding citizenship of black men to Attorney

General Edward Bates. While he was in the process of writing his opinion, Bates shared his views with Columbia University history professor Francis Lieber, who was considered an expert in political science. On December 1, 1862, Bates wrote:

> I am inclined to think that "Citizen," in our law, is a simple, common *noun*, that (by itself) is always one and the same thing—neither more nor less. If you take away any one of his essential qualities, then he is no longer a citizen. If you add anything to citizenship (as age, sex, or property) to qualify for office, you do not, in any degree, alter the original *noun, Citizenship*, but super-add another and independent title, which can as well exist without citizenship, as citizenship can exist without it. My forthcoming opinion will assert that the child in the cradle, viewed *as a citizen merely*, is the equal of his father, in the Senate—and has equal rights.[32]

Bates's lengthy opinion repudiated the principles of the *Dred Scott* decision and affirmed that every free person born in the United States was, "at the moment of birth, *prima facie* a citizen."[33]

The response to the Bates opinion came from all sides. The following are some examples:

> Every person born on the soil, man, woman, child, no matter what his color, is a citizen, and has a right to the protection of the Government. The right to vote has notthing [*sic*] to do with citizenship. In the barbarism which is promulgated by the Democratic press, it is preteneded [*sic*] that none but voters are citizens, and that none but they have a right to the protection of all our laws and institutions at home and abroad.[34]

> I see Mr. Bates is preparing an elaborate opinion on Negro citizenship. The wonder is that one should question it when the government in its diplomacy and the judiciary in its decisions have affirmed it, and that too in concurrence with the universal sanction of every publicist. It was left to these latter days to rest citizenship upon the fact of color and of the more or less curl of the hair rather than the essential facts of birth and allegiance.[35]

> We do not wish to do either Mr. Chase, or Mr. Bates, any injustice, but the shape in which the opinion of the latter is placed before the public, its statement and want of statement, create grave doubts whether the actual administration of the affairs of the Treasury Department required in this case any opinion of the Attorney-General upon the subject of negro citizenship. There is no aspect of *business in the whole affair*. It looks like a fixed-up, political stalking horse. The opinion itself is creditable in point of intellect,

although the argument is inartistic, and the style quite different from anything we have read before which has been attributed to Mr. Bates.[36]

In 1865, the same body that had banned black membership in American citizenry, the United States Supreme Court, admitted African American lawyer John S. Rock to argue before it. Francis Lieber wrote that there could no longer be "even the shadow of a doubt" that blacks were citizens entitled to protection by the federal government.[37]

This nation's ultimate rejection of a second-class legal status for freedmen in reconstructing the South was foreshadowed by the quiet action of Lincoln's administration in recognizing the citizenship of freeborn blacks. The Fourteenth Amendment represented the definitive codification of Lincoln's efforts to neutralize skin color in the determination of citizenship.

The framing and ratification of the Constitution, the development of a national government, and the adoption of the Bill of Rights all reflected a dominant concern with establishing one central government. Fearful of vesting one body with complete authority, the Founders structured the nation's government in such a way as to minimize the risks of abuse. But the enslavement of blacks and the ensuing Civil War demonstrated that individual states could also endanger individual rights and liberties. Against that backdrop, Congress proposed the Fourteenth Amendment in 1866. It was ratified on July 9, 1868, three years after Lincoln's death. The amendment established national citizenship as a basis for state citizenship. It also made the national government, rather than the states, the primary source and guardian of civil rights.

The opening sentence of the Fourteenth Amendment requires the states to surrender much, if not all, of the considerable power they previously held with respect to the definitions of state citizenship: "All persons born or naturalized in the United States, and subject to the jurisdiction thereof, are citizens of the United States and of the State wherein they reside."[38] This language essentially accomplished what Lincoln had long advocated—nullification of the *Dred Scott* decision.

In the constitutional controversy preceding the Civil War, Lincoln had emphasized his philosophy that government was based on the ideas of liberty and equality as expressed in the Declaration of Independence. In a speech given on August 7, 1858, Lincoln said:

Now, if slavery had been a good thing, would the Fathers of the Republic have taken a step calculated to diminish its beneficent influences among themselves, and snatch the boon wholly from their posterity? These communities, by their representatives in old Independence Hall, said to the whole world of men: "We hold these truths to be self evident: that all men are created equal; that they are endowed by their Creator with certain unalienable

rights; that among these are life, liberty, and the pursuit of happiness" . . .
They erected a beacon to guide their children and their children's children,
and the countless myriads who should inhabit the earth in other ages. Wise
statesmen as they were, they knew the tendency of prosperity to breed
tyrants, and so they established these great self-evident truths, that when
in the distant future some man, some faction, some interest, should set up
the doctrine that none but rich men, or none but white men, were entitled
to life, liberty and the pursuit of happiness, their posterity might look up
again to the Declaration of Independence and take courage to renew the
battle which their fathers began—so that truth, and justice, and mercy, and
all the humane and Christian virtues might not be extinguished from the
land; so that no man would hereafter dare to limit and circumscribe the
great principles on which the temple of liberty was being built.[39]

Lincoln's philosophy is reflected in the remaining language of the Fourteenth
Amendment, Section 1: "No State shall make or enforce any law which shall
abridge the privileges or immunities of citizens of the United States; nor shall
any State deprive any person of life, liberty, or property, without due process
of law; nor deny to any person within its jurisdiction the equal protection of
the laws."[40]

African Americans were not passive in the effort to gain equality. When
the Civil War broke out, former slave Frederick Douglass called on Lincoln to
free the slaves and recruit them as soldiers in the Federal army. He understood
that making blacks a part of the military effort presented the quickest and
surest way to ensure their liberation, along with the preservation of the Union.
Douglass argued that by supporting an all-white army, the Union was fighting
with "their soft white hand, while they kept their black iron hand chained and
helpless behind them."[41]

Lincoln was, at first, resistant to Douglass's suggestion, fearing that such
a policy would alienate a large part of the Union he was fighting so hard to
preserve. But as the war dragged on, the nation grew restless. Lincoln took
drastic measures in the name of national unification. The final Emancipation
Proclamation called for the enlistment of black troops. With this formal acceptance of freedmen as soldiers, Lincoln guaranteed a multiracial future for
this nation. He knew that no president could ask a man to fight for his country
and then tell him he could not call it home.

Douglass worked diligently to recruit black soldiers. When he grew frus-
trated at their mistreatment, he went to Washington to speak directly to the
president. From that meeting, Douglass secured a promise that black soldiers
would eventually be paid the same as white soldiers and that they would be
promoted as merited.[42] In response to Douglass's concern that black prisoners

were being murdered or enslaved by Confederates, Lincoln assured him that an order had already been issued stipulating that "for every soldier killed in violation of the laws of war a rebel soldier shall be executed."[43]

Eventually, the two leaders grew to respect each other. After leaving the Washington meeting, Douglass said of the president, "in all my interviews with Mr. Lincoln I was impressed with his entire freedom from popular prejudice against the colored race."[44]

In the end, more than 186,000 men enlisted in the United States Colored Troops, and by the close of the war, Lincoln was recommending commissioning black officers. In his 1863 message to Congress, the president reported, "So far as tested, it is difficult to say [black soldiers] are not as good soldiers as any."[45]

The friendship of Lincoln and Douglass endured until Lincoln's death separated them, but the respect Douglass had for Lincoln lingered on. About Lincoln's statesmanship, he said:

> Had he put the abolition of slavery before the salvation of the Union, he would
> have inevitably driven from him a powerful class of the American people and
> rendered resistance to rebellion impossible. Viewed from the genuine abolition
> ground, Mr. Lincoln seemed tardy, cold, dull, and indifferent; but measuring
> him by the sentiment of his country, a sentiment he was bound as a statesman
> to consult, he was swift, zealous, radical, and determined.[46]

In 1873, the United States Supreme Court issued a ruling in the *Slaughter-House* cases—the first case decided under the Fourteenth Amendment.[47] At issue was whether the privileges and immunities of national citizenship include the Bill of Rights or other fundamental rights, thereby limiting the reach of a state's authority. In a 5–4 decision, the Court held that those "privileges and immunities" were narrow—limited to the right to assert claims or transact business with the government, have access to seaports, receive federal protection when in a foreign country, peaceably assemble and petition for redress of grievances, file writs of habeas corpus, use navigable waters, and exercise those rights secured by the Reconstruction amendments. The Court ruled that fundamental rights enumerated in the Bill of Rights were not protected from state action. As a result, states retained much of the responsibility that they had traditionally exercised for the distribution and protection of fundamental rights and liberties.[48]

While the *Slaughter-House* ruling remains good law, contemporary jurisprudence has incorporated most of the Bill of Rights through the Fourteenth Amendment's due process clause, so that these guarantees now apply to the states. Although in the *Slaughter-House* decision the Court did not permanently disable the Fourteenth Amendment by rendering such a narrow interpretation, it deferred the amendment's full impact until well into the twentieth century.[49]

By the late nineteenth century, the Supreme Court began curbing state powers that it believed unreasonably interfered with an individual's natural rights. In light of the *Slaughter-House* cases, the Court found its authority to make such decisions in the "due process clause" of the Fourteenth Amendment, which prohibits states from "depriv[ing] any person of life, liberty, or property, without due process of law."

Throughout the 1900s, the Court's view of the Fourteenth Amendment continued to evolve. It ceased to view the due process clause as the basis for rights and liberties that limited state authority but rather as a vehicle for making the Bill of Rights applicable to the states. As the Court made this historic shift, the main question became whether the Fourteenth Amendment incorporated all or only some of those fundamental guarantees. Thus began a decades-long, laborious process of determining, on a case-by-case basis, which rights deemed by the Founders to be "unalienable" were attributable to state citizenship through the Fourteenth Amendment.[50] But black letter law became better established long before social practices reflected the change. For African Americans, equal under law did not translate into equal in fact.

During his presidency, Lincoln argued that "*equality*, in society, alike beats *inequality*, whether the lat[t]er be of the British aristocratic sort, or of the domestic slavery sort."[51] While establishment of the Thirteenth and Fourteenth Amendments brought the nation closer to fulfilling Lincoln's vision for society, the legal road remained pitted with potholes. Black Americans were still refused the right to vote.

Black Suffrage and the Fifteenth Amendment

As with all other issues regarding black rights, the matter of black suffrage remained contentious during Lincoln's presidency. During the early nineteenth century, blacks in New York, New Jersey, Pennsylvania, and Connecticut were prohibited from voting. Black men in Ohio were permitted to vote only if they had "a greater visible admixture of white than colored blood." [52]

As a young politician, Lincoln had explained his general position on suffrage during an 1836 session of the Illinois state legislature. He stated that he believed that the right to vote should be limited to white males who were taxpaying citizens or members of the militia.[53] Lincoln's deliberate exclusion of blacks from those he thought entitled to vote revealed his unwillingness to veer from the accepted position of all Illinois politicians.

But by January 1864, having guided the nation through a war in which the blood of blacks and whites was indistinguishable when shed on the battlefield, Lincoln began altering his ideas on voting rights. The president hoped that the inclusion of black soldiers in the defense of the Union would redefine the racial climate after the war. While not yet an advocate for universal suffrage,

Lincoln believed that black men who had served in the military should be afforded the right to vote. "When you give the Negro these rights, when you put a gun in his hands, it prophesies something more: it foretells that he is to have the full enjoyment of his liberty and manhood." The commander-in-chief felt morally obligated to acknowledge the contributions of his black soldiers: "They have demonstrated in blood their right to the ballot, which is but the humane protection of the flag they have so fearlessly defended."[54] Lincoln also believed that even this limited expansion of voting rights could start the process of national healing.

The nation as a whole, and Radical Republicans in particular, paid special attention to Lincoln's position on this topic.[55] In a private correspondence drafted to Michael Hahn, the first governor of liberated Louisiana, Lincoln became the first American president to advocate for limited black voting rights: "Now you are about to have a Convention which, among other things, will probably define the elective franchise. I barely suggest for your private consideration, whether some of the colored people may not be let in—as, for instance, the very intelligent, and especially those who have fought gallantly in our ranks. They would probably help, in some trying time to come, to keep the jewel of liberty within the family of freedom."[56]

The Hahn letter is more than an isolated articulation of Lincoln's efforts to promote black suffrage. In his last speech, given April 11, 1865, the president made the same argument: "It is also unsatisfactory to some that the elective franchise is not given to the colored man. I would myself prefer that it were now conferred on the very intelligent, and on those who serve our cause as soldiers." In the same speech, Lincoln praised the state's fledgling government for "giving the benefit of public schools equally to black and white, and empowering the Legislature to confer the elective franchise upon the colored man." He went on: "We encourage the hearts, and nerve the arms of the twelve thousand [Louisiana voters] to adhere to their work, and argue for it, and proselyte for it, and fight for it, and feed it, and grow it, and ripen it to a complete success. The colored man too, in seeing all united for him, is inspired with vigilance, and energy, and daring, to the same end. Grant that he desires the elective franchise, will he not attain it sooner by saving the already advanced steps toward it, than by running backward over them?"[57]

From the perspective of the Fifteenth Amendment, ratified five years later, Lincoln's advice to Louisiana and its new governor is an eerily prescient and profound statement of tolerance. By granting blacks suffrage rights, the Fifteenth Amendment represented the final component in a national effort to craft a colorblind Constitution. It states: "The right of citizens of the United States to vote shall not be denied or abridged by the United States or by any State on account of race, color, or previous condition of servitude."[58]

Yet even with the amendment's ratification, black suffrage remained a privilege rather than a right, subject to regulation by individual states. Only over time did the federal government redefine freedom to embody civil and political equality regardless of race.[59]

The Fifteenth Amendment contains guarantees that provide grounds for constitutional challenge if violated by the states. The final section of this amendment, as is also true for the Thirteenth and Fourteenth Amendments, grants Congress the "power to enforce this article by appropriate legislation."[60] Under this enabling provision, the federal government assumed responsibility from the states for protection of individual civil rights.

In his book *What Lincoln Believed,* author Michael Lind asserts, "If Lincoln had lived it is unlikely that he would have supported anything like the . . . Fifteenth Amendment."[61] The accuracy of this prediction, of course, is impossible to prove. It is true that Lincoln was a pragmatist, but his beliefs on the topic of black suffrage must be evaluated in the right historical context and within the framework of his "paramount goal" of preserving a united Union. As he did at the start of the Civil War, Lincoln evaluated all the potential outcomes before making a decision relating to black suffrage. It is perhaps the singular issue about which he spoke the least. Lincoln was acutely aware of the tenor in the society of his day with regard to free blacks and the supposed superiority of whites that made them exclusively qualified to vote.

In the same way that Lincoln's war aims evolved from unification to emancipation, toward the end of his administration he privately supported suffrage—albeit in a limited manner. Lincoln has been criticized for his reticence and reluctance on widespread black suffrage. However, always a cautious man, Lincoln was afraid that by forcing states to allow black suffrage he would exacerbate hostilities to such a degree that all his reunification efforts would be destroyed. The country was still binding its wounds from the Civil War, and a measure as drastic as unlimited black suffrage would not have commanded the country's support. But in his deliberate manner, Lincoln started to level the playing field for black Americans and illuminated the path to further reform.

Though his early death slowed the momentum for granting blacks the right to vote during Reconstruction, Lincoln's message echoed from the grave as the country struggled to realize complete equality.

Conclusion

"What I do about slavery . . . ," Lincoln wrote newspaper editor Horace Greeley, "I do because I believe it helps to save the Union; and what I forbear, I forbear because I do not believe it would help to save the Union."[62]

Lincoln's legislative, military, and rhetorical skills formed a seamless fabric of democratic leadership that protected and preserved the nation during its most acute crisis. While he is often considered a controversial figure in black American history, sometimes lauded for performing one of the greatest acts in American history—issuing the Emancipation Proclamation—and sometimes characterized as a racist who was simply spurred to action by more principled radical abolitionists, Abraham Lincoln remains a fitting hero to all who fight for equality.

By moving dramatically and repeatedly against slavery, Lincoln showed both a remarkable flexibility in the development of war strategy and an unflagging commitment to his presidential mission. The Emancipation Proclamation is perhaps the one document that marked forever his legacy of greatness and opened for posterity the door to substantial reconfiguration of national policy on equal rights. Statesmanship may have required delay, negotiations, and bargaining, but at the end of the day, black American men, women, and children knew because of Abraham Lincoln what it was to taste freedom. For the first time, black Americans could identify with the phrase "all men are created equal."

When Lincoln died, his secretary of war, Edwin M. Stanton, said, "Now he belongs to the ages."[63] The debate about the significance, prudence, and import of Lincoln's presidential actions is seemingly inexhaustible. Before us and after us, generations have pondered and will continue to ponder the man who, with extraordinary fortitude, set the American civil rights movement in motion. Lincoln's death marked the end of a beginning. But at the same time, his life heralded the beginning of a new America.

Notes

I would like to acknowledge and thank Andrea Krupp for her invaluable contributions to this article. I would also like to extend my thanks to Sara Gabbard, editor of *Lincoln Lore*, for her comments, Harold Holzer for his suggestions, and Michael Vorenberg for allowing me access to his notes. Meg Holzer provided research assistance.

1. *The Collected Works of Lincoln*, ed. Roy P. Basler, 9 vols. (New Brunswick, N.J.: Rutgers University Press, 1953–55), 2:222.

2. Ibid., 223.

3. Ibid., 318.

4. Second Inaugural Address, in ibid., 8:333.

5. Ibid., 4:240. In his speech in Independence Hall, Philadelphia, on February 22, 1861, the president-elect was not being hyperbolic when he invited assassination, as he had heard earlier that there was a plot to murder him when he changed trains in Baltimore on the way to Washington.

6. Speech at Peoria, Illinois, October 16, 1854, in ibid., 2:255.

7. The first debate at Ottawa, Illinois, in *The Lincoln-Douglas Debates: The First Complete Unexpurgated Text*, ed. Harold Holzer (New York: Harper Collins, 1993), 63.

8. Ibid., 77.

9. Seventh and final debate with Stephen A. Douglas at Alton, Illinois, October 15, 1858, in *Collected Works*, 3:315.

10. Lincoln to Horace Greeley, August 22, 1862, in ibid., 5:388.

11. Quoted in "Lincoln and Liberty," by Mark E. Neely Jr., in *Lincoln on Democracy: His Own Words, with Essays by America's Foremost Civil War Historians*, ed. Mario M. Cuomo and Harold Holzer (1990; New York: Fordham University Press, 2004), 249.

12. Reply to Emancipation Memorial Presented by Chicago Christians of All Denominations, September 13, 1862, in *Collected Works*, 5:420.

13. Preliminary Emancipation Proclamation, September 22, 1862, in ibid., 5:434.

14. Quoted in Randy Kennedy, "I Shall Never Forget the Weeping," *New York Times*, June 20, 2004.

15. Edward D. Bates to A. W. Bradford, May 10, 1862, Allan Nevins MSS, Henry E. Huntington Library, San Marino, California.

16. *Collected Works*, 5:537.

17. Annual Message to Congress, December 1, 1862, in ibid., 5:530.

18. Ibid., 5:529–37.

19. Ibid., 5:372.

20. Ibid., 2:132.

21. Ibid., 5:537.

22. *Ex parte Merryman*, 17 F.Cas. 144 (C.C.Md. 1861).

23. Lincoln to Winfield Scott, April 25, 1861, in *Collected Works*, 4:344.

24. James Dunlop, *Digest of the General Laws of the United States with References to the Acts Repealed, Supplemented, or Modified; and Notes of the Decisions and Dicta of The Supreme Court of the Union upon Their Construction* (Philadelphia: J. B. Lippincott, 1856), 711.

25. *Dred Scott v. Sandford*, 60 U.S. 393 (1857).

26. George Anastaplo, *The Amendments to the Constitution: A Commentary* (Baltimore: Johns Hopkins University Press, 1995), 173–74.

27. Speech in Springfield, Illinois, June 26, 1857, in *Collected Works*, 2:401.

28. Ibid., 2:404.

29. Ibid., 2:405.

30. Frank J. Williams, "'Institutions Are not Made, They Grow': Attorney General Bates and Attorney President Lincoln," *Lincoln Lore*, no. 1876 (Spring 2004), 2.

31. Under *Dred Scott*, blacks were not citizens and therefore not eligible to command ships under the American flag.

32. Edward Bates to Francis Lieber, December 1, 1862, Francis Lieber Papers, Henry E. Huntington Library.

33. J. Hubley Ashton, ed., *Official Opinions of the Attorneys General of the United States* (Washington, D.C.: W. H. and O. H. Morrison, 1868), 10: 382–413.

34. *Cincinnati Daily Gazette*, December 30, 1862.

35. John Appleton to William P. Fessenden, December 11, 1862, William Pitt Fessenden Papers, Western Reserve Historical Society, Cleveland, Ohio.

36. *New York Evening Express*, January 2, 1863.

37. Eric Foner, *The Story of American Freedom* (New York: W. W. Norton, 1998), 97.

38. U.S. Constitution, Amendment XIV, Section 1.

39. *Collected Works*, 2:546–47.

40. U. S. Constitution, Amendment XIV, Section 1.

41. Speech of Frederick Douglass on the War, delivered in National Hall, Philadelphia, January 14, 1862, reprinted in *Douglass' Monthly*, February 1862. See www.brandywine-sources.com.

42. William K. Klingaman, *Abraham Lincoln and the Road to Emancipation, 1861–1865* (New York: Penguin Group, 2001), 266.

43. *Collected Works*, 6:357.

44. Quoted in *Reminiscences of Abraham Lincoln by Distinguished Men of His Time*, ed. Allen Thorndike Rice (New York: North American Review, 1888), 193.

45. Annual Message to Congress, December 8, 1863, in *Collected Works*, 7:50.

46. Philip S. Foner, ed., *Frederick Douglass: Selected Speeches and Writings* (Chicago: Lawrence Hill Books, 1999), 621.

47. *Slaughter-House Cases*, 83 U.S. 36 (1873).

48. Donald E. Lively, *Landmark Supreme Court Cases: A Reference Guide* (Westport, Conn.: Greenwood Press, 1999), 12–15.

49. Ibid., 15.

50. *Palko v. Connecticut* 302 U.S. 319 (1937) (Fifth Amendment right against double jeopardy does not apply to states.); *Benton v. Maryland* 392 U.S. 925 (1968) (Double jeopardy provision is "fundamental to the American scheme of justice" and does apply to states.); *Adamson v. California* 332 U.S. 46 (1947) (Some but not all provisions of the Bill of Rights are incorporated through the Fourteenth Amendment and the right against self incrimination is not one of them); *Malloy v. Hogan*, 378 U.S. 1 (1964) (The right against self incrimination should be incorporated through the Fourteenth Amendment).

51. Cuomo and Holzer, *Lincoln on Democracy*, 159.

52. *Collected Works*, 6:365.

53. David Herbert Donald, *Lincoln* (New York: Simon & Schuster, 1995), 59.

54. William C. Davis, *Lincoln's Men: How President Lincoln Became Father to an Army and a Nation* (New York: Free Press, 1999), 164, citing *Collected Works*, 7:101 (Lincoln's letter to James S. Wadsworth) and Don E. Fehrenbacher and Virginia Fehrenbacher, eds., *Recollected Works of Lincoln* (Stanford: Stanford University Press, 1996), 468.

55. During the Civil War, the more zealously antislavery Republicans, who wanted the administration to move quickly to abolish slavery, came to be referred to as Radicals. Mark E. Neely Jr., *The Abraham Lincoln Encyclopedia* (New York: McGraw-Hill, 1982), 251.

56. *Collected Works*, 7:243.

57. Lincoln's last public address to the public from the White House balcony, April 11, 1865, in *Collected Works*, 8:403.

58. U.S. Constitution, Amendment XV, Section 1.

59. Foner, *Story of American Freedom*, 106.

60. U.S. Constitution, Amendment XV, Section 2.

61. Michael Lind, *What Lincoln Believed: The Values and Convictions of America's Greatest President* (New York: Doubleday, 2005), 222.

62. Letter to Horace Greeley, August 22, 1862, in *Collected Works*, 5:388. Author Richard Striner, however, warns that the first impression taken from this quote, that Lincoln only wanted to save the Union and did not care about ending slavery, is a "deception . . . swallowed by millions of readers who encounter Lincoln's letter to Greeley by itself, and without any knowledge of the president's overall purposes." *Father Abraham: Lincoln's Relentless Struggle to End Slavery*. (New York: Oxford University Press, 2006), 176. Striner contends that a deeper look at the context surrounding this famous letter reveals that

Lincoln's "entire career as a national leader makes that proposition untenable." Instead, Striner argues, the Greeley letter is "a stunning demonstration of Lincoln the tactitian," who expressed his "constitutional constraints" while "weighing all his options very carefully." Striner's Lincoln was "softening public opinion . . . getting things ready for his big and risky revelation" by couching his plans in the language of saving the Union (177). In fact, a draft of the Preliminary Emancipation Proclamation already rested in Lincoln's desk drawer when he composed the Greeley letter.

63. George S. Bryan, *The Great American Myth* (New York: Carnick & Evans, 1940), 189.

15 Picturing Freedom: The Thirteenth Amendment in the Graphic Arts

Harold Holzer

n unusual and "profound silence" gripped the bustling House of Representatives on January 31, 1865, as members of Congress began casting their history-altering votes on whether to approve the Thirteenth Amendment to the Constitution abolishing slavery. But as soon as the final tally was announced—119 yeas to 56 nays, more than enough to send the amendment on to the states for ratification[1]—the quiet chamber immediately erupted in a boisterous wave of "applause which came from all sides . . . the fullest expression of approbation and joy." To add to the din, a wall-rattling artillery salute echoed outside. Reporting that "the enthusiasm of all present . . . knew no bounds," a journalist on the scene expressed no doubt as to why this "grand . . . scene" so unfolded. All in the chamber knew that they were participating in "an epoch in the history of the country" destined to "be remembered by the members of the House and spectators present as an event in their lives."[2]

Few on hand would have been surprised if the nation's artists thereafter made certain that the "grand scene" was remembered by "spectators" outside the U.S. Capitol as well: the thousands of Americans who bought, displayed, and cherished mass-produced pictures of the major heroes and events of the day. Surely this was one such occasion.

In Civil War–era Washington—generations before photographers were permitted to record the momentous votes of the House and Senate, and more than a century before gavel-to-gavel television coverage of congressional deliberations became routine—great events were visually reported to the country in various ways. They were vivified in photographs of prominent leaders taken after the event, through woodcut illustrations in the picture weeklies, and in the medium of popular prints, the inexpensive engravings and lithographs designed for display on the parlor walls of private homes. These commemorative pictures might appear for sale within "only" a few weeks of the newsworthy occasions they portrayed. To modern audiences accustomed to instantly downloading news broadcasts on the World Wide Web, this may seem like an achingly sluggish response. But it was breathtakingly swift by nineteenth-century standards.

Yet, the Thirteenth Amendment—both the historic congressional votes that sent it to the states, and the ratification that ultimately made it law by the end of 1865—surprisingly failed to inspire America's engravers and lithographers to produce commemorative pictures either quickly or plentifully. Compared to the number of prints generated by the Emancipation Proclamation, the Thirteenth Amendment entered the history books with scant visual accompaniment. The relative dearth of celebratory Thirteenth Amendment graphics has long reigned as one of the major mysteries of Civil War–era iconography.

As it happened, several factors likely contributed to the scarcity of such tributes, and an understanding of them may not only help explain why so few of these prints exist but also help us judge whether or not their rarity should be interpreted as proof of public indifference, or even hostility, to passage of the amendment that ended American slavery forever.

What modern observers seldom take into account is that printmakers never enjoyed the luxury of focusing on a single subject, no matter how unprecedented: even as the Civil War raged, for example, printmakers like Currier & Ives of New York produced catalogues that offered many more lithographs of kittens, flowers, comic scenes, and portraits of comely little girls than of land and sea battles and uniformed generals.[3] The truth is, Thirteenth Amendment iconography was doomed before it could evolve because of the demands and exigencies of commercial publishing, coupled with some unexpected twists of politics, history, and what passed in the 1860s for marketing. These circumstances limited the Thirteenth Amendment as a subject for popular prints but did not necessarily reflect public attitudes toward the amendment itself.

One such circumstance was the exalted state of the Lincoln image in 1865, the year the Thirteenth Amendment became law. Although an old adage has long insisted that success has many parents, artists have traditionally found it easier to illustrate the triumphs of history through the accomplishments of individual heroes—especially in small-scale pictures like popular prints. With a few notable exceptions, the American Revolution, for example, more often than not inspired prints for private homes depicting only the era's greatest figure, George Washington, not the many military and civilian contemporaries who also helped guide the Colonies to independence. Similarly, where the subject of freedom was concerned, graphic artists preferred to convey the topic through portrayals of Abraham Lincoln, rather than the dozens of politically brave representatives and senators who risked their careers to endorse the Thirteenth Amendment.[4]

The compelling personal drama that just a few years earlier had culminated in Lincoln's writing and promulgating the Emancipation Proclamation—all but alone—made him the ideal focus for most artistic tributes to the end of slavery in America, especially after the president's death had elevated him into the realm of secular sainthood. Lincoln's assassination in April 1865, just weeks after the House vote, made him the focus of so many tributes, in so many genres, that artists contemplating new pictorial tributes to freedom proved understandably reluctant to do more than continue tapping the insatiable public hunger for images of the late president. Even—especially—in death, Lincoln continued to dominate the medium as the leader who had sacrificed his life not only to preserve the Union but also to end slavery.[5]

An additional factor served to intensify the focus on Lincoln. The artistic response to the Emancipation Proclamation had been both muted and delayed when Lincoln first issued the final order in 1863. By the time the Thirteenth Amendment was enacted two years later, tributes to the proclamation were still being generated and distributed; artists were still catching up to the nation's first blow at slavery, when the second, fatal blow was struck. This perplexing delay in the appearance of Emancipation Proclamation graphics has long been overlooked or disregarded. In 1950, in the first, and as yet the only, book ever dedicated to chronicling all the reprints of the Emancipation Proclamation, writer Charles Eberstadt contended that, as early as 1863, such keepsakes provided "an ever-present reminder of the war's true justification" and became an "important propaganda and morale factor" for winning the war. "Framed and displayed in thousands of homes and prominent places," Eberstadt went on to argue, "emancipation became a watchword of almost hysterical power and incalculable effect."[6]

Nothing could be further from the truth. A careful review of the copyright dates on engraved and lithographed tributes to emancipation puts the lie to Eberstadt's long-unchallenged argument. A handful of reprints of the document itself appeared in 1863; but the initial pictorial tributes bear the publication date of 1864, the year of Lincoln's campaign for reelection to the presidency, a campaign that did not begin until some twenty months after he had signed the final proclamation.[7] And the overwhelming number of Emancipation Proclamation prints—scenes that showed Lincoln signing the document or represented him literally unshackling slaves—came off the press after the president's assassination in April 1865, when suddenly such prints became popular with the public, at least enough to inspire production by the country's previously timid publishers.[8]

Many of the first prints may have been afflicted by the inhibiting constraints of what might be called "artistic racism": the reluctance of white publishers to issue pictures that depicted the great upheavals that changed the status of black people in America and that, therefore, seemed to require the portrayal of black men and women in artistic representations of their changed circumstances. Engravers and lithographers were first and foremost businessmen, and it is not difficult to imagine they had doubts that such pictures would become popular decorations in white American homes. With most free blacks lacking the financial resources to buy homes, much less pictures to hang in them, publishers probably calculated that graphics devoted to the liberation of the black race, including passage of the Thirteenth Amendment, would similarly have little appeal and would fail to sell on the white-dominated market.

While some prints defied these limited expectations, most such depictions, if they included blacks at all, relegated them to the fringes of the main scene, in the form of small cameo portraits of slaves being lifted from their knees either by the Great Emancipator or by a symbolic national figure like Columbia. Amidst this wave of art focused on the Emancipation Proclamation and the Great Emancipator, passage of the Thirteenth Amendment—by hundreds of national and state legislators—had little chance of inspiring vivid printmaking.

Both of the North's leading picture newspapers did manage to take note of congressional passage of the Thirteenth Amendment resolution—if incompletely. *Frank Leslie's Illustrated Newspaper* (fig. 1) and *Harper's Weekly* (fig. 2) each issued woodcut engravings in their February 18, 1865, editions, showing the House chamber from the back, with members on the floor and observers in the galleries cheering wildly and tossing top hats into the air. But neither woodcut identified the congressmen or showed the cabinet officials or Supreme Court justices who witnessed the exuberant scene as guest onlookers.

More tellingly, the galleries that day had included African American spectators, too, and they were absent from the pictures as well. As historian Michael Vorenberg has noted, one later wrote home to tell his father that "such rejoicing I never before witnessed . . . (white people I mean)," while another suppressed his excitement until he could steal away to an empty anteroom—where he started dancing, alone and unseen. But in a harbinger of things to come in the iconography of freedom, these witnesses were excluded from the early renderings—relegated to the symbolic, empty anterooms of pictorial invisibility. Like the Emancipation Proclamation before it, the Thirteenth Amendment was more often than not depicted as an act ennobling white people, not freeing black people.[9]

Confronting the abundance of white heroes—and determined to exclude blacks from visual reports of these events—printmakers not surprisingly turned to the man who had issued the Emancipation Proclamation and had won

Fig. 1. Artist unknown, "Exciting Scene in the House of Representatives, Jan. 31, 1865, on the Announcement of the Passage of the Amendment to the Constitution Abolishing Slavery for Ever," *Frank Leslie's Illustrated Newspaper*, February 18, 1865. Woodcut engraving. Courtesy of The Lincoln Museum, Fort Wayne, Indiana (Ref. 4610).

reelection to the presidency on a platform that called specifically for passage of this very amendment. Lincoln made the artists' task easier by stepping into the void to take his share of credit for the triumph.

On February 1, 1865, Lincoln signed his name to the resolution that submitted the Thirteenth Amendment to the states, a signature that was not required by law (the resolution had already been certified by Speaker of the House Schuyler Colfax and Vice President Hamlin).[10] Lincoln's unusual action provoked the Senate to pass a resolution on February 7 stating for the record that "such approval was unnecessary," since the Supreme Court had ruled years before that a president "has nothing to do with the proposition or adoption of amendments to the Constitution." That explanatory complaint was voiced on the Senate floor by none other than Lyman Trumbull—who represented Lincoln's home state of Illinois![11] But the rather belligerent rebuff did little to dampen Lincoln's effort to identify himself with the amendment. He went on to sign additional copies at will.

The president's enthusiasm was palpable. On the day he affixed his signature to the original resolution, he also received word from Springfield that Illinois had become the first state to ratify the Thirteenth Amendment. That same evening, when a crowd gathered outside the White House to serenade

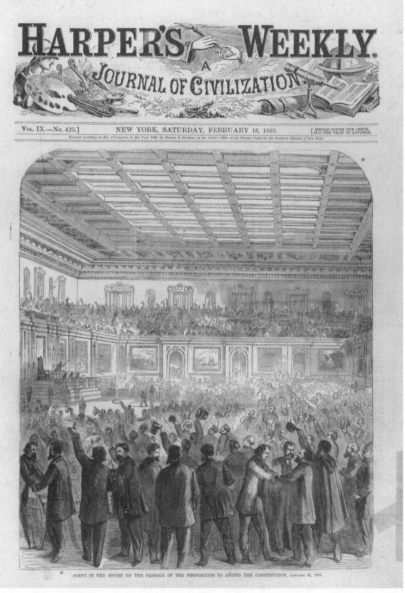

Fig. 2. Artist unknown, "Scene in the House on the Passage of the Proposition to Amend the Constitution, January 31, 1865," *Harper's Weekly*, February 18, 1865. Woodcut engraving. Courtesy of The Lincoln Museum, Fort Wayne, Indiana (Ref. 4601).

him, Lincoln appeared at an upstairs window to respond. After reporting with pride that Illinois "was a little ahead" of the other states, he added, to much applause, that the amendment "was a very fitting if not an indispensable adjunct to the winding up of the great difficulty . . . a King's cure for all the evils . . . [a] great moral victory." But he also took pains, the *New York Tribune* reported, to remind the audience that he "thought all would bear him witness that he had never shrunk from doing all that he could to eradicate Slavery by issuing an emancipation proclamation." Lincoln was not only making history, he was writing it. It should surprise no one that the printmakers obligingly illustrated this revolutionary cultural transfiguration just as Lincoln wanted.[12]

Was Lincoln directly complicit in an effort to make sure he was enshrined in public memory as the father of emancipation—both as proclaimed by his executive order and codified by constitutional amendment? Perhaps not, but he certainly did make sure that he was identified politically with both victories. It cannot surprise the student of iconography that graphic artists followed his lead. Just two and a half months later, his heroic death made his efforts seem all the more unassailable.

Amidst all the heroic portraits, murder scenes, deathbed pictures, and family composites thereafter devoted to the assassinated president, printmakers belatedly churned out their much-delayed "Great Emancipator" scenes as well. Around 1865, for example, Philadelphia lithographer L. Haugg[13] issued a print of the Emancipation Proclamation (fig. 3) that was crowned by a portrait of Lincoln and featured the entire text of the document surrounded by an American eagle and sculpted figures symbolizing Justice and Liberty, accompanied by the president's facsimile signature and the biblical exhortation from Leviticus 25:10: "Proclaim Liberty throughout the land unto all the inhabitants thereof." But the only direct visual reference to the emancipated slave in Haugg's print came in a small scene showing the figure Columbia, draped in the American flag and wearing a liberty cap (the classical symbol of manumission), shielding a bedraggled family of blacks from a mob of slave catchers and dogs.[14] It was but one example of a now-vigorous genre.

More than twenty years later, an eerily similar print from the Strobridge lithographic firm of Cincinnati demonstrated that very little had changed in emancipation iconography despite the coming of a new generation of artists and publishers.[15] The firm's 1888 print, "Abraham Lincoln and His Emancipation Proclamation," featured a flag-festooned portrait of Lincoln, along with the full text of the freedom-granting document and sculptural symbols of Justice and Liberty within carefully framed niches on either side of Lincoln's words (fig. 4). The only significant difference was that, now, blacks had been eliminated from the composition altogether.

Fig. 3. L. Haugg, "The Emancipation Proclamation." Lithograph, published by
F. W. Thomas for the Free Press, Philadelphia, ca. 1865. Library of Congress.

Haugg's and Strobridge's were but two of the myriad of separate-sheet
Emancipation Proclamation display prints that flooded the market in the
quarter of a century after its announcement, most of them dating to 1865,
the year of Lincoln's martyrdom. Some prints reproduced the document
in florid calligraphy (fig. 5), while others depicted Lincoln announcing
the proclamation to his cabinet (fig. 6), a subsidiary genre that was all but

Fig. 4. Strobridge Lith. Co., "Abraham Lincoln and His Emancipation Proclamation." Lithograph, published by Mrs. M. M. Pabor, Washington, D.C., 1888.
Library of Congress.

invented by artist Francis B. Carpenter, only to be pirated by rivals while the hapless painter struggled to get his own canvas adapted to a popularly priced engraving.[16]

Fig. 5. Swander Bishop & Co. (after a photograph by the Mathew Brady Gallery), "Emancipation Proclamations. Allegorical Portrait of Abraham Lincoln." Calligraphic lithograph, published by the Art Publishing Association of Philadelphia, Swander Bishop & Co., 1865. Courtesy of The Lincoln Museum, Fort Wayne, Indiana (Ref. 3313).

Many subsequent tributes to emancipation lauded Lincoln to the exclusion of all others. Perhaps the apex of this laudatory mood was marked by Charles Nahl's bravura 1865 mourning print (fig. 7). Describing Lincoln as "the best beloved of the nation," the lithograph showed him enshrined within a grand public monument, crowned by crape, an American flag, and symbolic owls testifying to the martyr's wisdom. Both white America, represented by the

Fig. 6. Currier & Ives (after Francis B. Carpenter), "President Lincoln and His Cabinet. In Council, Sept. 22nd, 1862. Adopting the Emancipation Proclamation, Issued Jany. 1st, 1863." Lithograph, New York, 1876. Library of Congress.

figure of Columbia, and black America, in the form of a half-naked former slave, weep openly. The dead of the Civil War litter the background, while the more prominent foreground is dominated by a slain dragon of rebellion and the evocative broken shackle of the liberated slave. Lying nearby is a pure white scroll, bathed in light, marked neither "Emancipation Proclamation" nor "Thirteenth Amendment," but, generically, "Emancipation Act"—as if all of the efforts toward liberty were part of a single, ongoing effort, for which Lincoln deserved both recognition and acclaim.

Among all of these visual tributes to freedom, there appeared but one widely circulated Thirteenth Amendment picture: a small carte de visite issued by Powell & Co., crowding within its tiny, 2½ × 3½ inch frame the separate miniature portraits of all the 157 members of Congress who supported the resolution in 1865, along with President Lincoln and the outgoing vice president, Hannibal Hamlin (fig. 8). This carte de visite, with its panoply of minuscule images making it more a curiosity than a viable tribute, is probably best remembered in a larger-format companion print published concurrently by J. M. Bradstreet & Son of New York labeled "Anti-Slavery Constitutional

Fig. 7. C[harles]. Nahl (after a photograph by the Mathew Brady Gallery), "To Abraham Lincoln, the Best Beloved of the Nation." Lithograph, published by L. Nagel, with Puck, the Pacific Pictorial, San Francisco, ca. 1865. Author's collection.

Amendment Picture" and described as the "Key to Powell & Co.'s Photographs of Abraham Lincoln, Hannibal Hamlin, and of the Senators and Representatives Who Voted 'AYE' on the Resolution" (fig. 9).

Bradstreet's "key" provided 159 names, numerically arranged, to identify all of the characters depicted in Powell & Co.'s carte de visite, accompanied by specific instructions on how to follow the concentric rings of portraits: "The

Fig. 8. Powell & Co., Congressional supporters of the Thirteenth Amendment with President Lincoln and Vice President Hamlin. Carte de visite photomontage, 1865. Courtesy of The Lincoln Museum, Fort Wayne, Indiana (Ref. 2603).

regular numerical order commences at the head of Speaker Colfax (No. 3) in the center, and turning to the right at No. 5, follows around in successive circles. The numbers are placed uniformly at the reader's right hand of the head to which they refer. The Senators are arranged in open order in two outer circles; the Representatives in close order around the center." Given pride of place, too, were the words of the simple, straightforward resolution they had all voted to approve:

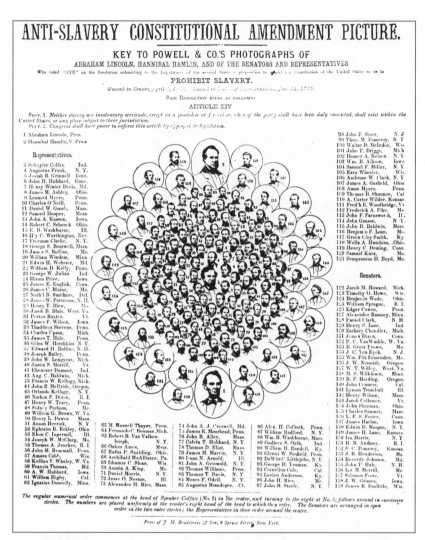

Fig. 9. J. M. Bradstreet & Son (after a photograph by Powell & Co.), "Anti-Slavery Constitutional Amendment Picture. Key to Powell & Co.'s Photographs of Abraham Lincoln, Hannibal Hamlin, and of the Senators and Representatives Who voted 'AYE' on the Resolution submitting to the Legislatures of the several States a proposition to amend the Constitution of the United States so as to PROHIBIT SLAVERY. . . ." Woodcut engraving, ca. 1865. Courtesy of The Lincoln Museum, Fort Wayne, Indiana (Ref. 2607).

Sect. 1. Neither slavery nor involuntary servitude, except as a punishment for crime, whereof the party shall have been duly convicted, shall exist within the United States, or any place subject to their jurisdiction.

Sect. 2. Congress shall have power to enforce this article by appropriate legislation.[17]

But the ultimate irony in this major pictorial tribute to the Thirteenth Amendment is that the very subject of the print—the historic amendment of the Constitution—was misidentified as "Article XIV."

No such error afflicted the recently discovered D. R. Clark broadside headed "Joint Resolution of the Thirty Eighth Congress of the United States of America Proposing an Amendment to the Constitution of the United States Abolishing Slavery" (fig. 10). The large sheet, recently donated to Lincoln College in Lincoln, Illinois,[18] features the facsimile signatures of 148 members of Congress who signed the resolution, beneath an extraordinary scene showing, among other things, a liberated slave clutching a framed, beardless likeness of Abraham Lincoln, while a freed mother teaches her child—a right denied African Americans under slavery (fig. 11). The rarity of this print suggests the limited market at the time for such celebratory prints. Had the market required more examples, more would certainly have been produced.

Like the Emancipation Proclamation before it, the Thirteenth Amendment was capable of inspiring not only heroic but also critical portraiture.[19] "The 'Freedom' of the South," published by Bromley & Co. in 1865, is the major example (fig. 12). The incendiary lithograph presented a supposedly horrific scene of a society turned upside down by the end of slavery. In the center foreground of the print, African American Federal soldiers and civilian freedmen hold at bay the bound figure of a kneeling woman identified as "South." The blacks are cruelly caricatured figures who speak in minstrel dialect with such phrases as "Dis chile am the government." Meanwhile, in the background, black men are shown courting white women ("dis darkey haben high ole time"), burning stately Southern buildings, and stealing from the U.S. Commissary with chants of "Ole John Brown he's a rotten in de grabe." Surveying the scene, white abolitionists Horace Greeley, Wendell Phillips, and Charles Sumner offer their approval ("Bless the Lord, the south is free, the great principle is established." "My thirty years work is done. I have lived to see 'the Union as it ought to be.'" "Oh, that these charming, elegant, intelligent freed men had the right to vote! Johnson must come up to the principle, or we'll crush him."). The final quote from the abolitionist trio clearly identifies the print as a Thirteenth Amendment, not an Emancipation Proclamation, graphic: reference is made not to Lincoln, but to his successor, Andrew Johnson, who held office when the amendment was ratified in December 1865.

Fig. 10. D. R. Clark, "Joint Resolution of the Thirty Eighth Congress of the United States of America Proposing an Amendment to the Constitution of the United States Abolishing Slavery." Engraving, published by Western Bank Note & Eng. Co., Chicago, 1868. Courtesy of the Lincoln College Museum, Lincoln, Illinois.

Fig. 11. Detail from D. R. Clark, "Joint Resolution of the Thirty Eighth Congress of the United States . . ." (Fig. 10). Courtesy of the Lincoln College Museum, Lincoln, Illinois.

Fig. 12. Broml[e]y & Co., "The 'Freedom' of the South." Lithograph, New York, 1865. Library of Congress.

Little is known of Bromley & Co., except that they had been responsible in the fall of 1864 for a series of virulently racist, anti-Lincoln campaign cartoons, all of which were designed to warn of the imagined perils of the biracial society that would evolve if Lincoln were reelected. The best known of these, "Miscegenation, or the Millennium of Abolitionism," was "a capital hit upon the new plank in the Republican platform," according to a period advertisement for the picture (fig. 13). "It represents society as it is to be in the era of 'Equality and Fraternity.' Lincoln, Sumner, Greeley, a female Lecturer, and a large number of 'colored ladies and gentlemen,' with white drivers and servants, show what society is to be in the millennium of abolitionism."[20]

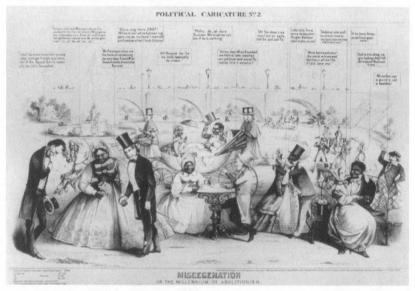

Fig. 13. Broml[e]y & Co., "Miscegenation, or the Millennium of Abolitionism." Lithograph, New York, 1864. Library of Congress.

During the campaign of 1864, Democrats had shamelessly and continually played the race card in their effort to capture the White House from Lincoln and the Republicans.[21] Bromley & Co.'s parallel artistic campaign of racist vitriol, distributed by the anti-Lincoln *New York World,* has been described in several earlier books as a pictorial outburst inspired by, but limited to, the roiling atmosphere of the national election. Now, with the discovery, proper identification, and this first publication of the firm's 1865 effort, "The 'Freedom' of the South," the printmaker's output may be further understood as a prolonged series of racist cartoons that did not end with Lincoln's victory in 1864 but flourished anew the following year, no doubt inspired by congressional approval of the Thirteenth Amendment resolution.[22] Still, the output of pictorial acknowledgment of the amendment remained almost nil.

Then, five years later, American iconography was transformed. Passage of the Fifteenth Amendment in 1870 not only guaranteed African Americans the right to vote but, perhaps more important to the nation's picture publishers, seemed to signal the emergence of the African American audience for popular prints. When chromolithographer Louis Prang of Boston issued a portrait that year of Hiram Revels, the first African American elected to the United States Senate—to the very seat that had previously been held by Jefferson Davis—an influential endorsement came from the civil rights leader Frederick Douglass, who predicted that such pictures would soon be cherished in the homes of former slaves. "Heretofore, colored Americans have thought little of adorning their parlors with pictures," Douglass observed. " . . . Pictures come not with slavery and oppression and destitution, but with liberty, fair play, leisure. And refinement. These conditions are now possible to colored American citizens, and I think the walls of their houses will soon begin to bear evidence of their altered relations to the people about them."[23]

Now, perhaps sated at last by scores of Great Emancipator images, print audiences—their ranks swelled by African American patrons—welcomed a number of tributes to the Fifteenth Amendment (figs. 14–16). Many paid unflagging respect to Lincoln by including him among cameo portraiture that typically celebrated abolitionist heroes like John Brown, William Lloyd Garrison, and

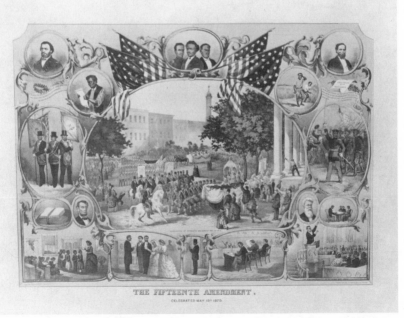

Fig. 14. James C. Beard, "The Fifteenth Amendment. Celebrated May 19th, 1870." Lithograph, published by Thomas Kelly, New York, 1870. Courtesy of The Lincoln Museum, Fort Wayne, Indiana (Ref. 3881).

Fig. 15. Metcalf & Clark, "The Result of the Fifteenth Amendment, and the Rise and Progress of the African Race in America and Its Final Accomplishment, and Celebration on May 19th, A.D. 1870." Lithograph, Baltimore, 1870. Courtesy of The Lincoln Museum, Fort Wayne, Indiana. (Ref. 3883).

Fig. 16. G. F. Kahl, "The Fifteenth Amendment and Its Results. Respectfully Dedicated to the Colored Citizens of the U.S. of America, A.D. 1870." Lithograph, published by Schneider & Fuchs, Baltimore, 1870. Library of Congress.

Fig. 17. E. C. Bridgman, "Liberty." Lithograph, New York, 1870. Courtesy of The Lincoln Museum, Fort Wayne, Indiana (Ref. 3882).

Wendell Phillips. These prints showed African Americans going to school, learning trades, marrying, preaching, and, of course, voting. But this sudden flood of pictures acknowledging the importance of constitutional reform did little to advance the image of the Thirteenth Amendment. In a typical print, "Liberty," the usual assortment of portraits and scenes is accompanied by only three texts: the Emancipation Proclamation, the new Fifteenth Amendment, and a speech by Hiram Revels, "the first colored United States Senator" (fig. 17). Once again, the neglected Thirteenth Amendment had been overshadowed by the intertwined rhythms of politics, newsworthiness, and commercial opportunity.

Unintentionally, the only reminder of that earlier constitutional upheaval came in the occasional inclusion in such prints of emblematic portraits of a politician who had heretofore escaped pictorial notice: Schuyler Colfax. The Speaker of the House when it voted to pass the Thirteenth Amendment, he was serving as vice president of the United States when the states ratified the Fifteenth Amendment. But aside from occasional portraits of Colfax, two themes dominated Fifteenth Amendment prints: the slow but steady transformation in the image of African Americans, from barely clothed slaves to soldiers, farmers, students, and free workers; and the ongoing pictorial acknowledgment of Abraham Lincoln's overarching role in securing freedom—even earning him credit for freedoms codified into law after his death.

Heroes provide artists with heroic scenes, and even if he never provided what might today be called a "photo opportunity" to consecrate the Emancipation Proclamation or the Thirteenth Amendment, Abraham Lincoln did offer a heart-wrenching substitute when the "deliverer" met the "delivered" shortly before his death in the old capital of the Confederacy. Thus, in 1865, the immediate and dramatic impact of emancipation could be powerfully depicted in J. C. Buttre's print, published by Benjamin B. Russell, "Abraham Lincoln

ABRAHAM LINCOLN ENTERING RICHMOND, APRIL 3? 1865
PUBLISHED BY B B RUSSELL & CO. BOSTON

Fig 18. J[ohn]. C[hester]. Buttre (after L. Hollis), "Abraham Lincoln Entering Richmond, April 3d, 1865." Steel engraving, published by B[enjamin]. B. Russell, Boston, 1866. Author's collection.

Entering Richmond, April 3d, 1865" (fig. 18). Whatever document had made freedom possible—the two-year-old Emancipation Proclamation or the soon-to-be-ratified Thirteenth Amendment—the credit falls squarely on Lincoln, who is seen being greeted by a throng of jubilant ex-slaves. With the old Virginia Capitol Building—designed by Thomas Jefferson—looming in the background, viewers could not help but conclude that Lincoln, above all others, had brought reality to Jefferson's promise that all men were created equal.

Over a period of years, but especially from 1865 to 1870, graphic artists helped create the enduring image of Abraham Lincoln as the Great Emancipator both for his wartime executive initiatives and the constitutional amendments they spawned. Such a focus inevitably relegated the Thirteenth Amendment to the status of iconographical coda. But understood within the context of the countless pictorial tributes to emancipation that appeared around the time the amendment was ratified, it could more accurately be understood as yet another stimulant to their proliferation, even if it failed to attract much separate pictorial notice. The Thirteenth Amendment was, in history if less so in iconography, the "great moral victory" for which the "best beloved of the nation" deserves eternal credit and gratitude.

Notes

1. The Senate had voted to approve the constitutional amendment on April 8, 1864.

2. *New York Times*, February 1, 1865.

3. "Uncolored Prints Published by Currier and Ives," Advertising brochure in *Currier and Ives: A Catalogue Raisonné* (Detroit: Gale Research, 1984), xlii.

4. Admittedly, there are exceptions to this rule. Trumbull's great painting of the *Declaration of Independence* spread the credit to all the leaders assembled in Philadelphia. And Francis B. Carpenter's 1864 painting, *The First Reading of the Emancipation Proclamation*, showed not only Lincoln but also members of his cabinet. But a clue to changing public taste may lie in where these paintings are displayed: Trumbull's scene hangs in the Capitol Rotunda, where it is widely accessible to the public. But by the time Congress acquired the Carpenter picture in 1876, it was relegated to a stairway leading to the Senate galleries. There it remains today.

5. See Harold Holzer, Gabor S. Boritt, and Mark E. Neely Jr., *The Lincoln Image: Abraham Lincoln and the Popular Print* (New York: Charles Scribner's Sons, 1984), 147–216.

6. Charles Eberstadt, *Lincoln's Emancipation Proclamation* (New York: Duschnes Crawford, 1950), 23.

7. The major exception was Ehrgott, Forbriger & Co.'s lithograph of a David Gilmour Blythe painting, *President Lincoln Writing the Proclamation of Freedom*, published in Pittsburgh in 1863, which, judging by its rarity (the sole known copy resides in The Lincoln Museum collection) was a commercial failure when it was issued. See Holzer, Boritt, and Neely, *Lincoln Image*, 105.

8. See Harold Holzer, Edna Greene Medford, and Frank J. Williams, *The Emancipation Proclamation: Three Views* (Baton Rouge: Louisiana State University Press, 2006).

9. Michael Vorenberg, *Final Freedom: The Civil War, the Abolition of Slavery, and the Thirteenth Amendment* (Cambridge: Cambridge University Press, 2001), 207, 209.

10. *The Collected Works of Abraham Lincoln*, ed. Roy P. Basler, 9 vols. (New Brunswick, N.J.: Rutgers University Press, 1953–55), 8:253–54.

11. John G. Nicolay and John Hay, *Abraham Lincoln: A History*, 10 vols. (New York: Century, 1890), 10:86. For more of the Senate debate on Lincoln's signature, see *Congressional Globe*, February 7, 1865, 629–31, reprinted in R. Gerald McMurtry, "Lincoln Need Not Have Signed the Resolution Submitting the Thirteenth Amendment to the States," *Lincoln Lore* no. 1604 (October 1971): 2–4.

12. *Collected Works*, 8:254–55.

13. Little is known about Haugg, except that he produced a series of train prints for Richard Norris & Son, Locomotive Builders, in 1856. See Harry T. Peters, *America on Stone: The Other Printmakers to the American People* (Garden City, N.Y.: Doubleday, Doran, 1931), 210.

14. Eberstadt claimed that the undated print was published "*circa* 1863," but though Haugg's portrait of Lincoln might have been based on a photograph of the president taken as early as 1861, there is no evidence that the lithograph appeared as early as 1863. See Eberstadt, *Lincoln's Emancipation Proclamation*, 49.

15. Actually, lithographer Hines Strobridge had direct ties to the Lincoln era by virtue of his wartime partnership with another Cincinnati printmaker, Elijah C. Middleton. Together they produced several prints of Abraham Lincoln's 1865 funeral in their home city.

16. On Carpenter, see Harold Holzer, Gabor S. Boritt, and Mark E. Neely Jr., "Francis Bicknell Carpenter (1830–1900): Painter of Abraham Lincoln and His Circle," *American Art Journal* 16 (Spring 1984): 75–78.

17. It has been commonly argued that the Civil War transformed the phrase "the United States are" to "the United States is," but the language of the Thirteenth Amendment—designed, perhaps, to ruffle as few states' rights feathers as possible en route to ratification—did not acknowledge this sea change. See, for example, Garry Wills, *Lincoln at Gettysburg: The Words That Remade America* (New York: Simon & Schuster, 1992), 145.

18. Omar Monzon, "Lincoln College Museum Acquires Rare Thirteenth Amendment Lithograph; Lincoln Group of New York President Garrera Provides Generous Donation," *Lincoln Newsletter* 25 (winter/spring 2006): 1, 6.

19. For a full account of the failure and ruin of the Confederate printmaking industry, see Mark E. Neely Jr., Harold Holzer, and Gabor S. Boritt, *The Confederate Image: Prints of the Lost Cause* (Chapel Hill: University of North Carolina Press, 1987), 3–10.

20. Advertising sheet, *Bromley & Co's Publications*, 1864, in the collection of the Library of Congress, and reprinted in Mark E. Neely Jr. and Harold Holzer, *The Union Image: Prints of the Civil War North* (Chapel Hill: University of North Carolina Press, 2000), 153.

21. See David E. Long, *The Jewel of Liberty: Abraham Lincoln's Re-election and the End of Slavery in America* (Mechanicsburg, Pa.: Stackpole Books, 1994), 153–69, 172–77.

22. For previous discussions of the Bromley (also occasionally spelled "Bromly") prints, see Bernard Reilly, *American Political Prints, 1766–1876: A Catalog of the Collections in the Library of Congress* (Boston: G. K. Hall, 1991), 542; and Harold Holzer, *Lincoln Seen and Heard* (Lawrence: University Press of Kansas, 2000), 122–23.

23. Peter Marzio, *The Democratic Art: Chromolithography 1840–1900—Pictures for a 19th-Century America* (Boston: David R. Godine, 1979), 104.

Contributors
Index

Contributors

Herman Belz / Professor of history at the University of Maryland. Author of *A New Birth of Freedom: The Republican Party and Freedmen's Rights, 1861–1866*; *Abraham Lincoln, Constitutionalism and Equal Rights in the Civil War Era*; and *A Living Constitution or Fundamental Law? American Constitutionalism in Historical Perspective.*

Joseph R. Fornieri / Associate professor of political science at Rochester Institute of Technology. Author of *Abraham Lincoln's Political Faith* and editor of *The Language of Liberty: The Political Speeches and Writings of Abraham Lincoln.*

Sara Vaughn Gabbard / Vice president and director of development at The Lincoln Museum, Fort Wayne, Indiana, and editor of *Lincoln Lore*, the museum's bulletin, which was recognized in 2005 and 2006 by the *Chicago Tribune* as one of the nation's fifty best magazines.

Allen C. Guelzo / Henry R. Luce Professor of the Civil War Era and professor of history at Gettysburg College. Author of *Abraham Lincoln: Redeemer President* and *Lincoln's Emancipation Proclamation: The End of Slavery in America*, both of which won the Lincoln Prize.

Harold Holzer / Cochairman of the U.S. Lincoln Bicentennial Commission and senior vice president for external affairs at the Metropolitan Museum of Art. Author or coauthor of twenty-six books, including *The Lincoln Image*; *The Lincoln-Douglas Debates*; *Lincoln Seen and Heard*; *Lincoln as I Knew Him*; and *Lincoln at Cooper Union,* winner of a 2005 Lincoln Prize.

James Oliver Horton / Benjamin Banneker Professor of American Studies and History at George Washington University, member of the Lincoln Bicentennial Commission, and historian emeritus at the National Museum of American History. Books include *Hard Road to Freedom: The Story of African America* and *Slavery and the Making of America*, which inspired a PBS series for which he served as on-air commentator.

Ron J. Keller / Assistant professor of history and political science at Lincoln College, curator of the Lincoln College Museum in Lincoln, Illinois, and chief editor, researcher, and writer for *The Lincoln Newsletter*. Coauthor and coproducer of the award-winning documentary *From Surveyor to President: A. Lincoln in Logan County*.

David E. Long / Professor of history at East Carolina University. Author of *The Jewel of Liberty: Abraham Lincoln's Re-election and the End of Slavery* and many articles on the life and times of Lincoln.

John F. Marszalek / Giles Distinguished Professor Emeritus of History and Mentor of Distinguished Scholars, Mississippi State University. Books include *Sherman: A Soldier's Passion for Order* and *Commander of All Lincoln's Armies: A Life of General Henry W. Halleck*.

Lucas E. Morel / Associate professor of politics at Washington and Lee University. Author of *Lincoln's Sacred Effort: Defining Religion's Role in American Self-Government*.

Phillip Shaw Paludan / Professor of history at the University of Illinois at Springfield. Books include *The Presidency of Abraham Lincoln* (winner of the Lincoln Prize); *A People's Contest: The Union and the Civil War, 1861–1865*; and *A Covenant with Death: The Constitution, Law, and Equality in the Civil War Era*.

Matthew Pinsker / Brian Pohanka Chair of Civil War History, Dickinson College. Author of *Abraham Lincoln* (American Presidents Reference Series) and *Lincoln's Sanctuary: Abraham Lincoln and the Soldiers' Home*.

Hans L. Trefousse / Distinguished Professor of History emeritus at Brooklyn College and the Graduate Center of the City University of New York. Books include *Thaddeus Stevens: Nineteenth-Century Egalitarian,* and, most recently, *First among Equals: Abraham Lincoln's Reputation during His Administration.*

Michael Vorenberg / Associate professor of history at Brown University. Author of *Final Freedom: The Civil War, the Abolition of Slavery, and the Thirteenth Amendment.* Works in progress include an edited volume on the Emancipation Proclamation and a book about the Civil War's impact on citizenship.

Ronald C. White Jr. / Professor emeritus of American religious history at San Francisco Theological Seminary and Fellow of the Huntington Library. Author of *Lincoln's Greatest Speech: The Second Inaugural* and *The Eloquent President: A Portrait of Lincoln through His Words.*

Frank J. Williams / Chief justice of the Rhode Island Supreme Court, chairman of the Lincoln Forum, member of the U.S. Lincoln Bicentennial Commission, former president of the Lincoln Group of Boston and the Abraham Lincoln Association, a major Lincoln collector. Author of *Judging Lincoln* and coauthor of *The Emancipation Proclamation: Three Views—Social, Political, Iconographic.*

Index

Italicized page numbers indicate illustrations. Individual military units are indexed under the state name.

The Lincoln Museum, Fort Wayne, Indiana

Founded in Fort Wayne, Indiana, in 1928 as the Lincoln Historical Research Foundation, The Lincoln Museum houses the nation's largest private collection of Abraham Lincoln memorabilia. Executives of Lincoln National Life Insurance Company (organized in Fort Wayne in 1905) were determined to establish a museum and research center in gratitude for Robert Todd Lincoln's agreement that his father's image should become the new firm's official logo. As one described the goal of this project: "No motive of commercialism or profit entered into our plans to assemble this wealth of Lincolniana—we seek merely to provide the means and the channel through which there may continue to flow an ever-increasing volume of information concerning Lincoln, especially to the youth of our land, that they may be influenced to think and to live as Lincoln did—'with malice toward none; with charity for all.'"

Lincoln scholar Louis Warren was hired as the first director. He started work on Lincoln's birthday, February 12, 1928, and published the first issue of *Lincoln Lore* on April 15, 1929, the sixty-fourth anniversary of Lincoln's death. Today, *Lincoln Lore* is the longest continuously published periodical devoted exclusively to Abraham Lincoln and his era.

The museum's ever-growing collection now includes more than eighteen thousand volumes, numerous Lincoln artifacts (including the inkwell he used to sign the Emancipation Proclamation, his pocketknife, legal wallet, and shawl), three hundred Lincoln manuscripts, more than ten thousand nineteenth-century photographs, prints, broadsides, and political cartoons, and the Lincoln family's personal photographs. The museum also houses extensive art and Civil War collections and hosts a number of exhibitions, educational programs, and lectures annually.

The Lincoln Museum is online at www.TheLincolnMuseum.org.